A Coat of Many Colours

Two Centuries of Jewish Life in Canada

A Coat of
Many Colours

Two Centuries of Jewish Life in Canada

IRVING ABELLA

KEY PORTER BOOKS

Canadian Cataloguing in Publication Data

Abella, Irving, 1940-
    A coat of many colours : two centuries of Jewish life in Canada

ISBN 1-55263-108-7

1. Jews – Canada – History.   I. Title

FC106.J5A23   1999   971'.004924   C99-931499-8
F1035.J5A23   1999

Frontispiece: Free-standing Ark that houses a collection of Sepharic Torahs in ornately
worked silver cases, from Shearith, Israel, the oldest congregation in Canada, founded in
Montreal in 1768. (Toronto Jewish Congress Archives-Shuls Project by Sheldon Levitt,
Lynn Milstone and Sid Tenenbaum)

The publisher gratefully acknowledges the support of the
Canada Council for the Arts and the Ontario Arts Council for
its publishing program.

We acknowledge the financial support of the Government of
Canada through the Book Publishing Industry Development
Program (BPIDP) for our publishing activities.

Canadä

Key Porter Books Limited
70 The Esplanade
Toronto, Ontario
Canada M5E 1R2

www.keyporter.com

Printed and bound in Canada

99 00 01 02 03   6 5 4 3 2 1

INTRODUCTION

Almost ten years have passed since this book first appeared—ten years of rapid growth for both the Jewish community of Canada and the literature about it. While *A Coat of Many Colours* is still the only single-volume history of Canadian Jewry published in the past twenty-five years, it has been joined by a plethora of other studies of Canadian Jews, particularly Gerald Tulchinsky's comprehensive two-volume work.

That there is a growing interest in Canadian Jewry should come as no surprise. After all, the Canadian Jewish community is the fastest-growing in the Diaspora, and it is certainly among the most affluent, educated and integrated ethnic communities in the country. While American Jewry is in decline and British Jewry is in a state of crisis, Canadian Jewry is flourishing.

Being a Jew in Canada today means being able to celebrate and participate freely in all of this country's wonderful possibilities. Canada at the end of the twentieth century is a generous country, far different from the benighted, xenophobic, anti-semitic country it was a generation or two ago. Then, Jews were excluded from almost every sector of Canadian society, and some were even excluded from the country itself by a government and a people who felt there were already too many Jews here.

This is an enormous country, with a tiny, though growing, Jewish population. And as for all Canadians, life for Jews is influenced by the vastness of the land. If Jews suffer from an excess of history, then Canadians suffer from an excess of geography—and Canadian Jews suffer from both. We are the world's largest small nation. That sense of both the country's smallness and its immensity has contributed to a sense of insecurity and marginality that has dominated the Canadian Jewish community for too much of this century.

Yet that too has changed. For Canada's Jews, life has never been better. The quotas, barriers and restrictions of an earlier period of Canadian history are all gone. Jews now hold positions in government, business, academe, the judiciary, medicine—indeed, in each sector of Canadian society—that were unattainable a generation or two ago. Day schools are full; new synagogues and giant community centres are being built; Jewish homes for the aged are the envy of other communities. Jewish organizations are more politically potent then ever before, and vast funds are raised both for Israel and for domestic needs. Indeed, Canadian Jews give more per capita to charities than any other group in the world.

In fact, there is no area of Canadian Jewish life that is not thriving—or so it seems. Book fairs and film festivals; special lectures and educational programs; cultural events, galas; they all clog the Jewish calendar.

And yet, like Jews everywhere, Canadian Jews worry.

Their worries, of course, are real. Can the Jewish community continue on into the next century with the same vigour and vitality with which it is leaving this one? Today's community worries more about rates of assimilation than rates of anti-semitism. Its greatest concern is for its children and grandchildren: will they remain Jewish? Are the seeds of its destruction implanted in its very success? Can Jewishness in North America survive freedom? Can it survive in an open, tolerant, multicultural society?

It is clear that Canadian Jews now confront a classic paradox of pluralistic societies. They want desperately to integrate fully into a society in which, until recently, they were not allowed; yet they know that such integration might not allow them to maintain themselves as a unique, vibrant, identifiable community.

Canadian Jews live in a society in which Jewish lives are not in danger. What is in danger, according to some scholars, is Jewish life. Burgeoning assimilation rates in the United States are a growing concern to Canadian Jews. In North America, living as a Jew is only one option among many. And when living as a Jew is a choice, the community must be able to offer its children more than simply an invitation to survive. When the brightest of our young ask what it is that Jewish survival will make possible, we should have answers for them—if we have any. What are we Jews about? What dream do we fulfil by surviving?

It seems to me that the time has come to dream a new dream, one that focuses on Canadian Jewish life as we would like it to look in the twenty-first century. For me, the dream flows directly from the historic mission of North America's Jewish community: to demonstrate that Judaism and Jewishness can succeed and flourish in a free, democratic, Diaspora environment. Classical Zionism insisted that emancipation was a failure, that assimilation was inevitable, and that only in Israel could Jewish life thrive. North American Jews responded that America was different. In the United States and Canada, they argued, Jews could achieve what they never did elsewhere in the Diaspora: equal treatment, economic prosperity, and at the same time a distinct spiritual and cultural identity.

That is the central question facing Canadian Jews today.

Can Judaism survive in an atmosphere of unprecedented freedom? If it does not, then the old-time assimilationists—and the Zionists—will be proved right. In the end, North America may not be so different. If that is the case, then Jewish life will not succeed anywhere outside of Israel. And that suggests the unthinkable: that Judaism cannot hold its own within a competitive, pluralistic religious environment.

The task facing Canadian Jewry is formidable. But as this book shows, Canadian Jews are a formidable people.

Irving Abella
Toronto, May 1999

CONTENTS

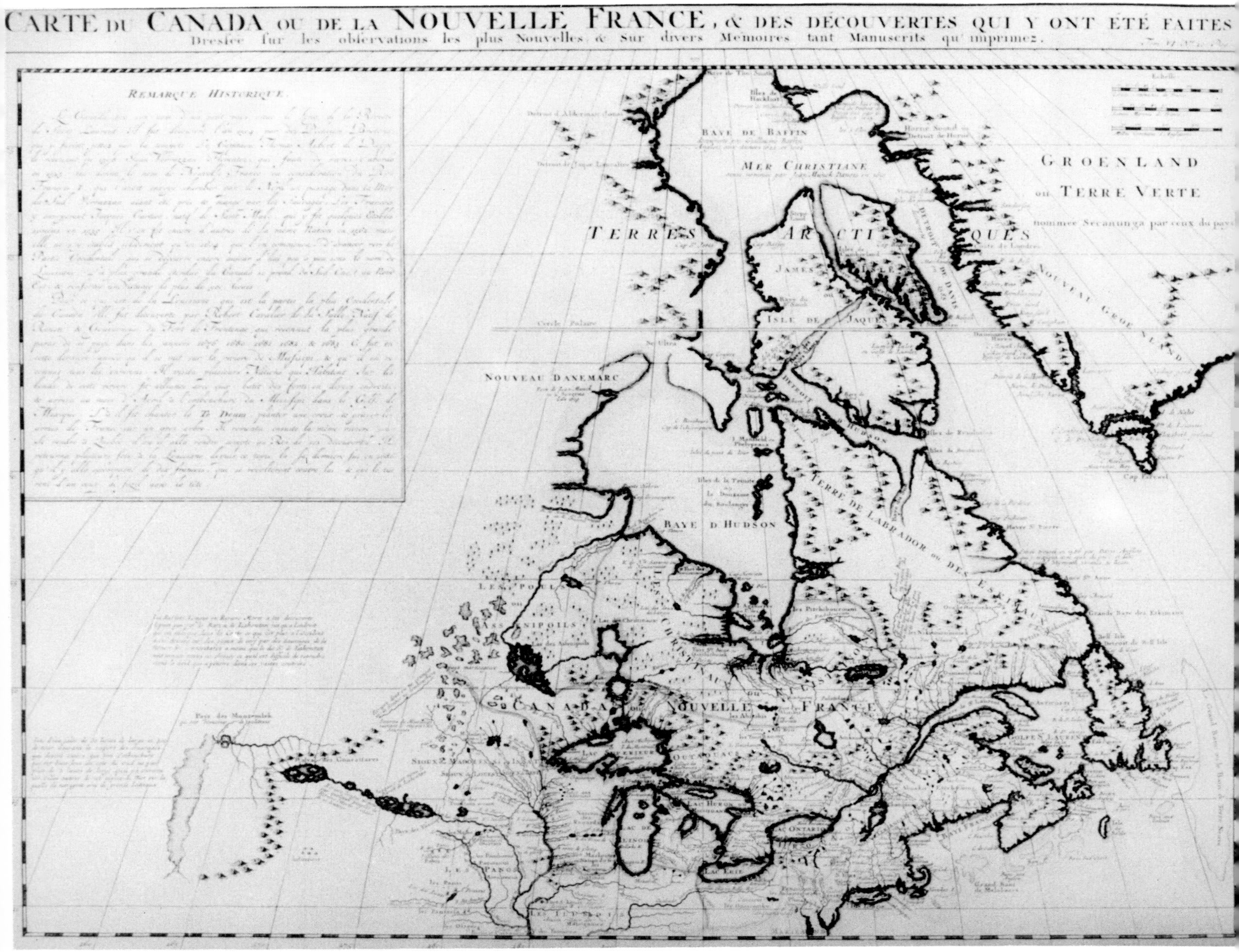

CARTE DU CANADA OU DE LA NOUVELLE FRANCE, & DES DÉCOUVERTES QUI Y ONT ÉTÉ FAITES

Dressée sur les observations les plus Nouvelles, & sur divers Memoires tant Manuscrits qu'imprimez.

REMARQUE HISTORIQUE.

GROENLAND ou TERRE VERTE

nommée Secanunga par ceux du pays

NOUVEAU GROENLAND

BAYE DE BAFFIN

MER CHRISTIANE

TERRES ARCTIQUES

JAMES

ISLE DE JACQUES

NOUVEAU DANEMARC

Cercle Polaire

BAYE D'HUDSON

TERRE DE LABRADOR ou DES ESKIMAUX

CANADA ou NOUVELLE FRANCE

ONTARIO

CHAPTER ONE

THE FIRST GENERATION

1 7 3 8 - 1 8 1 0

On September 15, 1738 a young Frenchman was summoned to appear before government officials in Quebec. He had just arrived from the French port of La Rochelle aboard the schooner *St. Michel*. He said his name was Jacques La Farge and that he had come to New France to find work. But there was something about him that aroused the suspicions of colonial authorities. Perhaps it was his youth, his polished manner or his ill-fitting clothes.

How different he was soon became apparent. Under questioning by the Maritime commissioner, La Farge admitted that not only was his name assumed — so was his gender. In reality, "he" was a she, a nineteen-year-old Jewess from France named Esther Brandeau.

Her story was intriguing. Born in Bayonne, France, the daughter of Jewish refugees from the Portuguese Inquisition, Brandeau was shipwrecked at the age of fifteen while on her way to visit relatives in Holland. Following her rescue she decided not to return home but to see as much of the world as she could.

Using the name Pierre Mausiette, she disguised herself as a boy and signed on as a ship's cook in Bordeaux. Apparently the kitchen was not for her and over the next four years she worked as a tailor,

Left: New France, 1719.

Right: Quebec, the capital of New France.

a baker, a messenger-boy in a convent and as a footman to a military officer. Her quest for adventure still not sated, she changed her name to Jacques La Farge and set out aboard the *St. Michel*.

It was clear that Brandeau could not remain in New France — Jews were not allowed into the colony. Church authorities in Quebec pleaded with her to convert to Catholicism. Despite months of persuasion, cajoling and threats, Brandeau would not yield. Exasperated authorities complained about her "frivolity" and "stubbornness." After a year of fruitless effort they gave up. Esther Brandeau, they concluded, would not convert and, therefore, could not remain. King Louis XVI was kept fully apprised of the bizarre situation and finally, in 1739, on his express orders, Brandeau was shipped back home at the expense of the French government.

French officials had better luck with another Jewess. Marianne Perious, born in a village outside of Bordeaux, arrived unannounced in New France in 1749, looking for adventure and a husband. Told she would be sent home if she did not convert, the illiterate Perious affixed an X to her baptismal papers; thus she became, at the same time, a Catholic and a citizen of the colony. There was such a scarcity of women in New France that any female, even a converted Jew, was welcome. But New France, it was clear, was no place for Jews who wished to remain Jewish.

Under the French, Canada's first colonizers, Jewish settlement was strictly barred; indeed all non-Catholic settlement was prohibited. Theirs was to be a totally homogeneous community — one language, one religion, one loyalty, one monarch. It could have been no other way. France was a theocracy, a union between church and state. Religious minorities had to conform, to accept the state religion or leave. Thus, from the moment French settlement began in the early 1600s, to the capture of Quebec by the British in 1759, Jews were forbidden to enter New France.

When Cardinal Richelieu founded the Company of New France in 1627 to develop and explore the French territories in North

Painting by Richard Paton showing the burning of the *Prudent* and the capture of the *Bienfaisant* at Louisbourg, July 26, 1758. Both ships were owned by Abraham Gradis and are now at the bottom of the Louisbourg harbour.

America, he stipulated that they be open only to French Catholics. No Jews, no Huguenots, no dissenters or foreigners of any sort were to be allowed admission. This order was reinforced by the infamous Black Code of 1685, which decreed that officials in every French possession in the world "drive out...all Jews...as enemies of the Christian name."

Nevertheless there is growing evidence that some Jews were able to side-step these prohibitions. Most did so by converting to Catholicism — or, like the Marranos, Jewish refugees from the Spanish Inquisition, by pretending to convert but secretly practising their religion. Others, like Esther Brandeau, simply hid their true identities.

Yet, it was a Jew who was providing much of the sustenance and financial support to keep the colony alive. It is one of the real ironies of Canadian history that some of the early colonizing efforts in this country were underwritten by a Jewish family which was barred from the colony because of its faith.

The Gradis family had escaped the Portuguese Inquisition and settled in Bordeaux. There they set up a trading company and prospered. Much of their trade was with French settlements in the West Indies, but by the 1740s New France was the centre of the family interests. In 1748, Abraham Gradis went into partnership with the corrupt intendant of Quebec, François Bigot, to supply goods to the colony. From all the evidence it was a good deal for everyone — especially Bigot, who put up no funds yet made enormous profits, so large, in fact, that he was later convicted of plundering the public treasury and ultimately forced into exile.

There is little evidence to indicate that the Gradis family acted criminally. Indeed there is much to indicate it did not. The charter of the company they had formed with Bigot, "La Société du Canada," stipulated that the family was to put up all the capital and take all the risks and yet share in only half the profits. In the end, the family took far less of the profits than it was entitled to.

Though historians will argue about the role and the importance of the Gradis family to New France before its submission to the British, it is clear that the colony was dependent on the provisions they provided. For a short period it was the family's ships that, almost unaided, kept the settlers from starving and provided the munitions necessary to defend the colony.

With his Portuguese Jewish colleagues Abraham Gradis delivered to New France through the 1750s massive amounts of food, supplies and munitions, as well as hundreds of soldiers and indentured servants. One French historian claimed that "Gradis did more for the protection of French interests in Canada than royalty itself." Though this is certainly an exaggeration, there is no doubt that at his own expense Abraham Gradis armed ships for the futile defence of Louisbourg and sent boatloads of troops through the British blockade to reinforce Quebec. The family firm was, as another historian has remarked, "almost a whole quartermaster corps in itself" in supplying French troops. The commander of French forces in Quebec, the Marquis de Montcalm, called Abraham Gradis his "right-hand man" and credited him as the person most responsible for allowing the French to hold out as long as they did against the superior British force. Even while many of Gradis' ships arrived safely and unloaded desperately needed reinforcements, weapons and foods, few made it back to France.

Through his contacts with fellow Jews in London, Gradis even arranged for the exchange of prisoners between the English and the French, and it was his firm that fed and clothed French prisoners in British custody. He lobbied intensively for the colony's interests with the largely apathetic officials in Louis XVI's court — but to no avail. There was not much interest in saving the colony, perhaps because government authorities knew the cause was hopeless.

They were right. The French could not match the overwhelming power of the British fleet. The fall of Quebec, they knew, was only a matter of time. Yet to the very end Gradis persevered. Despite massive losses, he was determined to reinforce the French province in North America. Clearly he acted out of a variety of motives. He undoubtedly wished to prove his loyalty to his adopted country, but just as important, his company had made huge profits in its dealings with the colonies, and Gradis was reluctant to see these disappear. Supplying de Montcalm, he decided, was still a worthwhile investment despite the heavy odds.

Though the Gradis company would survive, New France would not. In 1759 Quebec fell to the British under Brigadier-General James Wolfe. The Gradis family's contribution, however, was not forgotten. Twenty-five years after the battle on the Plains of Abraham, Louis XVI expressed his nation's gratitude to the family and offered them "full freedom" as citizens of France in the "new world." Unfortunately, they could not take advantage of this newly bestowed liberty since most of the New World was now in British hands.

Ironically, while the Gradis family was so deeply involved with strengthening the hand of de Montcalm, another Jew was just as heavily involved with the forces of Wolfe. Alexander Schomberg, the scion of a prominent Jewish family in London, was the commander of the frigate *Diana*, which took part in the attack on Quebec. What is perhaps most noteworthy about Schomberg is that in order to become a British officer, he had had to convert: Jews were not allowed into the British navy. It was thus as a Christian and not as a Jew that he played his role in making Canada British.

Nevertheless, the British were far more welcoming towards Jewish settlers than were the French. Aware of the Jews' fabled talents and expertise as traders, the British opened their overseas possessions to Jews and to a variety of other dissenters. As long as they were loyal to the Crown, they were welcome to settle in whatever colony they chose. Even while the right of Jews to hold citizenship in England was denied, under a special act of Parliament in 1740, they could be naturalized in the colonies.

British forces move up the river to fight the battle on the Plains of Abraham, 1759.

Detail from *View of Louisbourg in 1731* by Claude-Etienne Verrier.

And for a very good reason. In the eighteenth century supplying armies had become a common Jewish occupation — "the royal road to wealth" according to one historian. Since the British army was so active in this period, it relied heavily on Jews for its provisions. Many Jews who arrived in the New World — and especially in Canada — came as provisioners to the British army. They were usually the only private citizens accompanying the troops. On their arrival they often settled and branched out into other areas of trade and commerce.

It has always been thought that the first Jewish settlers in Canada arrived with the British army in Halifax in 1749. There is some evidence, however, that a few Jews had managed to evade the restrictions of the French and take up residence farther up the Nova Scotia coast at Louisbourg. Research now being undertaken at the fortress indicates that Portuguese Jewish merchants associated with the Gradis firm, likely the Roderigue family, led a secret Jewish life under the noses of the French government and Catholic church.

Most, of course, were eventually forced to convert — but some did not. According to the most recent historian of Louisbourg, Kenneth Donovan, local parish records reveal that there were some residents with typical Jewish names and even a "street of Jews" in the 1740s. Many of these were likely actively involved with the Gradis trading empire, which was perhaps Louisbourg's most important supplier in the years before its capture by the British in 1758. Thus it appears that there were Jews in Canada even before the British arrived.

There is some evidence, however, that at least one Jew arrived unexpectedly in Canada as early as the 1670s. A Jewish trader from Rotterdam, Joseph de la Penha, was driven onto the coast of Labrador by a sudden North Atlantic storm. He immediately claimed the territory for England, whose ruler, William III, also reigned over Holland. Twenty years later, as a reward for de la Penha's having saved his monarch's life at sea, William ceded Labrador to de la Penha and his descendants. The document granting the Jewish family Labrador still exists, though for various reasons the de la Penhas never took up the offer.

The first Jewish settlers who left conclusive evidence of their presence arrived in Halifax in 1749. A handful of enterprising Jewish merchants in the American colonies made their way to Halifax, fully expecting that the British presence and the protected natural harbour would ensure the town's growth and prosperity. The British governor of Nova Scotia, Lord Cornwallis, aware that the new colony needed supplies and credit to help it survive its first few difficult years, welcomed Jewish merchants and traders from New England.

By 1752 Halifax was home to about thirty Jews. Most were of German background and had originally emigrated to the American colonies. The most prominent of these were Israel Abrahams, Isaac Levy, Nathan Nathans and the four Hart brothers, Abraham, Isaac, Naphtali and Samuel. All were ambitious and energetic and made significant contributions to the developing colony. Levy was the first to attempt to exploit the Cape Breton coal fields. Abrahams began the potash industry in the colony, and the largest purveyor of goods in the entire region was the company of Nathans and Hart.

There were high hopes for the establishment of a Jewish community in Halifax in this period. Though Jews were then tolerated in England, they had suffered previous expulsions. Thus many looked with interest towards the colonies for new places where they might prosper and still remain true to their faith. In 1752 a Halifax newspaper reported that three ships had been chartered in England to bring over Jewish families, but nothing came of this.

And ultimately nothing much came of early Jewish settlement in Halifax.

The first activity of the Halifax Jewish community was to create a cemetery; all Jews must be buried in consecrated ground. In 1750 land was bought for this purpose, but a few years later it was sold as the site for a government workhouse. It was clear by then that Halifax

The founder of Halifax, Lord Edward Cornwallis, who as governor of Nova Scotia (1749-1753) welcomed Jewish merchants and traders from New England.

Left: Governor's House and St. Mather's Meeting House, Halifax, 1759. The first Jewish community in Canada was in Halifax; by 1752, there were approximately thirty Jews living in the city.

Right: The town and harbour of Halifax, as viewed from the opposite shore of Dartmouth, 1759.

was not going to contain a permanent Jewish settlement. Many of the Jews who had come there had either converted, married outside the faith or moved back south, especially after the outbreak of the American Revolution. Aside from this cemetery, there were no other signs of Jewish life or religion—no synagogue, no rabbi, no ritual slaughterer and eventually almost no Jews.

The most influential of those Jews who did remain in Halifax was Samuel Hart, a wealthy merchant who had made his fortune in Newport, Rhode Island. By the 1780s he was one of the leading merchants in the colony and owner of perhaps the most magnificent estate in all of Halifax. In 1793 he was elected to the Nova Scotia Assembly, and thus became the first Jew anywhere in the British Empire to hold a seat in a legislature. To do so, however, it appears that he had to swear an oath to carry out his responsibilities while adhering to "the one true faith as a Christian." Hart likely complied; his four children had already been baptized as Anglicans, though there is no evidence that Hart himself ever converted. In any case, Nova Scotia had had a Jewish legislator at least sixty years before a Jew was allowed to sit in the British Parliament.

There is some evidence that there were a few scattered Jews in Nova Scotia before 1800, aside from those in Halifax. Since none of their descendants remained Jewish, the documentation is sadly limited. But we do know that one of the original settlers of the Annapolis Valley was Jacob Calneck, a German Jew, who had been hired by the British to supply their Hessian mercenaries during the American Revolution. His reward was a substantial land grant in Nova Scotia. Evidence also suggests that some Jews followed the British army through New Brunswick and took up residence there.

Among the land grants made in this period at least another two were to Jews. In southwestern Nova Scotia, a Mr. Abraham and a Mr. Shepard took up land. But we do not know for certain what happened to them or to their families. Another Jew who settled in the colony, Nathan Levy, was of Dutch origin. He soon became a Lutheran, and some of his descendants still reside in Lunenburg County.

With the fall of Quebec in 1759 it was clear that all of British North America was at last open to Jews. Many took advantage of the new possibilities. Foremost among them was Samuel Jacobs, an Alsatian Jew, who had emigrated to the New England colonies and become a supplier to the British army. When war with the French began in the 1750s Jacobs followed the British troops into Canada. He settled for a time in Fort Cumberland, New Brunswick, where he was active in the timber and liquor trade. In 1759 he helped found a brewery in the recently captured French town of Louisbourg. Later that year, on his schooner *Betsey*, he followed the British fleet up the St. Lawrence to Quebec and was there immediately after the surrender of the French.

Though his ship was requisitioned by the British to carry food between Quebec and the Ile d'Orléans, Jacobs had sufficient resources to become actively involved in a series of business enterprises. He hired agents — most of whom were fellow Jews — in New York, and in Montreal, Sorel, Quebec and Three Rivers, to seek out contracts for his trading companies. By the mid-1760s Jacobs was one of the leading businessmen of the new colony and its largest importer. In St. Denis, on the Richelieu River north of Lake Champlain, where he eventually settled, Jacobs operated a general store as well as a distillery. In addition, he was supplying much of the

Samuel Hart.

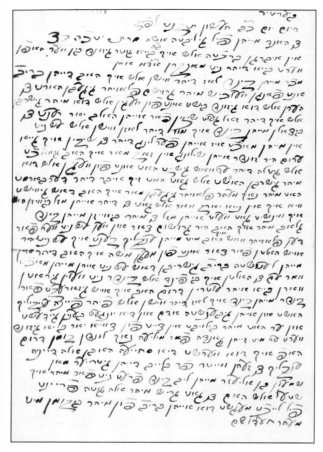

Samuel Jacobs' diary, *c.* 1798.

goods and capital to support the ventures of other Jewish traders who followed in his wake.

A truly remarkable man, Samuel Jacobs was exceptionally well read—a rarity in a pioneer community—and he had a huge library. He complained constantly to his many correspondents that he was desperate for more reading material. He also loved music and was particularly proud of his violin. Though he never denied his Jewishness—he often added his Hebrew name to his formal signature, and even wrote in Hebrew characters, though the language was English—he refused to join or contribute to a synagogue. Nor did he marry in the faith. His wife was a French Canadian and his five children were raised as Catholics. Nevertheless, he insisted whenever he was in court on swearing on a "Hebrew Bible." As he told a friend: "Tho' I am not a wandering Jew, yet I am a stirring one."

Samuel Jacobs was not the only Jew to take advantage of the opportunities created by the British army. Beyond Quebec there was a vast land awaiting development, a land full of lumber, furs, minerals and foodstuffs. And no one acted more swiftly to capitalize on these opportunities than the Jewish purveyors who arrived with the British troops.

First off the mark to explore the lands beyond Montreal was a consortium of German Jews who had arrived in Montreal with the British army in 1760. Founded by Ezekiel Solomons, his cousin Levy Solomons, Chapman Abraham, Benjamin Lyon and Gershon Levy, the partnership viewed the St. Lawrence as a vast highway of commerce that flowed deep into the heart of the continent. With Montreal as their headquarters, they were soon ranging throughout the Great Lakes region, bringing in supplies, trinkets and liquor to the Indians and bringing out vast quantities of furs. Long before any British soldier had ventured much beyond the safety of Montreal, Solomons, Abraham, Lyon and Levy were canoeing into uncharted territories. The risks were great, but so were the potential profits. These Jewish fur traders and their associates were seemingly prepared to challenge the Hudson's Bay Company for control of the Northwest.

In 1761 Ezekiel Solomons set out on what has been called "the most dangerous, the most adventurous expedition, in all of Canada's commercial history." He was determined to reach Fort Michilimackinac at the juncture of Lakes Michigan and Huron. If he was the first trader to arrive there and establish links with the Indians on the Great Lakes, the profits would be enormous — or so he and his partners thought.

Located on the straits between the two lakes, the fort was key to controlling trade of the upper Great Lakes. Under the French it had become a major fur-trade centre, but after they left, the area was open to exploitation by whoever arrived first.

Though Solomons and his group of traders were the first to reach the fort, after a number of wild adventures, they found it in the hands of the French fur traders and their Indian allies. No English troops had yet ventured so far into the interior, and the Indians surrounding the fort had always supported the French in their many wars with the British. Solomons was taken prisoner, and only the timely arrival of English troops saved him from certain execution.

After his rescue, Solomons took full advantage of the economic opportunity he had gained. He sent canoes laden with goods out from the fort to trade with Indians hundreds of miles away. In return for trinkets, blankets, dry goods and liquor, the Indians bartered hundreds of pelts, which Solomons then sent on to Montreal.

Unfortunately for Solomons and the other English traders, in 1763 the Indians under Pontiac rebelled against the British invasion. Solomons, Abraham and Levy were captured and held as hostages. While some of their colleagues were burned at the stake, they were more fortunate, and were among the few prisoners who emerged unscathed.

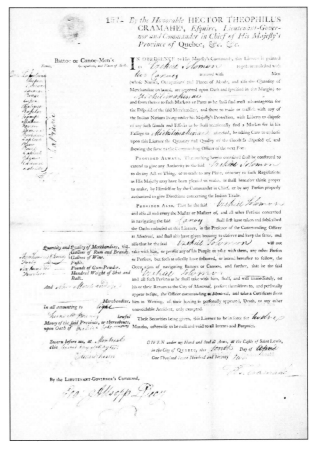

Upper: Ezekiel Solomons' fur-trading licence, 1772.

Lower: Levy Solomons.

Jacob Franks.

Undeterred, upon his release Solomons extended his fur-trading empire farther into the Northwest, well beyond Lake Superior. Though he and his partners suffered a variety of business reverses — they went bankrupt several times — they always recovered and went back into the wilderness.

Another intrepid adventurer was Jacob Franks, a member of the extended family of Bavarian Jews who had business interests in Philadelphia and New York, as well as in Montreal and Quebec. In the 1780s and 1790s Franks, who was well known for his integrity and fairness, set up a trading post on Lake Michigan, and he soon controlled much of the fur trade in the area. He also built the first flour mill and distillery in the upper Great Lakes region.

It is clear now that these pioneer Jewish entrepreneurs helped set the pattern for commercial trade along the St. Lawrence and Great Lakes. They opened up new routes, negotiated with the Indians and were among the first whites in many areas of the Northwest. Solomons, for example, was the first Jewish settler in Michigan, and he and Benjamin Lyon, along with a few other Jewish traders, operated successful businesses for years in Fort Michilimackinac. So colourful and eventful were their lives that these Canadian Jewish fur traders became the subject of partly fictionalized stories by such American authors as Stephen Vincent Benét and Francis Parkman.

There can no longer be any doubt that right from the beginning Jews were intimately involved in the business and trade of the new British colony. Though small in number they played a pivotal role in its development. There was scarcely an area of commerce in which they did not take part and in many of the new towns springing up in British North America there was a Jewish presence. Through their contacts with co-religionists, family members and former associates south of the border, they helped forge trade links with the new United States that emerged after the Revolution.

Jews also played an important political role, in a way that would not have been allowed them in England. Not only did they sign petitions and declarations calling for reforms and for a representative assembly, and complain against the Quebec Act, which would limit their entrepreneurial activities, they also began to assume government positions. John Franks was appointed fire inspector in Quebec in 1768, as was John Lewis in Three Rivers. Aaron Hart was made postmaster in Three Rivers and Uriah Judah its protonotary (chief court clerk). Canadian Jews were given militia appointments long before English Jews were permitted to become officers. And most of those appointed took their oath not as Christians but as Jews — another impossibility in the Mother Country.

Thus from the beginning Canada was more open and far more liberal than Great Britain. Jews — and others, of course, including Catholics and dissenters — had freedoms in Canada that they could only dream of in Britain. Remarkably, Jews in Canada in 1800 numbered fewer than 120 men in a population of over 300,000. Nonetheless their achievements and contributions were staggering. Perhaps their greatest difficulty was to remain Jewish. Theirs was a community with almost no women. Thus many lived with — and usually married — Indian or French-Canadian women, with whom they had children. And though the children often bore Jewish names, and were considered Jews by their contemporaries, almost all were brought up and lived their lives as Christians.

Montreal was, of course, the heart of the Jewish community. Most of those who arrived with the British chose to settle there, and in 1768 they met to found the country's first synagogue, Shearith Israel, literally "the remnant of Israel." Named after the first synagogue in New York, it would come to be known as the Spanish and Portuguese Synagogue and would be Canada's only Jewish congregation for the next two generations. For almost ten years the members of the synagogue met in a small house on St. James Street. Finally, in 1777 a building to house the congregation was put up on Notre Dame Street on land donated by the family of Lazurus David and with funds raised from most of the Jews living in the town. In 1778 Reverend Jacob Rafael Cohen

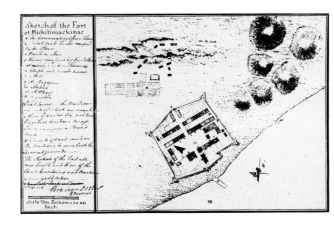

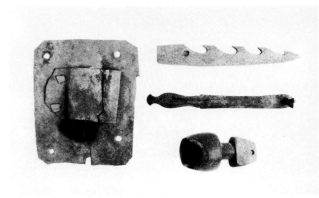

Upper: Sketch of Fort Michilimackinac, 1766, with an arrow showing the house occupied by Ezekiel Solomons and Gershon Levy.

Lower: Artifacts uncovered by archaeologists from Ezekiel Solomons and Gershon Levy's house at Fort Michilimackinac.

Left: Colonel David Salesby Franks, a Montreal merchant and president of the Shearith Israel Synagogue.

Right: Fortifications and town of Montreal, *c.* 1760.

arrived from London to become the community's spiritual leader. Unfortunately, Cohen soon became embroiled in a dispute with his congregation regarding his salary. After a prolonged court battle he resigned his position and in 1784 he accepted a post in Philadelphia. The community would have to do without a rabbi for many years.

Although the Montreal Jewish community was larger, a more vibrant one was taking shape in the small town of Three Rivers, largely as the result of the efforts of one man, Aaron Hart. In the history of Canadian Jewry, no settler in this period was more important or left a greater legacy. Almost alone among the Jewish settlers of the time, the Hart family remained Jewish. Few of its members intermarried; most were brought up with a solid Jewish background and education and almost all played a role in the Jewish life of their times. For most of the past two centuries the descendants of Aaron Hart have taken their place in the forefront of the Jewish community.

Not much is known of Aaron Hart's background. Of German parentage, he was probably born in London in 1724. Some time after 1740 he emigrated to the New World, and from a document attesting to his membership in a Masonic lodge we know he was in New York in

1760. At about that time, he joined up as a provisioner with the British forces under Generals Haldimand and Amherst as they marched on Montreal. He was not, as some early historians would have us believe, a British officer — no Jew was — and he certainly did not ride into Montreal alongside Amherst, as other early versions claim. But he was loyal, and he apparently did a good enough job as a supplier to become known to both Amherst and Haldimand.

With the surrender of the French in Montreal, the British no longer had need of Hart's services. Recognizing the enormous potential of the new colony, Hart decided not to return to New York but to set up shop in Three Rivers, a small French town between Quebec and Montreal. He thus became one of the first English-speaking settlers in that area.

More important, within a few years he became the leading businessman outside of Montreal. He opened up a thriving fur-trading business with the Indians who found his store at the convergence of the St. Maurice and St. Lawrence rivers far more accessible than those in Montreal and Quebec. As well he was deeply involved in the liquor trade, in exporting grain directly to England and in acquiring vast tracts of land, the most noteworthy of which was the picturesque seigneury of Bécancour. At the time of his death he was perhaps the largest landowner in all of Lower Canada. In addition to being the first postmaster of Three Rivers, he was the paymaster for British troops in the area. In effect, Hart was a conglomerate with business interests in a variety of areas: real estate, fur, liquor, foodstuffs and lumber.

Why was Hart so successful? Most historians agree that he was the right man in the right place at the right time. Charming, shrewd, energetic and honest, he happened to arrive in Three Rivers just when the old feudalism of the French regime was collapsing. There were enormous financial possibilities but few to take advantage of them. Through his connections with the British army, which controlled the area, and his commercial interests beyond Three Rivers, Hart was able to capitalize on those opportunities. There were few other British

Upper: Three Rivers, *c.* 1760.

Lower: Aaron Hart (1724-1800), the most influential of the early Jewish settlers in Canada.

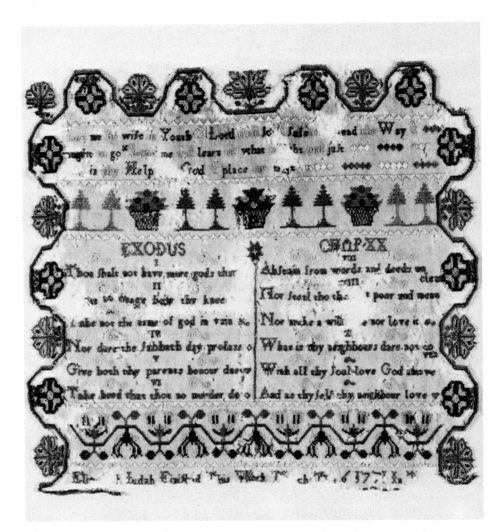

An embroidered sampler made by Elizabeth Judah, Quebec, in 1771 when she was eight years old.

businessmen to challenge his primacy, and though most of his dealings were with non-Jews he could always count on his fellow Jewish merchants, Samuel Jacobs, the Solomonses and others, for support. In the words of one scholar these Jews formed "sort of a mutual aid society." Few in number, they were frequently linked through marriage, had common problems and a common guild spirit. Though they were often bitter rivals and quite litigious, it is clear that more often than not they supported one another, though most were envious of Hart, who was by far the most successful — and the most Jewish — of them all.

It was his stubborn adherence to his religion that made Hart so important to Canadian Jewish history. Determined to marry within the faith, in 1768 Hart returned to England to wed his cousin Dorothea Judah, the sister of one of his business partners. They had eleven children, seven of whom survived into adulthood — all of whom received a traditional Jewish upbringing. Indeed his sons Ezekiel, Moses, Benjamin and Alexander were sent to New York and Philadelphia to stay with Jewish families and to receive a religious education.

To augment the Hart clan in Three Rivers, two of Dorothea's brothers, Uriah and Samuel Judah, settled nearby, as did the children of Hart's brother-in-law, Naphtali Joseph. The extended Hart–Judah–Joseph family would dominate Jewish society in Quebec for the next century.

Although he lived less than a day's travel from Montreal, there is no evidence that Hart had anything other than business dealings with the Montreal Jewish community. He never became a member of the Shearith Israel Synagogue and never contributed to it. Indeed he built his own synagogue — and, of course, cemetery — in Three Rivers. He was, as one historian observed, "a community by himself."

Hart had difficulties with his French neighbours. Unable to adjust to the new economic circumstances following the Conquest, many of the old seigneurs and landowners found themselves deeply in debt and mortgaged far beyond their resources. As a result, Hart was able to buy their lands at a fraction of their value. Although his acumen and opportunism were resented, Hart was scrupulously honest in his dealings with the French and gave a good deal of money to local charities, particularly to the Ursuline convent nearby, whose nuns thought him to be a veritable saint. Not only did he extend to them a generous line of credit — without charging interest — and provided free goods and services, but he earned the sisters' gratitude for what they described as "the piping hot meals which he used to send" during some bitterly cold winters. So generous was he to the church that on his death one

Upper: The Hart family home in Three Rivers.

Lower: Alexander Hart of Three Rivers, son of Aaron Hart.

Moses Hart.

local humorist remarked that "Hart had done more for Catholics in Three Rivers than the Pope himself."

Though Aaron Hart never sought political office, he did ally himself with fellow British businessmen in protesting the heavy hand of the British government and in calling for a more representative form of government. But he knew full well that, even in a colony as free as Canada seemed, there were still restrictions — especially for Jews. Prophetically he warned his son Ezekiel, who was eager to enter politics: "You will be opposed as a Jew. You may go to law, but be assured, you will never get a jury in your favour nor a party in the House for you." Thus even the Seigneur of Bécancour understood that despite his prestige, wealth and philanthropy, there were limits beyond which a Jew could not yet venture. By 1800 the handful of Jewish settlers had already achieved much, but a great deal more remained to be achieved.

Ignoring his father's admonition, Hart's eldest son, Moses, decided to test the political waters. He announced his candidacy for election to the Assembly in 1796. He was not elected, nor would he be in the other two or three elections in which he later presented himself as a candidate.

Following the death of their father in 1800, the Hart children began branching out on their own. Alexander, the youngest brother, moved to Montreal and set up the family business there, probably to get out of the shadow of his older siblings. Moses stayed in Three Rivers, where he founded a transportation company and a bank. He was also something of a writer, publishing a work on religion in 1815. Despite his electoral setbacks, Moses was chosen first high constable of police in Three Rivers. But the seat in the Assembly he so coveted never came. Rather it went to his brother Ezekiel; or, more accurately, it almost went to Ezekiel.

The Three Rivers by-election of 1807 is a seminal event in Canadian Jewish history. On the death of the sitting member, John Lees, three candidates besides Ezekiel Hart offered themselves for election: Matthew Bell and Thomas Coffin represented the minority English-speaking population; Pierre Vézina was a popular French-speaking militia officer.

The election was held on Saturday, April 11, with the other sitting member of the riding, Judge Louis Foucher, calling on the voters to rally behind Coffin and castigating Hart for his pretensions, inexperience and Jewishness. Only Ezekiel's brother Benjamin, the most eloquent of Aaron's children, rose to defend his brother.

Nonetheless, there was much goodwill towards the Hart family in the community and, as a result, Ezekiel won a swift but decisive victory — perhaps too swift. He refused to sign the election papers following the election as it was still the Sabbath. As he told the electors: "I cannot do work on the Sabbath day; wait at least for the setting sun." When officials begged him to sign in order to validate his victory, he did so, but only after striking out the words "In the year of our Lord 1807" and simply signing "Ezekiel Hart, 1807" at the bottom. Thus Ezekiel became the first — and only — Jew elected to the legislative assembly of either Upper or Lower Canada.

There was no doubt in Hart's mind that despite his Jewishness he was entitled to the seat. Indeed the chief justice of the province, James Reid, reassured Hart that questions of his eligibility were "wholly groundless" as the restrictions on Jews in Great Britain "do not extend to this Province." "Your right to be elected," he added, "and to sit as a Member of the House, I consider to be equal to that of any other member in it."

Armed with Reid's letter, as well as a legal opinion from the attorney-general of England reassuring him that as far as the Crown was concerned there was no legal objection to the eligibility of a Jew to be elected and to sit in the Assembly as long as he swore the "usual oaths," Hart arrived in Quebec on April 16 and immediately took his seat. Coincidentally, on that same day, the Assembly was dissolved. When the House met again on January 29, 1808, a member asked if Hart had taken "the Oaths in the customary manner."

Upper: Legislative assembly, Quebec.

Lower left: Believed to be Mrs. Ezekiel Hart.

Lower right: Ezekiel Hart (1770-1843).

Letter from Ezekiel Hart to James Phillips and Sons regarding the opposition to Hart's seat in the House, 1808.

When the members were informed that Hart had taken the oath on the Pentateuch, the Old Testament, with his head covered, the House adjourned in disarray.

On the next day a resolution was introduced by the province's attorney-general, Jonathan Sewell, that Hart not be allowed to take his seat since he had "not taken the oath in the customary manner." After two days a petition on behalf of the defeated candidate for Three Rivers, Thomas Coffin, was presented to the House stating that since as a Jew Hart could neither sit in the House nor take the appropriate oaths, Coffin should replace him as the member for Three Rivers.

On February 12, Hart presented his own petition claiming that he had indeed taken the appropriate oaths, but that if there were any objections, he would swear the oath "in the usual form." The House did not give him that opportunity. By a vote of 21 to 5 Hart was barred from the Assembly on the grounds that anyone "professing the Jewish religion cannot take a seat nor sit nor vote in the House." Thus for the remainder of the session the duly elected member from Three Rivers was unable to represent his constituents.

In April of 1808, the newly appointed governor of Lower Canada, James Craig, dissolved the House. On May 17, Hart was re-elected by the voters of Three Rivers. To ensure that he could enter the House, Hart this time took the oath on the New Testament with his head uncovered. The stratagem did not work. A resolution was introduced in the House stating that a Jew who swore "on the Holy Evangels which could not bind him...did thereby profane [the Christian religion]." There was much debate on the oaths question until finally the Assembly voted 18 to 8 that anyone "professing the Jewish religion...cannot sit nor vote in this House."

On May 8, 1809, Hart was informed that his seat was officially vacated. A week later Craig, angry at the House for a variety of reasons, dissolved it and asked London for advice on the status of Hart. Almost a year later the British government informed him that "a real Jew could not sit in the Assembly as he could not take an oath upon the Gospels."

What does the Hart case tell us about the role of the Jew in Canadian society in the early 1800s? There are those historians who argue that Hart's religion was not the issue; the fact that he supported the English was. Yet his election was opposed by both English and French members. It is also true, however, that his constituents — mostly French Canadian — elected him twice, though they knew that he was a Jew. Ultimately a variety of factors coalesced to ensure his defeat. Hart was caught in the middle of a conflict between the executive and the legislature and between English merchants and French-Canadian farmers for political power. Combine this unfortunate situation with the anti-semitism of the period, and Hart's election was likely doomed from the start.

Despite the efforts of the founding fathers of Canadian Jews, the Jew still had not achieved full political rights in Canada. Such entitlement would have to wait another generation.

It is possible to romanticize and exaggerate the achievements of the earliest Jewish settlers in Canada, but it is not possible to ignore them, as previous generations of historians have done. Because the Jews were so few in number, their accomplishments have scarcely been recorded. A colourful, intrepid group, the Harts, Jacobses, Solomonses, Abrahamses and others arrived in Canada to find a teetering, bankrupt feudal society. Within a generation they had helped revivify it. They provided goods other Canadian settlers needed, created new trade patterns and relationships, helped raise the standard of living and, thereby, helped attract new immigrants. They did not do this by themselves, of course — rather they acted in alliance with the far more numerous English merchant class — but they played a key role in building and extending the commercial empire of the St. Lawrence, and helped lead the struggle for equality and political rights more than two centuries ago.

Public Act . VIII. And be it further enacted by the authority aforesaid, that this Act shall be taken and deemed to be a public Act, and as such shall be judicially taken notice of by all Judges, Justices of the Peace, and all others whom it shall concern without being specially pleaded.

CA P. LVII.

An Act to declare persons professing the Jewish Religion intitled to all the rights and privileges of the other subjects of His Majesty in this Province.

> 31st March, 1831 —Presented for His Majesty's Assent and reserved "for the ' signification of His Majesty's pleasure thereon."
> 12th April, 1832,—Assented to by His Majesty in His Council.
> 5th June, 1832,—The Royal Assent signified by the proclamation of His Excellency the Governor in Chief.

Preamble. WHEREAS doubts have arisen whether persons professing the Jewish Religion are by law entitled to many of the privileges enjoyed by the other subjects of His Majesty within this Province: Be it therefore declared and enacted by the King's Most Excellent Majesty, by and with the advice and consent of the Legislative Council and Assembly of the Province of Lower Canada, constituted and assembled by virtue of and under the authority of an Act passed in the Parliament of Great Britain, intituled, " An Act to repeal certain parts of an Act passed in " the fourteenth year of His Majesty's Reign, intituled, "*An Act for making* " *more effectual provision for the Government of the Province of Quebec, in North* " *America,*" and to make further provision for the Government of the said " Province of Quebec in North America." And it is hereby declared and enacted by the authority aforesaid, that all persons professing the Jewish Religion *Persons pro-fessing the Jewish Reli-gion to be en-titled to all the civil rights of British Subjects.* being natural born British subjects inhabiting and residing in this Province, are entitled and shall be deemed, adjudged and taken to be entitled to the full rights and privileges of the other subjects of His Majesty, his Heirs or Successors, to all intents, constructions and purposes whatsoever. and capable of taking, having or enjoying any office or place of trust whatsoever, within this Province.

CHAPTER TWO

THE STRUGGLE FOR EQUALITY
1810 - 1840

Moses David, the son of Lazarus David of Montreal, was one of the first Jewish children born in Canada. Striking out on his own while still in his early twenties, he had made his way to the largely unexplored but fur-rich areas around Fort Michilimackinac and Detroit to trade with the Indians. When the British ceded Detroit to the Americans in the early 1790s, the intensely loyal David moved across the river and applied for a grant of land in Sandwich, Upper Canada — now Windsor.

It was no easy matter for a practising Jew to become a resident in Upper Canada. No one had ever done it before. Earlier, when Levy Solomon, another Montreal Jew, had applied for land around Cornwall, the chief justice of the province had informed the governor that it was his opinion that "Jews cannot hold land in this province." Those who had converted, however, did not face the same obstacles. Samuel Jacobs' son, John, had received a land grant in the Niagara area — but he was a Catholic. Similarly, John Lawe, the Anglican son of a Jewish mother, had been given land around Niagara.

But Moses David was a real problem for the authorities. How could they reject him? He was, after all, well known in the area and

Left: The 1831 Bill of Rights, which granted Jews equality under the law in Lower Canada, as presented for approval to His Majesty William IV, King of England.

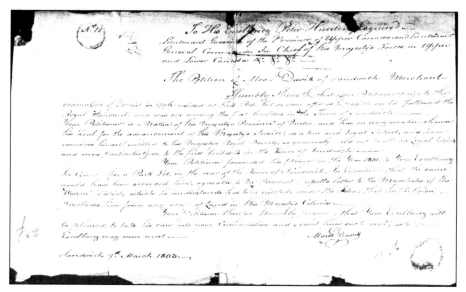

David David (upper left) and his brother Samuel (lower left).

Upper right: Moses David's land request, March 9, 1803.

had served loyally in the militia. Nevertheless, for several years, while others in his regiment were being granted land, nothing was available for David. Again and again he wrote to the Executive Council complaining of the delay in processing his application. Finally, in 1803, some six years after his first request, the council reversed the chief justice's decision. David received his land and was permitted to become a permanent settler. Jews, it appeared, were now allowed to settle in Upper Canada.

No great surge of Jewish settlers followed David's success, but a few did come. Though most historians are convinced that there were no permanent Jewish inhabitants in Upper Canada before the 1830s, there is now strong evidence, largely uncovered through the research of Sheldon and Judy Godfrey, that some of the traders and suppliers who travelled through the province did on occasion take up residence. Certainly we know of Jews in Sandwich, York, Kingston, Uxbridge and in the Niagara–Hamilton area. There even appears to have been a village aptly named Jewsburg, founded by German Jew Samuel Liebshitz, a miller who had settled in the area around today's Preston. Likely there were other Jews in Upper Canada about whom we know nothing. Most intermarried, converted and integrated into the Christian community, leaving little trace of their Jewish heritage.

There is no greater proof of the Jews' commitment to their new land than the War of 1812. While it seems that many inhabitants in both Upper and Lower Canada were quite indifferent to the American invasion, the tiny Jewish community responded to the crisis with total unanimity, even though many had originally settled in the Thirteen Colonies. Though complete statistics are not available, it appears that almost all of the Jewish men eligible for military duty volunteered to fight for the British. A glance at the list of officers in the Canadian militia reveals such names as Hart, Franks, Joseph, Michaels, David and others. David David, Moses' brother, commanded a regiment on the American border, and Jacob Franks was key to the British efforts at Fort Michilimackinac. Ezekiel Hart, having overcome his grievance against the Assembly, began the war as a lieutenant and ended it as a captain.

However, not all Jews were allowed to serve. Ezekiel's younger brother Benjamin applied for a commission in the militia, but was rejected by the commanding officer of his district, who told the governor that "Christian soldiers would not tolerate a Jew in their midst." Benjamin was so determined to fight that he joined the infantry as a private and saw action against the American army moving on Montreal. As well, at his own expense — and at the request of the governor — he equipped and paid for volunteers to defend Fort William Henry on the Richelieu River. The feisty Hart eventually got into the militia — as a lieutenant — but not until 1820, and after he had moved to Montreal.

Despite the rebuff to Hart — probably caused by the local commanding officer's personal animus against the Hart family — it is clear that there were few restrictions against Jews holding military office, which they still could not do in the Mother Country. English Jews were astonished to get letters from their relatives signed "Captain" or "Lieutenant." But the Jew of Canada had long-standing links with the

Benjamin Hart, son of Aaron Hart.

army. Many of the original Jewish settlers in Canada had arrived with British forces; army life was not unfamiliar to their children, many of whom were used to the rigours of frontier life. Most had had military training, had spent months in the bush and were skilled in weaponry.

The retreat of the Americans from Canada and the signing of a peace treaty in 1815 were celebrated by Canada's Jews. They had proven their loyalty and their fighting mettle. Small in number though the Jewish community was, no community had given more of itself. Yet no community felt more aggrieved after the war. Despite their efforts, no official recognition was given to their religion. Canadian Jews were in a legal limbo. Because births, marriages and deaths could only be registered in an Anglican church—the rights of the Catholic church had been protected by the Quebec Act and other statutes—Jews were being born, getting married and dying without an official record. As far as the state was concerned, no Jews had been born or had died since 1759. In the matter of wills and inheritances, Jews faced a serious legal encumbrance: if they could not die, then how could their children—who were not "legally" born—inherit their property?

Jews were not alone in this legal limbo. It was shared by members of the Church of Scotland, as well as by Methodists, Wesleyans, Quakers and others. Like the Jews, their numbers were small and they could do little against the enforced monopoly of the Church of England. But the French Canadians could. They, too, lived under the thumb of Anglicanism and did not like it one bit. Though they were guaranteed their own religion, culture and way of life, they were anxious to strike a blow against the English and to undermine the monopoly of the church. The French members of the Lower Canada Assembly, straining at the bit, angry at the powers exerted by the English governor and his appointed council, awaited only the right moment and cause.

The latter was unwittingly provided by Benjamin Hart. For some time, he had been trying to revivify the old Shearith Israel

Synagogue, which had fallen into disrepair. Indeed, Hart was providing his own home as a temporary place of worship until a new synagogue could be built. A committed Jew, Hart published a "manifesto" calling upon all of Montreal's Jews — about fifty men and women — to join together to underwrite the new building. It was a Jew's duty, he admonished, "to worship, to perpetuate being Jewish and to bring up Jewish children" — none of which was possible without a proper place of worship.

The problem for the community was that the old synagogue and all of its artifacts and holy books were in the hands of the executors of the David family, who had originally provided the land. The lack of official records for Jews was making it difficult to extricate the synagogue from the estate. Litigation had achieved little. What was needed was new and fairer legislation. In December of 1828, Hart and his Jewish friends petitioned the Assembly to change the law. They asked that their religion be officially recognized, that the community be allowed to administer its affairs and that it be given the right to keep an official register of births, marriages and deaths.

The Assembly, dominated by French Canadians, was only too happy to respond. It had already, a year earlier, regularized the position of the Church of Scotland. It seemed that anything that would weaken the Anglican establishment was acceptable to them. They dealt with Hart's petition with exceptional alacrity. Within a few months of receiving it, they passed a bill giving the Jewish community everything it had asked for. Two years later the bill received royal assent and by the end of 1831 Canadian Jewry had at last achieved legal recognition. They could now legally be born, get married and die, and they could finally build their synagogue. But they could still not sit in the Assembly or accept appointments that required swearing the official oath to serve "in the true faith of a Christian." Since almost all positions required the oath — though for some it had been waived or ignored in the past — no Jew could accept any public office. Having won the battle for religious rights, the

Samuel Hart's petition to the House of Assembly of Lower Canada, January 31, 1831, stating that "all persons professing the Jewish Religion are excluded from office in a manner very public and mortifying."

Lord Aylmer.

Jewish community now girded itself for the equally serious struggle for political rights. Once again, a Hart led the fight.

Samuel Bécancour Hart was the eldest son of Ezekiel, and Benjamin's nephew. Who more appropriate to challenge the law that disqualified Jews than the son of the only man in Canadian history to have lost his seat in the legislature because he was Jewish?

The campaign began innocently enough. On July 23, 1830, the new governor of Lower Canada, Lord Aylmer, clearly not cognizant of the ways of the province, offered Hart the position of magistrate and justice of the peace for Montreal. In Aylmer's mind, it was a well-deserved honour. He saw it as a belated recognition for Hart's efforts in the War of 1812, during which he had distinguished himself on the field of battle at Lundy's Lane, a particularly bloody skirmish. As well the new Seigneur of Bécancour was a highly successful businessman and a lieutenant in the militia.

Only after he had approached Hart did Aylmer consult his attorney-general. His chief legal officer's response was chilling: "[As] a Jew…cannot take the oaths that are required by a Justice of the Peace…[Hart] cannot therefore be appointed to that office." This opinion was supported by Aylmer's Executive Council, which consisted almost entirely of English Canadians.

Unfortunately for the government, it was too late. While they were still discussing the legitimacy of the selection, Hart's acceptance arrived. Aylmer could do little but inform him that his name was being removed from the list of appointments because he was a Jew. The fiery Hart was beside himself. The province had already humiliated his father; it was not going to humiliate him.

He immediately addressed a petition, through Aylmer, to William IV, complaining bitterly that Jews in Canada were "excluded from office in a manner very public and mortifying." He added that he "could not bear [this] in silence without forfeiting every claim to his own esteem and to the good opinion of his fellow subjects." This was an age, he reminded the king, "of liberality and universal tolerance."

The activities and behaviour of the king's officials, he charged, were "illegal" and he pleaded for relief for both himself and his fellow Jewish subjects.

At the same time, some of Hart's "fellow Jewish subjects" sent a personal appeal to the legislature protesting the iniquitous laws that prevented Jews from holding public office. Their petition was presented to the Assembly by John Neilson, owner of the *Quebec Gazette* and a leader of the reform element among the English-Canadian members. At the same time, Denis Viger, an activist in the French party, submitted this petition to the legislative council, along with Hart's address to the king.

Viger's role is significant. In 1809, he had joined the majority of French-Canadian members in voting to expel Ezekiel Hart. Now, it seemed, he had changed his mind. More important, he was closely allied with — indeed, he was related to — the outstanding French-Canadian leader of the time, Louis-Joseph Papineau, who had also voted against Hart in 1809. As speaker of the Assembly, Papineau commanded much influence and could always count on his French-Canadian colleagues to throw their votes behind any bill he favoured. Thus Papineau's support was absolutely crucial.

The bill guaranteeing Jews their political rights moved quickly through the Assembly. It was introduced on March 16, 1831 by Neilson, and passed through all readings of the House by March 31. On June 5, 1832 it was given royal assent and proclaimed the law of the land.

Though the bill did not entirely resolve the question of the extent to which Canadian Jews were free to partake fully in Canadian society — that would come later — it was nonetheless a landmark in the quest for political equality. The title of the bill was "An Act to declare persons professing the Jewish Religion intitled to all the rights and privileges of the other subjects of His Majesty in this Province." Despite the grand title, the bill was not, as some have described it, "the Magna Carta of Canadian Jewry," although it certainly went a long way to resolve the grievances of Canada's one hundred or so Jews. With the possible exception of Jamaica, Canada became the first colony in the British Empire to emancipate its Jews — a step Britain would not take for another twenty-five years. Indeed, at almost precisely the moment the Lower Canada legislature was voting to give Canadian Jews full political rights, the Parliament in England was defeating a bill to give British Jews those very same rights.

The act was almost revolutionary in its implications, a milestone in the battle for civil rights. However, with the exception of the handful of Jews, no one at the time took much notice of it. Perhaps most knowledgeable Canadians sensed that the battle was not yet won.

They were right. Shortly after the passage of the bill, Samuel Hart was again invited to become a magistrate, as were two other prominent Montreal Jews, his uncle Benjamin Hart, and the past president of the Montreal synagogue, Moses Judah Hays.

But those opposed to granting equal rights to Jews — and there were clearly some in the highest circles of the government — were not prepared to give up their cause without a fight. The attorney-general of the province warned Benjamin Hart and Hays to save themselves embarrassment by declining the offer, since they could not swear the appropriate oath. Similarly, the clerk of the courts in Three Rivers let it be known that he would only administer the oath of office to Samuel Hart if he swore "on the true faith of a Christian." Thus it seemed that they were still barred from holding public office.

The two Harts chose different tactics to overcome the traditional obstacle of the oath. The Three Rivers Hart chose defiance; the Montreal Hart, compliance. After consulting his son Aaron Philip Hart, a freshly minted lawyer, Benjamin Hart, along with Hays, declined the appointment. It was the young Hart's legal opinion that despite the new legislation, Jews could still not swear the oath. Benjamin then petitioned the government, once and for all, to deal with the prickly problem of the oath, and urged his nephew to do the same.

Samuel Hart would not hear of it. He had once before been forced to give up his nomination; he would not be forced to do so a second time. A different strategy was called for. He canvassed all the commissioners of oaths in Three Rivers until he found one who would administer the oath without appending "the disagreeable phrase." A local French-Canadian commissioner, an old friend of the Hart family, readily agreed, and in October of 1833 Samuel B. Hart took his place as a magistrate for Three Rivers. It appeared that a Jew could take public office in one part of the province, but not in another. Clearly the matter had to be dealt with again by the Assembly — or by the government in England.

In response to Lord Aylmer's plea for help, the Colonial Office in London replied that the problem was a matter for the Lower Canada legislature. Immediately the Assembly appointed a special commission under a well-known friend of the Jews, Dr. René Kimber — whose son-in-law was of Jewish origin — to report on the legal ramifications of the oath problem.

The Assembly, which thought it had already dealt with the issue, was now determined to expedite matters with as much speed and finality as was legally possible. After a few meetings, the Kimber Commission reported to the House that it saw no problem with the law giving Jews full political freedom. As far as it was concerned, Jews need not swear "on the true faith of a Christian." Any personal oath was acceptable. As the commission stated, had Benjamin Hart and Moses Hays not "put their own interpretation on the statute," they would likely "now be serving as magistrates in Montreal." From the point of view of the Assembly, the matter was definitely concluded.

It remained only to deal with Benjamin Hart and Moses Hays. For some reason they decided not to take up their appointments as magistrates until London approved. On August 5, 1837, Queen Victoria herself put her signature on a document appointing Hart and Hays to the magistracy. It had taken four years since their initial nomination, but they could finally take their seats on the

Louis-Joseph Papineau.

bench. At long last, the Jew in British North America was fully emancipated.

For many years, historians have debated as to how it was possible to pass such a progressive piece of legislation in Canada. Few Canadians were concerned about the political disabilities of a group numbering well under a hundred men. (Jewish women, like all Canadian women at the time, had no political rights at all.) Why were the bills passed so quickly and with so little dissent?

Some historians argue that the legislation was a reflection of the times. The 1830s were a decade of reform throughout the western world. Jacksonian democracy was sweeping through America, and it probably had some impact north of the border. In Europe, liberalism and revolution seemed to be the order of the day. Thus to some, the bills emancipating the Jews, along with the Rebellions of 1837, were simply Canada's response to the new ideas circulating throughout Europe and North America.

Others see the legislation as part of the ongoing struggle between the French and the English for political power in Quebec. According to this interpretation, the French party was using the Jewish issue to undermine the English. Any measures that would lessen the power of the Anglican church and tweak the noses of the haughty English-dominated Executive Council were welcome. If the rights of minorities such as Jews were advanced, then so much the better. Some historians make the case that the Catholic church supported the struggle of the Jews for religious liberty because they believed any gain made by the Jews was a gain for the Catholics as well.

The support of Papineau was most important for the passage of these laws. It seems clear that without him there would have been no legislation. He was the most charismatic French-Canadian leader of the nineteenth century — and the most egalitarian. Though he had voted against Hart in 1809, by the 1820s he had totally recanted. Promoting the rights of minorities became his passion. As he said in a speech in 1827: "Diversity of religious opinion which creates no re-

sistance to the laws ought not to be submitted to the oppression of laws enacted merely to prohibit and punish it; [and] that the same freedom…which I claim for myself, for my countrymen…I allow to those whose belief is different." No one else spoke with such eloquence on this issue; indeed, few in Quebec over the next century would speak with such conviction.

Championed by Papineau, the Jewish cause was guaranteed success. While some English Canadians in Lower Canada — especially those concerned with the prerogatives of their church — were discomfited, the issue was not serious enough for them to oppose the French-Canadian majority in the Assembly. There were far more serious matters just over the horizon.

Thus the struggle of the two Harts — Benjamin for his synagogue and Samuel for his appointment to the bench — came at precisely the right moment for Canadian Jewry. A decade or two later, when there was no Papineau to speak out, the bills might not have been passed. Indeed, there is little doubt that they would not have been approved by any Quebec legislature for the next century. Ironically,

Left: The Hart family, *c.* 1880.

Upper right: The diary of Bernard Samuel Judah, the son of Samuel Judah and husband of Aaron Hart's daughter, Catherine. He wrote this diary during a trip to Vincennes in 1827.

Lower right: Phoebe David Hart, wife of Aaron Ezekiel Hart.

⁕BIRTHS.⁕

NAME OF PARENTS.	NAME OF CHILD.	DATE OF BIRTH.	WHERE BORN.

A page (beginning in 1903) from a record of the Hart family births, as recorded by Alan Judah Hart.

despite this great political victory, no Jew would sit in the Quebec Assembly for the next eighty-five years, though in the 1840s Henry Judah, Dr. Kimber's son-in-law and a converted Jew, took over his father-in-law's seat.

Only weeks after the appointment of Hart and Hays, there was rebellion in Lower Canada. The grievances of the French could no longer be contained; for years they had been battling increasingly autocratic rule by the British-appointed governor and his Executive Council. The Assembly, which the far more numerous French Canadians controlled, had little influence over the governor. And the more impotent it became, the more militant became its French-Canadian members. Eventually rebellion broke out as some of the more radical *Patriotes* took up arms against the government.

The Jews were caught in the middle. They admired Papineau, the leader of the rebellion, and were appreciative of the French support of their cause. On the other hand, they were Anglophones and intensely loyal to the Crown. They shared the *Patriotes'* demand for reform, but none supported rebellion. The Three Rivers Harts, especially Ezekiel, were close to Papineau and his colleagues; indeed Papineau even dined at his home just before the outbreak of violence. But though some Jews supported the rebels, none fought with them — with one singular exception. Levi Koopman, an enigmatic Jew who had taken on the name Louis Marchand, perhaps to signal his separation from the Jewish community, joined in the attack on the British troops. He would later be a leader of the intensely Catholic St-Jean-Baptiste Society in Montreal.

Even though the rebellion in Lower Canada was not entirely a French-English conflict — there were members of both communities on either side — when the call for troops was issued, Jews responded enthusiastically. Dozens volunteered. The list of those fighting for the government included a number of Jews with ranks such as captain, lieutenant and major, and Jews were present at most of the major battles of the uprising.

34

Those who could not fight also played a role. As a magistrate, Benjamin Hart spent much of the rebellion issuing warrants for the arrest of the rebels, giving patriotic speeches to the troops, reading the riot act whenever and wherever he felt necessary, and even on occasion arresting rebels himself. Ironically his son, Aaron Philip Hart, who served bravely in the militia, was the lawyer for some of the rebels following the rebellion. There is little doubt that the senior Hart's activities enraged the rebels. So infuriated were they that a secret group of *Patriotes* calling themselves *Les Chasseurs* even conceived a plan to murder him. "All the Jews," their circular stated, "with Benjamin Hart at their head are to be strangled and their properties confiscated." There is no way of knowing how serious this threat was, or even how many members the organization had. Certainly there is no evidence that the leading *Patriotes* were aware of this group or of its plans. But the Montreal newspapers uncovered this bizarre scheme and published a report of it. When Benjamin Hart became aware of their threats, he simply redoubled his efforts on behalf of the Crown. After the rebellion was over, he vainly petitioned the British government to grant him a knighthood for his activities.

As the decade closed, the enemies of the Jews — and there were not many in Canada at this period — had no choice but to accept defeat. The Jew had been accepted as a citizen, and his political and religious rights were fully protected. This had been done with a unanimity rare in the Lower Canada Assembly. Scarcely a voice had spoken out against the legislation.

The proclamation of religious and political freedoms was not simply a victory for the Jews. It was a victory for future generations of Canadians and helped build the foundation of this country's religious and political freedoms. Upon it would be constructed a whole series of acts, judgments and amendments guaranteeing full liberty to every Canadian. And all because Benjamin Hart wanted to build a synagogue and Samuel Hart wished to become a justice of the peace.

Aaron Hart's niece Lalla Hart (left) in front of the Hart family home in Three Rivers, with two of Aaron Hart's grandchildren.

Three Rivers, L. Canada 18

HART'S BANK.

On demand for value received I
Promise to pay ONE DOLLAR to the order
of

Three Rivers L. Canada 18

HART'S BANK.

On demand for value received I
Promise to pay THREE DOLLARS to the Order
of

Three Rivers L. Canada 18

HART'S BANK.

On demand for value received I
Promise to Pay FIVE DOLLARS to the Order
of

CHAPTER THREE

THE GOLDEN AGE

1840 - 1860

If there was a golden age of Canadian Jewry, one could make a strong case for the period before Confederation, particularly the 1830s and 1840s. An era largely free of the anti-semitism and nativism that would mark this country for the next century, these years were a period in which there were countless opportunities and a few obstacles for Canadian Jews and a time when restrictions and quotas were unknown to them.

Though small in number — by 1841 there were about two hundred people — Canadian Jews were playing a prominent role in their society. There were Jewish doctors, lawyers, military officers and even bank presidents. In 1835 Moses Hart founded the Hart's Bank, which issued its own currency. David David was a founding partner of the Bank of Montreal and served on its board of directors for years — the last Jew to do so for more than a century.

If there was a family, aside from the Harts, that embodied the status of Canada's Jews in the mid-nineteenth century, it was the Josephs. Not surprisingly — almost everyone in the community was interrelated — they were relatives of the Harts. The first of this family to arrive in Canada, Henry Joseph, was Aaron Hart's nephew. He

Left: Bank notes issued by the Hart's Bank, founded by Moses Hart in Three Rivers, 1835.

Right: Rachel Solomon, Henry Joseph's wife.

Upper: Henry Joseph (1775-1832).
Lower: Henry Joseph's house in Berthier, Quebec.

arrived from England some years after his uncle and set up shop as a fur trader and provisioner in Berthier, near Montreal. He soon was the proprietor of one of the largest chains of trading posts in the colony. He was adventurous, especially in business, and was well ahead of most of his competitors in providing goods and services. Indeed, he earned the description "father of Canada's merchant marine" for being the first businessman to charter ships directly between Canada and England, and for conducting an extensive shipping trade in the St. Lawrence and the Great Lakes. One Joseph trade expedition into Lake Huron reportedly numbered over a hundred boats.

Though he was successful in business, Joseph's major concern was to retain his religion while so many around him were losing theirs. It was a difficult task. Like all pioneer societies, Canada had far more single men than women — especially Jewish women. And since few were prepared to travel back across the Atlantic to marry, as did Aaron Hart, most took French-Canadian or native women as their wives. Joseph was fortunate; he married the daughter of Levy Solomon of Montreal. Even so, maintaining a Jewish way of life was a struggle for the Josephs.

They lived in a small town isolated from other Jews. There was no synagogue, no rabbi, no kosher food, no Jewish friends or relatives to visit — indeed, there was nothing Jewish for miles. Still, they did everything possible to bring up their children as Jews. Joseph taught himself the laws of ritual slaughter, so that the family could eat kosher food. He worked out a calendar, so that he and his children would be aware of Jewish holidays. Both he and his wife spent a good deal of time teaching their children everything they knew about Judaism. Their efforts were rewarded; most of their children married into the faith, one daughter to a rabbi.

Onerous as it was, it was nonetheless possible, as the Joseph family showed, for Canadian Jews to remain Jewish. It was far less difficult for the next generation to play a full role in their society. One Joseph son, Abraham, helped found the Banque Nationale and was president of the Stadacona Bank. Another son, Jacob Henry, was a founding partner of the Union Bank and the Bank of British North America; as well, he helped create Canada's first telegraph company and was a partner in the Newfoundland Telegraph Company, which participated in laying the first transatlantic cable. His brother Jesse headed the Montreal Gas Company and the city's Street Railway Company and — along with Jacob — was a prime mover in establishing the colony's first railroad company, the St. Lawrence and Champlain. Finally, the youngest son, Gershom, was the first Jew admitted to Upper Canada College and the country's first Jewish Queen's Counsel.

Though the Josephs were truly exceptional in their achievements, they were not alone. The Harts, the Hayses and, to a lesser extent, the Davids and others also clung to their religion while making their imprint on their new land. Being Jewish was no hindrance to career success, nor was it an obstacle to entering the upper ranks of Canadian society. As the diaries and social columns of the period make clear, many of Quebec's Jews were unusually active socialites. They attended a vast array of balls, musical evenings and plays. When the Duke of Kent, the father of Queen Victoria, visited Canada, he was entertained by Aaron Hart. Indeed an invitation to a Hart — any Hart — or Joseph soirée was highly coveted. Mrs. Henry Joseph once hosted a party in her home for over two hundred guests, including the Governor General and his family. The records of the period indicate that the Jewish families in Montreal and Three Rivers entertained regularly — and in turn were entertained by government officials and the colony's English merchant princes. Jews belonged to all the best clubs and were also active in the Masons; they sat on the boards of charitable institutions and were deeply involved in philanthropy.

Nor did being Jewish restrict one's ability to hold office. In 1849, for example, two of the key positions in Montreal were held by Jews; Moses Judah Hays was chief commissioner of police and Samuel Benjamin was an alderman. Abraham Joseph sat on the Quebec city

The Joseph brothers: (clockwise from upper left) Jacob Henry, Abraham, Jesse, Gershom.

Left: Hannah Hyman, the daughter of a Russian immigrant, William Hyman, and his wife Amelia Hart. William Hyman was the mayor of Cap-des-Rosiers, Quebec, for most of his life, as well as the proprietor of a chain of stores along the Gaspé coast. The company, William Hyman and Sons, operated for 123 years, before the last store closed in 1967.

Right: Montreal, 1830.

council. William Hyman was elected mayor of the completely French town of Cap-des-Rosiers in the Gaspé in 1858, a position he would hold until his death thirty years later. His sons would later serve as mayors of nearby villages. Aaron Hart David was dean of medicine at Bishop's College, attending physician at the Montreal General Hospital and secretary to the Central Board of Health of Canada in the 1840s. He served indefatigably during the horrific cholera epidemics of that decade.

It was during this period that the first Jewish charitable society was organized, the Hebrew Philanthropic Society. Its purpose was to provide assistance to "deserving cases," most of whom were recent immigrants. Until the late 1840s, such an organization had been unnecessary as there was no evidence of any Jewish poor. The arrival of destitute Jewish immigrants, largely from Germany, was a new phenomenon that would become increasingly familiar over the next two generations. In 1849 the number of those Jews landing in Canada was still tiny, no more than thirty, but they needed help and the Jewish community mobilized to do what it could.

The man behind the first Jewish charity was Moses Judah Hays, magistrate, owner of the Montreal Water Works, founding stockholder of the Bank of Montreal and president of the synagogue. There was scarcely an aspect of Montreal civic life in which the dynamic Hays was not involved. For sixteen years he was chief of police. He was proprietor of one of the city's most popular hotels, and attached to it he built a theatre that played an unusual role in Canadian history: when rioters angry at the government for compensating victims of the 1837 Rebellion burned down the nearby Parliament building in April of 1849, the government simply moved into the Hays Theatre on Dalhousie Square and carried on as if nothing had happened. As a newspaper described it: "Functionaries set up their writing desks in the wings where…earlier Viennese dancers performed with the cellists of the German orchestra." If as police chief Hays could not stop the rioters, as a landlord—and a patriot—he could at least house the homeless legislators. His theatre was the Parliament of Canada until June of 1849—and Hays probably loved every minute of it.

Certainly there was much for Hays to do as police chief. Though crime was not yet a serious problem, cholera was. Hordes of Irish immigrants pushed aboard fetid British ships had brought the disease with them and it spread unimpeded throughout Montreal and Quebec City. Thousands died. Hays and his force did what they could to care for the victims and to quarantine the immigrants, but to little end. The epidemic took the life of Henry Joseph and one of his children, and claimed others in the community as well.

For the Montreal Jews the most important event of these years was the building of a new synagogue in 1838—planned, organized and supervised by Hays. For the tiny community it was a monumental effort requiring substantial funds and labour. Even Sir Moses Montefiore, the eminent British financier, contributed to the synagogue. Though almost the entire community was of Western and Eastern European background and therefore followed the

Upper: The Hays Hotel, Montreal.
Lower: Moses Judah Hays.

41

Left: Alexander Abraham de Sola.

Right: Hammered brass *hanukkiyah*, a ritual candelabra used during Hanukkah, brought to Quebec in 1882 by Annette Pinto when she married Montefiore Joseph, a descendant of one of Canada's earliest Jewish families.

Ashkenazi form of Judaism, the Shearith Israel Synagogue followed the Sephardi, or Southern European ritual — largely perhaps to mimic the great Spanish and Portuguese synagogues in New York and London. In any case, there was clearly a certain cachet to belonging to a Sephardi congregation. There must have been, since not one single member of the congregation was of Sephardi origin.

It appears that the first Sephardi to belong to the synagogue, perhaps even the first Sephardi to take up permanent residence in Canada, was its rabbi, the twenty-one-year-old Alexander Abraham de Sola, who took over the pulpit in 1847. Descended from a long line of rabbinical scholars on both sides of his family, de Sola was the spiritual leader of the community for the next thirty-five years. Born in London, he was English to the core, and often travelled back to the Mother Country for intellectual recharging. He married the youngest daughter of Henry Joseph and was immediately ushered into the elite circles of the Montreal social set.

No better choice of rabbi could have been made. The community was desperate for spiritual as well as intellectual leadership, and de Sola provided both. He became a leader in the non-Jewish scholarly community as well, authoring several books. He was a professor of Hebrew and rabbinical literature at McGill, and, when that university awarded him an honorary degree, he was perhaps the first Jew in any English-language country so honoured. With the completion of the

synagogue and the arrival of de Sola, the Montreal Jewish community had finally come of age.

At about this time another Jewish community was beginning to take shape some 350 miles to the west. By 1834 the newly named city of Toronto had a population of some nine thousand of whom one was a known Jew. There were likely others as well, but no record of them has survived. Arthur Wellington Hart, son of Benjamin and grandson of Aaron, had arrived in Toronto in 1832 to represent his family's business interests. Perhaps the city disappointed him, for by 1838 he was gone. But by then other Jews had taken up residence in Toronto and they formed the foundation of what would become Canada's largest Jewish community.

In 1835 two Montreal brothers came to Toronto to make their fortune. Goodman and Samuel Benjamin opened up a dry-goods business on King Street not far from Hart's office. They did so

King Street East, Toronto, 1856. Judah George Joseph's jewellery and optical business appears in the middle of the block, to the left of the Colonist building.

43

Jacob Maier Hirschfelder.

well that in 1837 they were given the contract to supply coats to the British troops involved in putting down the rebellion led by William Lyon Mackenzie. But they, too, found Toronto inadequate, and eventually returned to Montreal and played a prominent role in that city's Jewish community; in 1849 Samuel became Canada's first Jewish alderman.

Finally, in 1838, a Jew arrived who found Toronto perfectly acceptable; he became the city's first documented permanent Jewish resident. Judah George Joseph — no relation to the Montreal Josephs — had emigrated from his native England in 1820 and settled in Cincinnati. At the age of forty-two, for reasons that are unclear, Joseph moved his family first to Hamilton and then to Toronto, where he set up a jewellery and optical business on King Street. As an observant Jew, he would become the anchor of the nascent Toronto congregation.

He was soon joined by a number of other Jews who arrived mostly from England and Germany, where the situation for Jews was growing increasingly precarious. We don't know why they came to Toronto, since most Jewish immigrants were making their way into the inviting arms of the United States. But a tiny handful were landing in Montreal, and an even smaller number went on to Toronto.

During the 1840s, Toronto's population doubled. Industries were springing up and splendid opportunities awaited enterprising newcomers — especially those with money. In those ten years, however, fewer than thirty Jewish families moved to the city. Yet even this scanty group included a few remarkable figures.

From Germany came Samuel and Marcus Rossin, who established a profitable jewellery business — so profitable that in the 1850s they built the Rossin House, one of the country's largest and most sumptuous hotels, which accommodated the Prince of Wales on a royal visit to the city in 1860.

Two other German brothers who settled in Toronto were Abraham and Samuel Nordheimer. The former, a pianist from New

York, had been hired by Governor General Sir Charles Bagot to become the family's music teacher in Kingston. There the two brothers opened a music store, which they transferred to Toronto in 1844. They prospered and integrated thoroughly into Toronto society — too thoroughly, perhaps, as Samuel married into the Boulton family, members of the city's old Family Compact, and became an Anglican. He also acted as German consul in Toronto. Abraham remained Jewish and became one of the mainstays of the community until he returned to Germany in the 1860s.

Perhaps the strangest Jew to arrive in this period was Jacob Maier Hirschfelder, who taught Hebrew and Oriental Languages at the University of Toronto for forty-five years beginning in 1843. Although Jews were barred from teaching at the university, Hirschfelder had earlier — no one knows when or how — become an Anglican, which allowed him to join the faculty of King's College. He published extensively on the Bible, but had nothing to do with Toronto's tiny Jewish community. As historian Stephen Speisman points out, the professor "moved socially in the upper structure of Christian society."

Left: Judah George Joseph.

Middle: Lewis Samuel, one of the founders of the Toronto Hebrew Congregation, which later became the Holy Blossom Congregation.

Right: Abraham Nordheimer.

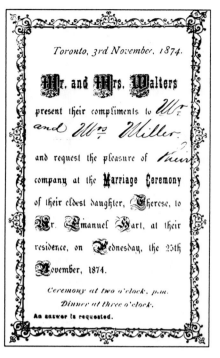

Wedding invitation, Toronto, 1874.

It was not until 1849 that Toronto Jewry committed its first act as a community. Spearheaded by Judah Joseph and Abraham Nordheimer, the city's Jews formed the Hebrew Congregation of Toronto, in order to purchase land for a cemetery in the eastern outskirts. This was the first legal recognition that there did indeed exist a Jewish community in Toronto; making the community a reality would take a few more years.

As Jewish immigrants continued to arrive throughout the 1850s — there were about seventy-five families in Toronto at the end of the decade — it became evident that a synagogue was necessary. Among the newcomers was a young Englishman, Lewis Samuel, who had previously lived in upper New York State and in Montreal. After the death of his two children from cholera in Montreal, Samuel and his wife decided to begin a new life in Toronto. They established a metal business on Yonge Street, which would eventually become one of Canada's largest.

Samuel was an observant Jew who could not live in a city without a synagogue. On his initiative, a group of community leaders decided to organize a congregation. Thus in June of 1856 the Toronto Hebrew Congregation was founded. To its members it was known as the Sons of Israel Synagogue, though some years later it took on the unique name it still bears, Holy Blossom.

Until the 1870s the congregation met on the third floor of a chemist's shop at Yonge and Richmond. By then it had reached a membership of 250 and these premises were inadequate. Again the energetic Lewis Samuel led a campaign, this time to put up a new building. Largely through the generosity of local Christians — who contributed more than a quarter of the funds — and of congregations in Montreal, New York and Boston, enough money was raised to complete a four-hundred-seat sanctuary on Richmond Street.

The official opening of the synagogue was a singular event in Toronto's history. Early on the morning of a cold, blustery January day in 1876, crowds of curious Torontonians watched a remarkable

Toronto Jan.ʸ 3ʳᵈ 1876.

The President and Executive of the Toronto Hebrew Congregation extend their cordial invitation to you and Ladies to witness The Dedication of the New Synagogue Richmond S.ᵗ East on Thursday January 20ᵗʰ next at one o'clock P.M.

The Consecration Sermon will be delivered by the Rev.ᵈ Professor A. De Sola L.L.D. of Montreal after which a Collection will be taken up in aid of the Building Fund.

Alexander Miller. Hon. Sec.ʸ

P.S.

Please present this invitation at the door.

procession take shape outside the chemist's shop at Yonge and Richmond. A parade led by several venerable men carrying the Torah, covered by a huge canopy on sticks held by several other men, headed eastward. Behind them was a long line of men and women walking to the new synagogue.

The newspapers of Orange Toronto gave the event front-page coverage. They praised the Jewish community for its loyalty and

Left: Invitation to the dedication of the Holy Blossom Synagogue on Richmond Street, 1876.

Upper: The opening of the new Holy Blossom Temple on Bond Street in 1897 was front-page news in Toronto.

Lower: The Holy Blossom Temple on Bond Street.

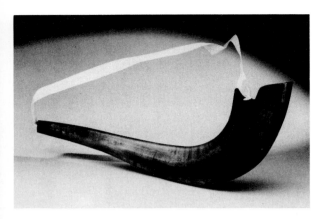

Upper: *Shofar*, or ram's horn, that is sounded on Rosh Hashanah and at the conclusion of Yom Kippur, brought from Romania to New Glasgow, Nova Scotia in the early 1900s.

Lower: Table used to prepare the body for burial, New Glasgow, *c.* 1912.

industry, and graphically described almost every detail of the exotic ceremony — the Hebrew prayers, the chanting of a choir of men and women, and the strange music provided by an organ, which had been rented for the occasion. If the ceremony was unfamiliar to a Christian audience, it was just as alien to Orthodox members of the audience, who did not know what to make of the organ or of women participating in the services. It appeared to the knowledgeable that the liberalized customs of the new Reform movement were making rapid headway among Holy Blossom members.

Toronto was not the only community in Upper Canada to play host to the advance guard of Jewish immigrants in the years before Confederation. By the 1850s, Lancaster, just west of the Quebec border on the St. Lawrence River, was a hub of activity. Neighbouring Indian lands had been opened up for white settlement and farmers, speculators and merchants were flooding in. Among them was a handful of Jewish families. In nearby Cornwall, several more Jewish families took up residence. By the 1860s, Hamilton was home to enough Jews to have its own synagogue, the Anshe Sholom. Jews could also be found in London, Windsor and smaller communities throughout the province.

One of these was George Benjamin of Montreal, who took up land in the eastern part of the province near Belleville. Liked and respected by his neighbours, over a period of twenty years Benjamin was elected to several municipal positions, culminating in 1857 in his election to the legislature as the member for North Hastings. He may have been the first Jew to sit in a Canadian assembly, although we can't be certain because at some time in his life he became a Christian; it is unclear whether this was before or after his election. For a short time in 1862, Benjamin even served in the cabinet of John A. Macdonald.

The 1850s and 1860s proved to be a favourable period for the renewal of Jewish life in the Atlantic provinces as well. Throughout the 1800s there had been a continuous Jewish presence in the

Saint John, New Brunswick,
c. 1829.

Atlantic provinces, but most of them were itinerant pedlars and
farmers in isolated areas who married into the Christian majority.
It was not until Confederation in 1867 that the Nova Scotia Jewish
community, which had begun with so much promise 115 years before
in Halifax only to wither away in a few decades, was rejuvenated
by the arrival of a handful of Jews. But it was in New Brunswick—
and especially in Saint John—that the Jewish presence was most
pronounced. In the 1850s, Solomon Hart and his brother-in-law

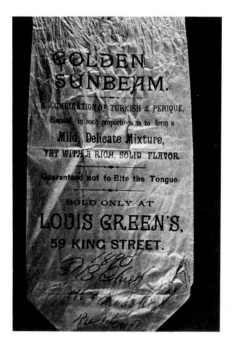

Left: Advertisement for Louis Green's tobacco store in Saint John.

Elizabeth Hart (middle) and Louis Green (right); theirs was the first Jewish wedding in Saint John, 1882.

Nathan Green moved their families up from the United States. The latter was the sole agent in Canada for the American Tobacco Company, and was so successful that within a few years of his arrival he was given the city's highest citizenship award. The fifteen members of this extended family struggled valiantly to preserve their Jewishness. There were scarcely any Jews for hundreds of miles — the closest Jewish communities were in Boston and Montreal. It was to the former that the Saint John Jews looked for succour and support. Their meat had to be imported from Boston, and when an outbreak of anthrax in the United States compelled authorities to bar American meat imports, the Jews became vegetarians.

In 1879, Saint John planned to hold the first Yom Kippur service in the Atlantic provinces. Jewish services require that ten men be present, but only nine could be found. Hart immediately began a search among all the hotels and inns in the city and its environs to see if any Jew was passing through the area. Luckily — the community thought it was an act of God — a young Jewish salesman on his way to Boston for the holiday was prevailed upon to remain in town and perform the coveted honour of being the "tenth man."

Outside of Saint John and Halifax there were hardly any Jews in the Atlantic provinces prior to the 1870s. There were none in Prince Edward Island, and it was not until the 1890s that the first Jews officially settled in the British colony of Newfoundland, although there are indications that Jews had been there for some time. Many believe that the colony's first postmaster in the early years of the century, Simon Solomon, was a Jew. There is also much evidence that in the early and middle decades of the nineteenth century Jews were heavily involved in the cod fisheries, and in the seal fur and coastal trading industries. A Mr. Levi, for example, was the premier seal trader in the 1830s in Carbonear.

The majority of Canada's Jews in the 1860s — about five hundred out of a total Jewish population of just over 1,100 — lived in Montreal. By 1870 they had built another synagogue. For some time a number had been unhappy with the Spanish and Portuguese Synagogue's Sephardi ritual. A group broke away in 1846 to found its own congregation of "English, German and Polish Jews." Without funds, resources or spiritual leaders, the congregation met in tiny rented quarters and made little headway for ten years. But the arrival of new immigrants provided it with the necessary base to expand. In 1859 a new building was put up on St. Constant Street (now de Bullion), which could seat approximately two hundred worshippers. Unfortunately, representatives of the Shearith Israel Synagogue refused to participate in the dedication of the new Shaar Hashomayim Congregation in July of 1859, despite repeated invitations and the efforts of a delegation that met with Rabbi de Sola. For years, relations between the two synagogues would be strained.

As Montreal Jews in the middle of the nineteenth century looked back at almost one hundred years of Jewish settlement in that city, they had much to be thankful for. The community was growing; its members could be found in almost every sector of the

Solomon and Alice Hart, founders of the Saint John Jewish community. After emigrating to New York from England, the family moved to Saint John, where they had 12 children, 6 of whom survived to adulthood.

Yom Kippur (the Day of Atonement) prayers at the Spanish and Portuguese Synagogue of Montreal, *c.* 1860.

economy and society; and its spirtual leader, Rabbi de Sola, had become one of the great thinkers and writers in North America, contributing scores of articles to leading journals. Jews were well represented on the city council, on its judiciary and in all its financial institutions. It was therefore in a celebratory, self-congratulatory and somewhat patronizing mood that Montreal's Jews gathered together on November 1, 1855, to commemorate the election of David Salomons as Lord Mayor of London, England.

52

For British Jewry, Salomons' election was a momentous event. After centuries of struggle, British Jews finally had achieved a degree of political freedom. Speaker after speaker at this festive occasion reminded his audience of how much more emancipated Canadian Jewry was. They praised themselves and the Canadian authorities for the huge strides made by the colony's Jewish community over the years.

Montreal Jewry, in particular, had every reason to be proud of its accomplishments and of its status. The celebration of November 1, 1855, would be unique in Canadian Jewish history. Rarely again would there be a gathering in which Canadian Jews came together simply to congratulate themselves and look forward to an unclouded future.

CHAPTER FOUR

PIONEERS ON THE PACIFIC

1 8 5 8 - 1 8 9 0

While Montreal Jewry was celebrating its status, some three thousand miles to the west another Jewish community was about to take shape. Indeed by 1858 Victoria would be home to British North America's second-largest Jewish community, hard on the heels of Montreal and, at least until the 1870s, well ahead of Toronto.

For years the Hudson's Bay Company had had a complete monopoly on trade and settlement on the Pacific coast. It maintained a small trading post in the sleepy village of Victoria on Vancouver Island and a larger one on the Columbia River on the mainland. In the late 1840s, bowing to threats of war from the Americans, the British ceded the Columbia River and everything between it and the forty-ninth parallel to the United States. Having lost most of its best land, the Hudson's Bay Company retreated to its base in Victoria to make the best of a sorry situation.

Anxious to preserve its control of the fur trade in the area, the company discouraged settlement over the next ten years. Except for a few Scottish miners brought in to work on some newly discovered coal deposits, almost no one came to the island. Then, late in 1857, word came from the mainland that an intrepid prospector had found

Left: Main Street, Barkerville, British Columbia, 1868. (British Columbia Archives and Records Service HP10110)

Right: Frank Sylvester. (British Columbia Archives and Records Service HP4173)

Victoria, B.C., *c.* 1861. (British Columbia Archives and Records Service HP25310)

some grains of gold in his pan while working on the Thompson River. This news was followed by that of another discovery in the nearby Fraser River.

The news electrified Victoria. Within a few months almost everyone who could made his way across the Straits of Georgia to try his luck. But Victoria would not remain empty for long. Once the news reached the rest of the world, thousands of fortune-seekers descended on the tiny village. By the middle of 1859, Victoria was a booming metropolis full of new stores, saloons and banks. Tens of thousands of prospectors and entrepreneurs arrived, bringing in their wake the usual camp-followers — prostitutes, barkeepers, gamblers and criminals. Most stayed only long enough to arrange transportation to the mainland, but some remained in Victoria.

Among the new arrivals were approximately one hundred Jews, most of whom were veterans of the California gold rush of the previous decade. Like the Jews who had accompanied the British into Quebec a hundred years before, Victoria's Jews were a colourful group — adventurous, courageous, entrepreneurial and aggressive. Most had emigrated from Germany and Central Europe, where the lot of Jews had grown precarious as a result of the failure of the revolutions of 1848. Several thousand — San Francisco alone had a thousand Jews in the 1850s — made their way over land or by sea around the treacherous waters at the bottom of South America to

California. There they formed one of the largest Jewish communities outside Europe.

Some were miners and prospectors who had come to make their fortunes like everyone else. Others were traders who supplied the miners from stores in almost every mining community in the state. It appears that most were successful and became leaders in their towns and camps. There they established synagogues, cemeteries and benevolent societies. As one American scholar described them: "The typical Jewish settler was a young man without opportunity in his homeland who had a compulsion to find a prosperous new life." They proved to any doubters that Jews were as capable as anyone else in settling and thriving in a region that had been a wilderness only a short time earlier.

When the news of the Fraser River gold find reached California, thousands headed north. San Francisco's docks were crowded with miners trying to book passage to Victoria. Many had failed to make their fortunes in California and were buoyed by the hope of striking it rich in British Columbia, while others had prospered in California but were drawn. by the allure of new opportunities. Many of the state's most useful citizens — too many, according to the press — left for the north. A newspaper in the small town of Jackson, for example, lamented the departure of the president of the town's synagogue: "Gone to Frazer [sic] — John Levinsky started for Frazer [sic] River yesterday morning. Mr. Levinsky...was one of our most prominent merchants and highly esteemed citizens. We wish him good health and abundant prosperity."

The first Jew on record to arrive in Victoria was twenty-one-year-old Frank Sylvester, aboard the S.S. *Pacific*, which docked on July 17, 1858, after a six-day voyage from San Francisco. But at least one Jew had been in British Columbia before him. Adolph Friedman, a Latvian, settled on Hudson's Bay Company land near today's Tacoma, Washington, in 1845. He was only nineteen when he arrived, and

The S.S. *Pacific*, the ship that brought miners and prospectors to British Columbia. (British Columbia Archives and Records Service HP14233)

he spent the rest of his life as a prosperous merchant supplying settlers, fishermen and miners across the border in British Columbia. Eventually he married a cousin whose family had emigrated to Victoria.

There is even some speculation — conjecture would perhaps be a more appropriate word — that Jews had been in British Columbia much earlier. Evidence, not very persuasive but, nonetheless, intriguing, exists that Jewish traders from China were among the first whites in North America. Some early travellers among the West Coast Indians noted similarities between their religious customs and those of the Jews. A Catholic missionary among the West Coast tribes excitedly "discovered" Hebrew words in every native dialect in the Pacific Northwest. Others at the time believed that North American Indians were themselves descendants of the Ten Lost Tribes of Israel.

As boat after boat followed the S.S. *Pacific* into Victoria, out of each emerged a Jew or two prepared to do whatever was necessary to succeed. Sylvester, for example, built a store on Victoria's main street, but could not survive the cut-throat competition, so he headed up the Fraser. After a series of harrowing misadventures in the Cariboo, he returned to Victoria empty-handed and within a short time became a successful provisioner and a mainstay of the young city.

By September of 1858 there were enough Jews in Victoria to hold high holiday services. Two years later land for a cemetery was bought and in 1863 a synagogue was built. But many of the new arrivals did not stay long. They fanned out into the mining camps and new towns along the Fraser and in the Cariboo. There they became miners or, more often, suppliers and provisioners. They were a truly remarkable group. The historian of British Columbia Jewry, Cyril Leonoff, writes: "They proved remarkably adaptable to the frontier...they did not hesitate to travel great distances over tortuous routes, endure appallingly primitive conditions, inhospitable climate and face physical dangers in pursuit of markets and profits. In a developing land of opportunity, the Jewish merchants were often successful where others less knowledgeable and motivated were quickly discouraged."

In 1861 this unique Jewish community attracted an equally unique visitor. Benjamin II (his real name was Joseph Israel Benjamin), a Romanian Jew, had devoted his life to searching for the Ten Lost Tribes. He adopted the name of Benjamin of Tudela, after the famous Jewish adventurer of the twelfth century, and began his travels. After publishing a book on his journeys through Asia and North Africa, he continued his search in the late 1850s in North America. Benjamin II was particularly taken with the Victoria Jewish community. He reported that though they had been there for only two years, they were "really responsible for the founding of the city of Victoria," since they alone of all the thousands of new arrivals "stood fast, pitched their tents and set up their booths for they…recognized that [Victoria] had a bright future commercially." Above all, as he wrote in his book *Three Years in America*, he was impressed with their commitment to their faith. He depicted movingly their efforts to create a benevolent society, to observe the holy days and to build a synagogue.

Victoria's Jewish cemetery, the oldest in western Canada.

Though Benjamin II's diaries provide a revealing portrait of the activities of the nascent Victoria Jewish community, they rather exaggerate the role of its members. Jews were not really responsible for the founding of Victoria — there were not enough of them. But they did represent a substantial proportion of the education, talent, initiative and business enterprise in the colony. Their experiences in California and their commercial connections to San Francisco stood them in good stead. They knew about mining, what the miners needed and where to get it.

Most representative of these British Columbia Jews was the Oppenheimer family. The five brothers, David, Charles, Meyer, Isaac and Godfrey, were born in Bavaria, emigrated to America in 1848 and settled in the 1850s in San Francisco, where they founded a successful mining supply business. As soon as they heard of the Fraser River gold

Left: David Oppenheimer (1832-1897).

Right: Cariboo Road, *c.* 1880.
(British Columbia Archives and Records Service HP4350)

strike, Charles was sent north to investigate. His reports must have been bullish, for within a year the entire Oppenheimer clan emigrated to British Columbia.

Charles opened up a trading firm in Victoria and at Point Roberts on the mainland. The family set up branches at Yale, the head of navigation on the Fraser, and in Fort Hope and Lytton in the interior. When gold was discovered in the Cariboo in 1862, the Oppenheimers opened up a trading post in Barkerville, named after the prospector who first struck it rich there. The town soon became the largest community in British North America west of Toronto, with the Oppenheimers' store its major commercial concern.

Access to the Cariboo was extremely difficult. With no roads or navigable rivers, the trek into the region was a challenge for prospectors carrying only their packs. How were they to be supplied? How was the gold to be transported out? Clearly a road was a necessity for the economic viability of the region.

Leading the campaign to construct a road were the Oppenheimers. More than anyone else in the Cariboo, they needed a transportation link for their various enterprises. They lobbied Governor James Douglas and organized petitions from the region's inhabitants. Eventually Douglas agreed, and in 1862 the famous Cariboo Trail was begun. Planned by the Royal Engineers, the wagon road paralleled the Fraser and Thompson rivers. Naturally, the Oppenheimers won the contract to construct the initial portions.

In 1868, in one of the many fires that swept through the towns and mining camps of the region, Barkerville burned to the ground. It was said that the Oppenheimers lost upwards of $100,000 in buildings and inventory. Shrugging off the loss, they built a bigger, better store. And to prevent further losses — and perhaps to score some useful public relations points — David Oppenheimer imported a shiny new fire engine from San Francisco, and his brother Isaac became the captain of the fire brigade.

The Colonial Hotel on the Cariboo Road, Soda Creek, B.C., *c.* 1868.

Isaac Oppenheimer, fire chief, Barkerville, B.C., *c.* 1869.

The Oppenheimers were not the only Jews in the Cariboo. In Cayoosh, Soda Creek, Williams Creek and the other towns springing up around gold finds, Jewish merchants such as Carl Strouss, Felix Neufelder, Abraham Hoffman and others opened up trading posts and general stores. Some of their customers were Jewish, too. Among these was a young university-educated London Jew named Morris Moss.

One of the more colourful characters in Canadian history, the twenty-one-year-old Moss arrived in Victoria in 1862 via San Francisco, where he had worked for some years for a fur company. Erudite, handsome and cultivated, he was an immediate hit with the more refined element of the city. Certainly he was far different from the hard-living, hard-drinking miners who were arriving daily. He fit well into the literary meetings, concerts, balls and even fox hunts that the city's gentry loved so much.

But Moss had other ideas. To him Victoria with all its airs was too effete, too urban. Had he wanted that type of life, he would have stayed in London or even San Francisco. A noted horseman, a crack shot and an avid sailor, Moss craved excitement. With the discovery of gold in the Cariboo, he saw his opportunity. He would trace a new route to the gold through Bentinck Arm, one of the many inlets on British Columbia's coast. It was a dangerous, mostly unexplored route through hostile Indian territory, but after a series of terrifying adventures, he arrived safely. Convinced that he had discovered a better and thus more profitable route, Moss set up a trading post along the way near the Indian village of Bella Coola, from which he did manage to run several pack trains full of supplies to the miners in the Cariboo. Sadly, the trading post proved to be a fiasco as smallpox wiped out the neighbouring Indian tribes. Nonetheless, as a reward for his activities Governor Douglas appointed Moss a justice of the peace, and asked him to take on the responsibilities of government agent for the Northwest coast.

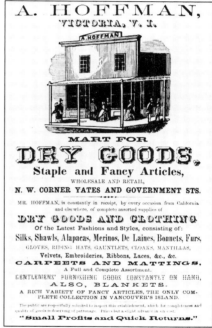

Disaster struck Moss's next expedition in December of 1862. His schooner, the *Rose Newman*, which was full of supplies for the miners, was sunk by a savage winter storm. Moss and his two-man crew managed to swim through the frigid waters to shore but found themselves on a deserted island. For ninety days they survived, three Robinson Crusoes on a wind-swept pile of rock. Fortunately they managed to salvage some food, flour, molasses, a musket and a keg of gunpowder from the boat. With the gunpowder they were able to build a fire, which they kept burning for the next three months. Eventually they were discovered by a hostile Indian tribe who held

Left: Carl Strouss. (British Columbia Archives and Records Service HP7281)

Upper right: Abraham Hoffman. (British Columbia Archives and Records Service HP3063)

Lower right: Advertisement for Abraham Hoffman's dry-goods store, *c.* 1850.

Mrs. H.A. Belasco and her son David.

them captive for another month, before they were rescued by a group of friendly Bella Coola Indians. Four months after he left Victoria, Moss returned poorer, wiser but, nonetheless, alive.

In spite of these setbacks, Moss was still not prepared to settle down. At the request of Frederick Simpson, the new governor of British Columbia — there were now two colonies on the Pacific coast, as the mainland had achieved its independence from Vancouver Island in 1866 — Moss led a punitive expedition to put down an Indian uprising in the northwestern region of the colony. From 1864 to 1867, as Indian agent for the government and its deputy collector of customs, he travelled extensively through every part of British Columbia. He tried prospecting again and discovered a promising find which he named the Hebrew Mine, but he earned little if anything from it. He even went prospecting near Alaska, but he was thirty years too soon; the discovery of gold in the Klondike in the 1890s would prove that his instincts had been right, even if his timing was not.

Eventually Moss returned to Victoria, ostensibly to settle down. He developed the largest sealing business in British Columbia before American coast guard vessels seized his ships, claiming the United States had a monopoly in the industry. He also became president of Victoria's synagogue and its B'nai B'rith lodge. He married the daughter of a prominent Jewish merchant, but domestic restraints were too much for Moss. Not long after the birth of their son, Moss disappeared, never to be heard from again. It was reported that he died some years later in Colorado.

Other Jews took part in the Cariboo gold rush and left empty-handed. Humphrey Abraham Belasco, a failed actor from San Francisco, landed in Victoria in 1858. His acting was no better, it seems, in Victoria's Royal Theatre Company, so he opened up a fruit store, which also failed. Belasco then left his wife and child in Victoria and headed off to seek his fortune in the Cariboo — again with not much success. His son, David, inherited his father's love

Morris Moss (seated) with his wife and their son, *c.* 1885.

for the theatre and took walk-on parts in Victoria's various theatre companies from the age of five. Though the elder Belasco wished his son to become a rabbi, there was no way he could keep David off the boards. Several times while he was still in short pants, he ran away to join a circus or a travelling theatre troupe. Eventually David Belasco became one of the world's leading playwrights (he wrote the play *Madame Butterfly*), producers and theatre impresarios, and built the Belasco, one of New York's finest theatres.

Less fortunate than Moss and Belasco, who at least returned from the Cariboo with their lives, were two other Jewish provisioners, "Dutchy" Harris Lewin and David Sokolski. On their way back from the Cariboo after a successful business expedition, they were ambushed by several thugs, shot three times each at close range and robbed of at least twelve thousand dollars, their jewellery, their watches and even their hats. This outrage became known in the

Left: Simon Leiser.

Right: Simon Leiser's wholesale grocery business, *c.* 1880. (British Columbia Archives and Records Service HP15100)

area as the "Massacre of the Jews." Though a posse was formed to hunt the killers, and a reward of three thousand dollars was raised among the Cariboo miners, the perpetrators went unpunished for years. Eventually they were found in Montana and hanged there for other murders they had committed south of the border.

Neither Morris Moss nor Humphrey Belasco, nor, of course, the unfortunate Lewin and Sokolski was representative of Victoria's Jewish community. Most were far more successful in their ventures and certainly more stable in their private lives. Historian David Rome has described them as "a remarkable group of men containing future mayors of major cities…members of the legislature, founders of industries, shipping men, manufacturers, pioneers, miners, real estate men and actors. The unusual quality of the group can be fully appreciated by a comparison with the achievements and records of any similar group…from any Jewish community in Canada."

Perhaps more representative was the Boscowitz family, whose first store, opened in 1858, developed into one of Canada's largest fur and sealing concerns. They also developed the massive Britannia copper mine. The Sutro family from Germany became leaders in the province's tobacco and banking business. Simon Leiser's tiny grocery

Victoria, B.C., *c.* 1862, showing Gambitz's dry-goods and drapery store on the left.

grew into the largest wholesale business in British Columbia. Such success stories were not unusual for Victoria's Jewish settlers.

Striking, as well, was how committed these men and women were to their faith and to their co-religionists elsewhere. Indeed the first reported meeting of the community occurred in 1858, only days after the arrival of the first Jews in Victoria. Its purpose was to send money to help the Jews of Morocco, and nearly $185 was collected. In August of 1858, exactly six weeks after Frank Sylvester stepped ashore, another meeting was held at the home of Kady Gambitz, founder of the Hebrew Sick and Burial Society of Shasta, California, who had just opened Victoria's first dry-goods store. The purpose of this meeting was to arrange services for the high holy days.

A year later an invitation appeared in Victoria's newspapers calling on the city's "Israelites" to meet together "for the purpose of procuring a suitable place for a Burying Ground." With money provided by Lewis Lewis, a Jewish merchant in the mining town of Yale, a small plot of land was bought and dedicated in February of 1860. One year

Selim Franklin (left), member of the legislative assembly for Vancouver Island, and Lumley Franklin, mayor of Victoria.

later, it received its first occupant, a German Jew, Morris Price, whose "throat was cut from ear to ear" by Indians in his store at Cayoosh Flats (now Lillooet) along the Fraser River.

In 1859 the first Jewish organization in western Canada, the Victoria Hebrew Benevolent Society, was founded largely through the efforts of Abraham Blackman, who had been active in the congregation of Stockton, California, before his arrival in Victoria. A teacher in a San Francisco synagogue, Julius Silversmith, who arrived in Victoria in 1858 to set up a private school, was made responsible for dispensing the society's funds to needy Jews. In effect he was western Canada's — if not Canada's — first professional social worker.

Without a synagogue, the community held its religious services in various rented rooms, including those at the aptly named Star and Garter Hotel, owned by a congregant, Lewis Davis. At a meeting at the hotel in August of 1862, the assembled leaders of the community decided it was time to build a proper place of worship. But not just a simple synagogue: this was to be a grand edifice designed by the architect who had planned many of the best of San Francisco's Nob Hill homes.

The building was a masterpiece, an "almost perfect little religious structure" in the words of one scholar. It was one of Victoria's first brick edifices, and people came from miles away to see it. Impressive as well was the ceremony of the laying of the cornerstone on June 2, 1863. Many of Victoria's stores closed so that their owners could participate. Led by the band from a visiting British naval ship, a long procession that included members of the St. Andrew's Society, German and French societies, the Freemason lodges, the chief justice of the colony, the mayor, and hundreds of others along with most of the city's two hundred or so Jews marched to the synagogue. The Jewish community even gave out cigars to those playing in the band. In the words of the newspaper the *British Colonist*, the event "must be a source of infinite gratification" to Victoria's Jewish community as it showed "in acts more powerful than words, the high estimation in which they are held by their fellow townsmen of the city of Victoria."

Perhaps there was no better proof of this "high estimation" than the success of individual Jews in the colony's political life. The first wave — it was more like a ripple — of Jewish immigrants produced a member of the colony's legislature, a member of the Canadian Parliament and mayors of Victoria and Vancouver. Two of these elected officials came from one remarkable family, the Franklins.

Born in Liverpool, Selim and Lumley Franklin arrived in Victoria in 1858 from San Francisco, where they had been prosperous merchants until a fire destroyed their store. Within a short time, Selim was appointed the first government auctioneer in British Columbia. Both brothers were active in Victoria's theatre community, helped found the Philharmonic Society and, according to the *British Colonist*, both rendered passable solo singing performances. But what interested the Franklins most was politics.

In January of 1860 the dapper, articulate Selim Franklin announced his intention to run for one of the two Victoria seats in the Assembly. No one took his candidacy seriously since his major opponent was the well-known Amor de Cosmos, editor of the *Colonist* and later premier of British Columbia. To everyone's surprise, Franklin emerged triumphant by a margin of fifteen votes. Though de Cosmos attempted to have the election overturned on the grounds that Franklin had "fraudulently" bought the votes of the city's tiny black population, there is no evidence that his Jewishness was an issue. Scarcely any mention was made of it during the campaign.

Only after the election, when Franklin attempted to take his seat in the House, did his faith become an obstacle. The problem confronting Franklin was the same one that had bedevilled Ezekiel Hart some forty years before — the troublesome matter of the oath. In 1859, when Governor Douglas introduced a bill to naturalize the growing number of aliens in the colony, the oath of allegiance included the troublesome phrase "on the true faith of a Christian."

The act incorporating the Congregation Emanuel, Victoria, 1864.

Henry Nathan Jr., MP, Victoria,
B.C., 1872.

Immediately the *British Colonist* was up in arms. De Cosmos despised Douglas and saw the bill as an opportunity to embarrass him. Douglas, a *Colonist* editorial charged, was "behind the age in which he lives" and had issued a proclamation "with an illiberality worthy of a bigot," which would bar all Jews from becoming citizens. The colony, it cautioned, must not "have the stain of religious bigotry and persecution fastened upon it."

Even before the *Colonist* attack, however, Douglas was having second thoughts on the bill. On the advice of Matthew Ballie Begbie, the first judge of British Columbia, a new Oath Act was introduced exempting Quakers and Jews from taking the Christian oath. It seemed the issue was resolved — until the Vancouver Island Assembly met in March of 1860.

On March 3, Selim Franklin was sworn in as a member of the Assembly. Immediately a member of the House objected that Franklin had not taken the prescribed oath. When Franklin refused a request from the Speaker to append to his declaration "upon the true faith of a Christian," he was not allowed to take his seat for two weeks. It was not until the chief justice of the colony, David Cameron, ruled in Franklin's favour that the matter seemed to be resolved. But the introduction of a new bill later in the session was required to remove the obstacle of the oath from Vancouver Island's Jewish citizens for good. What was most gratifying to the Island's Jewish community was that during the entire affair, with one or two exceptions, there were no anti-semitic outbursts either in the Assembly or in the press. Indeed the members of the House went on record repudiating intolerance.

In 1866, after a spotty legislative career, Franklin resigned from the Assembly in protest against the forced union between the Island and the mainland. The year before, however, his brother Lumley had been elected mayor of Victoria, the first Jewish mayor of a major city in British North America. He was a forceful advocate of the movement to bring British Columbia into Confederation.

Even more active in the Confederation movement was the colony's most prominent Jewish politician, Henry Nathan, a well-off Victoria merchant who settled on the Island in 1862. In 1870, after the merger with the mainland, he was elected to the last British Columbia legislature before the colony became part of Canada. After British Columbia joined Confederation in 1871, he was acclaimed Victoria's first member of Parliament—and became the first Jew to sit in the House of Commons. A Liberal, he had an excellent relationship with Prime Minister John A. Macdonald and was active in pushing for a transcontinental railway—indeed he was a director of what was to become the Canadian Pacific Railway Company.

The coming of the railway doomed Victoria's pretensions of becoming Canada's premier city on the Pacific. Already badly battered by the end of the gold rush—the gold disappeared almost as suddenly as it had been discovered—the economy of Victoria could not withstand the fatal shock of Vancouver, its sister city across the Narrows, being chosen as the terminal of the transcontinental railway. In any case, there was no way Victoria could compete with the magnificent deep-sea harbour and vast timber resources of Burrard Inlet, around which Vancouver would take shape. With the arrival in Vancouver of the CPR's passenger train, Victoria's decline was complete. Most of the city's commercial and financial interests soon

Upper: A view of "Gastown," where Louis Gold established Vancouver's first Jewish business, in 1872.

Lower: Oppenheimer Bros. wholesale grocery company in Vancouver, 1889.

shifted across the Straits of Georgia to Vancouver — and with these, of course, went many Jews, most notably the Oppenheimer brothers.

More than any other family, the Oppenheimers were responsible for Vancouver's early growth. They owned huge tracts of land in the city, established a steamship line, developed the city's first streetcar line and organized the city's other major landowners to give part of their property to the CPR to ensure that the railway would choose Vancouver as its Pacific terminal. Indeed the Oppenheimers themselves gave up a third of their land holdings in the city, so that the CPR would locate in Vancouver.

Two of the brothers, David and Isaac, were members of Vancouver's city council, and in 1888 David was elected mayor, serving for four years. He built the bridges that united the city, laid sidewalks, developed the town's water supply system, organized its transit system, founded the YMCA and astutely procured the land for Vancouver's downtown treasure, Stanley Park. No wonder he was called the "Father of Vancouver."

Though not as active a community as that of Victoria, by 1887 Vancouver Jews had purchased land for a cemetery, and by the early 1890s two congregations were functioning, the Reform led by Rabbi Solomon Philo, who was part of the Jewish exodus from Victoria, and a traditional Orthodox group presided over by Zebulon Franks, a hardware merchant whose father was a rabbi in the Ukraine. The

Upper left: The first synagogue wedding in Vancouver, 1914.

Upper right: Morning prayers at the Schara Tzedeck Synagogue in Vancouver, c. 1927.

Lower: Zebulon Franks (left) in his Vancouver hardware store, 1902.

Mayor David Oppenheimer (third from right) with government dignitaries on a trip to Howe Sound, 1889.

former consisted mostly of Jews who had spent some time in the United States; the latter of Eastern European immigrants, who were beginning to arrive in larger numbers.

Thus by the turn of the century there were two functioning Jewish communities on the Pacific coast. But there were Jews elsewhere in British Columbia as well. Frederick Heinze, a German immigrant from Montana, built the smelter at Trail, which eventually became the huge Cominco mining empire. Jews lived in Chilliwack, Prince Rupert and Prince George. Characters such as the trapper "Johnny the Jew" and the miner "Silver King Mike" certainly gave the British Columbia Jewish community a different flavour from its counterparts elsewhere in Canada, a flavour it would maintain throughout the next century.

Despite their small numbers, the Jews on the Pacific coast in the latter years of the nineteenth century contributed as much to the development of their region as did the founding fathers of Canadian Jewry to central Canada a hundred years before.

CHAPTER FIVE

CONQUERING THE PRAIRIES

1880 - 1910

On June 2, 1882, one of the first Jewish settlers of Winnipeg received a letter from a relative in Russia. Terrifying in its detail, it described the condition of Jews following the assassination of Czar Alexander II in March of 1881: "Our lives and wealth are every minute in danger…Such persecutions and cruelties never happened before in this civilized generation. Men and women have been slaughtered; the female sex have been ill-treated on the public streets…Children have been cast into wells and rivers and drowned; living infants have been torn in pieces and thrown upon the streets. Many women sick in bed from confinement, have been so abused that they died…There is no other way to remedy these evils than by escaping…"

The letter was passed around among the handful of Jews in Winnipeg at the time. All were distraught and felt helpless by the extent of the horror. None could foresee how traumatic for them and the entire Jewish community of Canada would be the pogroms some ten thousand miles away.

The first Jewish settler in Manitoba had come only four or five years before. Edmond Coblentz, an Alsatian Jew, arrived in the province

Left: John and Rachel Heppner family, Wapella, Saskatchewan, *c.* 1896.

Right: Edmond (right), Aachel (middle) and Adolphe Coblentz, *c.* 1877.

Sir Alexander Galt.

from Pennsylvania in 1877. Perhaps he learned of the new settlement from his Mennonite neighbours whose co-religionists had settled in western Canada. In any case, he must have liked what he saw, for his two brothers and their families joined him within the year. At the same time, one of the many pedlars who travelled through western Canada, Reuben Goldstein, also decided to settle in Winnipeg.

Though the Coblentzes and Goldsteins were the first Jews to take up residence in Manitoba, they were certainly not the first to have been there. According to some historians, Ferdinande Jacobs, an apprentice with the Hudson's Bay Company who spent twenty-seven years on the Churchill River from 1732 to 1759 and returned as the company's chief factor in 1760 for another fifteen years, was Jewish. But aside from his name and a passing remark in a traveller's diary in 1815 that an Indian woman he encountered was "the daughter of a Governor called Jacobs (a Jew)," there is little evidence that Jacobs was Jewish; indeed, there is plenty that he was not. However, there are many indications that Jewish traders were regularly traversing Manitoba throughout the period before 1880 — often travelling down the Red River from St. Paul, Minnesota, with their goods and returning with furs.

By 1880 the fur traders, natives and Métis were gradually being pushed farther west by waves of Mennonite, Icelandic and other settlers. Among the latter, according to the census of 1881, were thirty-three Jewish men and their families. Almost all were of German or English background. They settled immediately in Winnipeg as merchants, salesmen, hotel-keepers, pedlars and land dealers. They did so well that within a year or two of their arrival the *Winnipeg Sun* described them as "shrewd, far-seeing [and] successful... doing well, not only making a living but saving money." Though the community had a part-time rabbi, Abraham Benjamin, aside from the high holidays there was little community or religious activity.

And then the Russian Jews arrived.

Main Street, Winnipeg, 1874.

It was clear that by the summer of 1882, Jews remained in Russia at their own risk. The notorious May Laws of the czar ordered Jews out of their homes and villages. Many were only too happy to leave, not only because of the grinding poverty and pervasive restrictions that made their lives a misery, but because the massacres of Jews in Bialystok, Kharkov, Odessa, Kiev and other towns and villages were painful reminders of the dangers of remaining. Tens of thousands had left already; thousands more would soon follow. Penniless, hungry, homeless, they poured into Austria not knowing where fate would take them.

The western world was slow to respond, but when it did, it did so in a fury. Mass meetings were called in Europe and North America. For Canadian Jewry, the most important of these was held at Mansion House, the seat of the Lord Mayor of London. There, before a large crowd, influential British political and religious leaders made passionate speeches denouncing the inhumanity of the Russians. It was a moving event and everyone came away determined to help in any way possible. One of those at the meeting was Alexander Galt, Canada's first high commissioner to Great Britain.

A major part of Galt's responsibilities was to encourage immigration to Canada and to look for ways to ensure the country's economic development. Even before the Mansion House meeting, he had informed the banker, Lord Rothschild, that Canada would be interested in "removing the agricultural Jews" to Canada, hoping not only to find some suitable immigrants but to interest Rothschild and his affluent friends in investing in Canada. Russian Jews, Galt told Prime Minister John A. Macdonald, were "a superior class of people" who had "sufficient means to establish themselves in Canada." In any case, he added, since American Jews were "actively promoting emigration to the United States...what was good for them could not be bad for us." To ensure that Canada would play her proper role in this refugee movement, Galt agreed to serve on the Mansion House Committee that had been created to find countries which would accept the Russian Jews. "We might have a lot of them thrown up on our shores unprovided for," Galt explained to Macdonald. "By being on the Committee I can prevent this."

The prime minister liked the idea of bringing some Jews into the West and instructed immigration officials to make land available. "The Old Clo move is a good one," he said, referring to the stereotypical Jewish old-clothes pedlar. "A sprinkling of Jews in the North-West would be good," he added. "They would at once go in for peddling and politicking, and be of as much use in the new country as cheap jacks and chapmen." The contemptuous attitude of Macdonald pales beside that of the Governor General, the Marquis of Lorne. Responding to an appeal to help alleviate the sorry plight of Russian Jews, Lorne dismissed them as "a very dirty lot," but added that if British Jewry "will subscribe liberally and settle his Russian brother, why shouldn't the Canadian government get the benefit of the transaction."

Both Macdonald and Lorne were reflecting a widely shared attitude. Canada, they hoped, would be peopled by settlers of Anglo-Saxon or Nordic origins. Galt's task had been to recruit Britons and

The S.S. *International* at the immigration sheds in Winnipeg, *c.* 1870.

Northern Europeans, not Russian Jews. But while Eastern Europeans were not exactly what Canadian officials had in mind, most of the "preferred" immigrants were going to the United States, and Canada had little choice. In any case, taking some Jewish refugees would please Rothschild and other wealthy Jewish investors. Determined to get some of the Russian Jews, Galt assured the Mansion House Committee that it was his government's opinion that the empty lands of the Canadian west would be a perfect home for the refugees. The committee agreed, and on April 24, 1882, 240 refugees left Liverpool with tickets to Winnipeg in their hands.

Despite Galt's assurances, nothing was done to prepare for the arrival of the Russian Jews. After a horrifying three-week journey on the stormy Atlantic, the bedraggled Jews landed at Quebec, numbly underwent examination at the hands of imperious immigration officers and were bundled aboard trains heading west. In Montreal they were provided with, in the words of one nine-year-old refugee, "a splendid dinner" by the Jewish community. Similarly in Toronto they were welcomed by representatives of the Jewish community, and fed and clothed. As a result of these kindnesses, some of those scheduled to continue to Winnipeg decided to make their new homes in Toronto and Montreal instead.

In May of 1882, a vanguard of twenty-four Russian Jews arrived in Winnipeg. Although they were warmly greeted by their fellow Jews, a downturn in the local economy meant there was little work for the

H.L. Weidman and family, early Russian immigrants to Winnipeg, 1899.

new settlers, and apparently no land. Despite Galt's promises, no land grants were made; the Russian Jews were housed in dingy immigration sheds, with little hope of finding better accommodation for some time. Frantically, Winnipeg Jewry wired their counterparts in Toronto to stop the remaining Russian Jews from continuing their journey.

It was too late; on the very day the telegram was sent, the wires were carrying a message to Winnipeg from Mark Samuel of Toronto that the final contingent had already left Sarnia aboard the steamer *Ontario* bound for Duluth, Minnesota, on the westernmost shore of Lake Superior. On June 1, the refugees arrived in Winnipeg aboard a train from Duluth.

Though the Winnipeg Jewish community — all thirty or so of them — made efforts to help, there was little it could do. It raised funds — close to four hundred dollars from its members — and lobbied extensively among non-Jews to provide jobs and assistance. And though some jobs were available to the refugees, there were not nearly enough. Few of the Russian Jews spoke English or had the skills required for most of the work opportunities. Nor could they expect any help from the Canadian government. Aside from contributing some food and tents, even as more Jews were arriving, Ottawa washed its hands of the problem. The responsibility for "settling and providing" these refugees, it told concerned Winnipeg officials, lay with Canadian Jewry.

Although Winnipeg Jewry made enormous sacrifices, there was already a growing tension between the two groups. The Russian Jews were very observant — hungry as they were, they would not eat the meat provided by the more liberal "Deutsche Yuden" or German Jews of Manitoba, whose religious practices they did not trust. When an infant died in the immigration shed, they would not permit the child to be buried in the community cemetery, which they felt was not properly consecrated.

For the refugees, every day was a struggle. Were it not for the Canadian Pacific Railway, most would have found it impossible

Winnipeg, *c*. 1900.

to survive. Desperate for workers, the CPR was prepared to hire any man who could withstand the rigours of laying tracks, digging trenches and building bridges across the prairies. It even provided the observant Russian Jews with kosher food and their own sleeping cars, exempted them from working on the Sabbath and allowed them to return to Winnipeg for religious holidays — although some who preferred to remain near their work raised money to purchase a Torah and a *shofar*, a ram's horn, to celebrate the high holidays in a tent provided by the CPR.

Not only did these workers have to deal with horrific working conditions, but they had to deal with rowdy fellow workers, many of whom did not appreciate working with Jews. The first detail of Jews was set upon by a mob of club-carrying thugs; their quarters were ransacked, their food stolen and many were beaten. It seemed like Bialystok all over again.

Yet the veterans of the Russian pogroms had no choice but to persevere. Finally, a resolute Russian Jew whose head had been smashed by a club took his assailant to court. There a sympathetic judge admonished the attacker and sentenced him to jail. For

Manitoba Jewry, the case was a vindication; for Russian Jewry, it was proof that Canada was a far different place from their homeland.

Nevertheless, many saw no hope in Manitoba. As one refugee wrote movingly in a Russian-Hebrew newspaper: "I know not in what to dip my pen, in the inkstand before me, or in the flow of tears running from the eyes of the unfortunates who have come here with me, in order to describe their lamentable condition. One hears nothing but weeping and wailing over the prospect of wasting one's youth and spending it vainly in this desolate spot known as Winnipeg. We are exiled to wilderness." Though he recanted a few months later and told readers that he had "exaggerated somewhat" and that, in fact, the "situation has improved," there is no question that for the bulk of the refugees life was almost unendurable.

Few immigrants to Canada were as badly prepared for their new lives as the Russian Jews who believed they had been promised large tracts of free land by the federal government. The Dominion Immigration Agent even pleaded with Ottawa to send the refugees back east before another winter set in. Attempts by the Russian Jews to acquire land proved futile. When a site acceptable to both the government and the immigrants was finally found, the settlers of a nearby Methodist colony refused to allow the refugees to move in because, in the words of the land agent, "they didn't want any Jews there."

By 1883 this attitude had become widespread. The newspapers that had earlier welcomed the Jewish refugees now turned against them. "A more helpless and useless lot of creatures never crossed the Atlantic," editorialized one. "Though the river is at their door, they do not seem to know what cleanliness is," said another. "It would be criminal to send more of them here," declared a third. Only massive relief efforts by the tiny Jewish community and church groups allowed the new immigrants to survive the terrible winter of 1883.

It was soon clear to everyone involved that the movement of Russian Jewry to western Canada had not been a great success. The government of Manitoba pleaded with Ottawa to stem the flow, and Galt asked the Mansion House Committee to suspend the movement. Even Canadian Jewish leaders such as Mark Samuel in Toronto wrote to their British counterparts recommending that Russian Jews be sent elsewhere.

Canadian Jews were understandably discomfited by the sudden arrival on their shores of their Eastern European co-religionists. Their appearance, way of life, poverty, religious practices and inability to speak English were an embarrassment to a community struggling to integrate and be accepted. Established Jews feared that their hard-won respectability and their newfound status would be tarnished — if not destroyed — by the Russian Jewish immigrants. The sooner they moved out of Montreal and Toronto and on to the farmlands promised them, the happier Canadian Jewry would be. Settling Eastern European Jews on the land became the community's highest priority.

It was also high on the list of Galt's priorities. For two years he had pleaded in vain with federal authorities to turn over to the Jews some of the unused land granted to the Mennonites. The policy of the government had originally been to encourage homesteading by offering tracts of land to groups such as Mennonites, Scots, Icelanders and others. By the 1880s, with immigration to Canada at a standstill, it was decided to give the land to private companies that would then bring over settlers. But in truth there was not much land to give away: so much had been turned over to the CPR and the Hudson's Bay Company — approximately thirty-five million acres — that there was some concern whether there was any arable land left on the prairies. Over three million acres in western Canada had been given to other private companies, but they did nothing with them, and Galt told the prime minister that the companies should be ordered to sell the land to "bona fide settlers" or to "leave it." In the end, after attracting only about one thousand homesteaders, the companies gave the land back to the government.

NOTICE TO FARMERS.

A large number of the German Agricultural population of Russia are desirous of leaving their homes and finding a new field of occupation for themselves and their families, if they are assisted in their transportation.

The amount of passage to Winnipeg to be paid on arrival at that point will be as follows :—

For all from twelve years upwards   -   - $45.00
For those from five to twelve years of age   -   22.50
For those from one to five years of age   -   15 00

It is guaranteed that no Jews will be brought out under this scheme.

Parties wishing to take advantage of this opportunity should address themselves without delay to the

DOMINION GOVERNMENT IMMIGRATION AGENT, WINNIPEG.

or any other Government Immigration Agent,

Stating the number of families they want and when they will require them ; not less than a month's time to be reckoned for the voyage.

WINNIPEG, March 7th, 1892.

A government program to encourage agricultural settlement in the west, though not for Jews, 1892.

Upper: Abraham Klenman, reading a Yiddish newspaper, Wapella.

Lower: Mrs. Klenman in her kitchen, c. 1915.

Finally, in 1883, a government official travelled through large parts of the west with representatives of the new immigrants in Winnipeg, looking for a suitable locale for Canada's first Jewish settlement. A site near Moosomin, Saskatchewan, some 220 miles due west of Winnipeg, was decided on. Why this inhospitable tract was chosen over other more propitious possibilities is not certain. But hopes were high when twenty-seven Jewish families left Winnipeg early in May of 1884 to begin their new lives as farmers. Their optimism was reflected in the name given their new settlement: New Jerusalem. But this was no land of milk and honey.

Each family had been given 160 acres by the Canadian government and four hundred dollars by the Mansion House Committee. This was not nearly enough. The land was almost completely unproductive; what crops it grew were destroyed by hail, frost and drought. Few of the settlers had any farm experience, and none had ever faced the sub-zero temperatures and paralysing blizzards of a prairie winter. Yet they persevered. Though crop after crop failed, they kept on planting. They even built a synagogue and a school, but both collapsed when the self-appointed "rabbi" of the colony had his feet amputated due to frostbite and he left for warmer climes. Only in 1889, after their crop was destroyed by fire — the settlers suspected arson — was the colony abandoned, as a sadder but wiser group of Jews made their way back to Winnipeg.

The Moosomin failure may have reinforced the prejudices of some that Jews could not farm — Galt denounced the settlers as "vagabonds" who at the first sign of trouble "turned to their natural avocation for peddling" — but, in truth, many other agricultural colonies were collapsing at the same time. Lacking experience, skills, financial support and above all the co-operation of Mother Nature, settlers throughout western Canada in those years had little hope of success. The prairies were becoming dotted with ghost towns and abandoned farms.

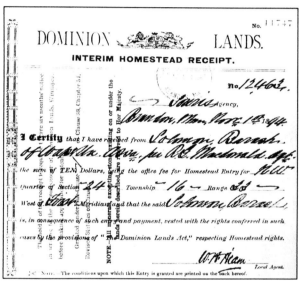

But not all the settlers gave up. In 1888 another Jewish colony, Wapella, was established, just fifteen miles north of Moosomin. It was the brainchild of an influential English Jewish financier, Herman Landau, who was convinced that Canada — "where the climate was similar to the one they were born under, and where religious tolerance had become the religion of the country" — was the answer to the plight of Russian Jewry. Landau sent out a group of eleven Jews who had agricultural training, led by John Heppner. Though settlers in the Wapella area protested — the local Conservative party organization complained to the government that Jews were "a most undesirable class of settlers" — a homestead inspector reported that Landau's Jews were "industrious and hardworking" and would be "beneficial to the country." In fact, most of those who arrived with Heppner soon left, but they were replaced by others — most notably Abraham Klenman and his son-in-law Solomon Barish, both of whom had farmed in the old country. Among the new arrivals as well was Ekiel Bronfman, whose family would leave its mark on both the country's Jewish and business communities.

Upper left: Mr. and Mrs. Solomon Barish in their home, Wapella.

Upper right: Tug-of-war, Barish Farm, Wapella, 1912.

Lower: Solomon Barish's land receipt, Wapella, 1894.

Upper: Edel Brotman, the first Jewish religious leader at Wapella, with his wife, Leah.

Lower: The Kalman Isman family homestead, Wapella, built in 1889. (Richard Kaplun, the fourth generation of the family, today farms this land.)

Wapella was a breakthrough. Its success proved to all the many doubters that, given half a chance, Jews could make a go of it as farmers. For years Wapella was a thriving Jewish community with its own congregation and, in Edel Brotman, a settler who arrived in 1889, a legitimate rabbi. It became Canada's longest-surviving Jewish farm colony — Klenman's son lived there until the 1960s — and served as a training ground for other would-be Jewish farmers.

By the early 1890s the persecution of Russian Jewry had become even more widespread. With their homes, shops, farms and jobs taken away, their schools and synagogues destroyed, thousands poured across the Russian borders in search of a haven. Thousands of others from Romania, Galicia, Poland and other Eastern European states were also fleeing their countries. Canada was not their first choice — indeed many did not know it existed — but the refugees did not control their own fate. As they moved westward, they were shunted from one immigration committee to another, each trying to push them farther west — from Vienna to Hamburg to London, then to New York or Montreal, and finally onward to whatever western community would take them, or whatever lands were available.

Most, of course, wanted to go to the United States. America meant freedom, opulence, security. Thus, those who found themselves getting off ships in Halifax, Quebec City or Montreal through no choice of their own were dumbfounded. Somehow they had been tricked. Jewish relief agencies in Canada complained to their counterparts in Europe that "unscrupulous steamship agents…[tell] an emigrant desiring to go to Chicago…that the steamer will land him at Montreal and that the fare from Montreal to Chicago is only 60¢." Many of these immigrants stayed only long enough to find a way to cross the border, but others remained to build new lives in Canada — not always by choice. By 1891, the United States had introduced stringent immigration restrictions, and many of the Jews turned away at American ports were dropped off in Canada.

As the situation of Russian Jewry deteriorated, Herman Landau again swung into action. He persuaded the eminent German financier and philanthropist Baron Maurice de Hirsch to subsidize the settlement of Jewish refugees in the New World. In 1891, de Hirsch founded the Jewish Colonization Association (JCA) to sponsor the resettlement of Russian Jews in agricultural colonies in North and South America. Though the baron's main interest was in Argentina, he did agree to underwrite Landau's proposal to fund large-scale settlements in Canada as well.

The support of de Hirsch was a godsend to Montreal's Jewish community. Almost alone it had had to bear the costs of housing, feeding and settling the thousands of Jewish immigrants who were arriving in Canada. The Young Men's Hebrew Benevolent Society (YMHBS) had been founded in 1863 by a group of young, single, Jewish males to assist "needy or unfortunate co-religionists…and to relieve the elder members of the families from the onerous task of attending to the wants of the poor." As the pressures of immigration mounted, married men were allowed to become members, and a ladies' auxiliary was formed in 1877. The society was constantly short of funds. Even the arrival of the small numbers of indigent Jews in the 1870s had put such a strain on its treasury that the society had pleaded with Jewish organizations in London to stop sending Eastern European Jews. Rabbi de Sola had personally interceded with charity officials in London to call a halt to the practice of shipping poor immigrant Jews to Canada.

All the rules changed following the outbreak of the pogroms in Russia. Montreal Jewry realized it would have no choice but to accept as many Jews as were sent to Canada. The YMHBS organized a non-denominational Jewish Relief Fund and rapidly raised over five thousand dollars. All the Jewish organizations in Montreal and Toronto (including the newly created Anglo-Jewish Association) combined to form the Jewish Emigration Aid Society (JEAS) under the leadership of the YMHBS. Yet it, too, buckled under the strain of

Upper left: Baron Maurice de Hirsch.

Upper right: Baroness Clara de Hirsch.

Lower: The Baron de Hirsch Institute, Montreal.

Asher Pierce and his sisters,
c. 1890.

dealing with so many refugees. Though it tried manfully, the JEAS simply did not have the resources to feed, shelter, clothe, rehabilitate and minister to every Jewish immigrant who arrived. Nonetheless, it was a landmark organization for Canadian Jewry — the first of many groups that would co-ordinate Jewish activities at a time of crisis.

Montreal Jewish leaders realized only too well that concentrating all the refugees in their city would cause serious problems for its own Jewish community. They did not want to create a ghetto and they feared an upsurge of anti-semitism from the surrounding population. Their goal was to provide a temporary haven for the new immigrants where they would have some time to recover from the horrors of the pogroms, the overseas voyage and the trauma of arriving friendless and homeless in a thoroughly alien society. As soon as they were on their feet, they would be sent west. That some of the immigrants did not wish to leave the relative comforts of Montreal for the rigours of the Canadian wilderness was a source of conflict between them and their Canadian benefactors.

Nevertheless, Montreal Jewish leaders persevered. In 1882 they delegated a respected businessman, Lazarus Cohen, to meet the federal Minister of Agriculture, John Henry Pope, to get his support for a program to settle Jewish refugees in the Northwest. Pope was non-committal. Over the next ten years there was a series of meetings between government officials and Jewish representatives. Finally, in 1892 a large delegation of YMHBS leaders met with Prime Minister John Abbott, who served for only a short time following John A. Macdonald's death. They pushed on him a request to create a colony of some ten thousand Jews on the Canadian prairies. Apparently Abbott thought it a splendid idea, even promising "special concessions," but as with so many other proposals, not much came of it — at least, not until the Montreal Jewish activitists determined to interest Baron de Hirsch in the scheme.

The baron was aware of Canada's problems. He had already sent twenty thousand dollars to the nearly bankrupt YMHBS to establish a Jewish school and a house of refuge. For the baron this amount was a pittance — it is estimated that the de Hirsch family gave over $100 million to charity — but for Montreal Jewry it was a godsend. Unfortunately, building shelters for Jewish immigrants, now arriving at a rate of one thousand a year, was no answer to the Montreal community's problem. In September of 1891, they again pleaded with the baron to underwrite Jewish settlements in the Canadian west, and sent over a small delegation to meet with him.

Their arguments were persuasive. In 1892, the baron's Jewish Colonization Association gave the YMHBS thirty-five thousand dollars to establish a farm colony in western Canada. Immediately the society hired two non-Jewish experts to choose an appropriate area for the new settlement. Though they preferred the lands around Regina and Prince Albert, in the end they chose an area in southeastern Saskatchewan, near Oxbow, where some Jewish settlers led by Asher and Jacob Pierce had already taken up residence both to farm and to set up stores to service a new CPR branch line. It would be "more beneficial," the experts thought, to be close to an existing Jewish community as well as near the railway. Thus, in May of 1892, the new colony of Hirsch was officially founded.

The first four years of the colony were exceptionally difficult. About fifty immigrant families arrived from Montreal and Winnipeg to homestead. Few had any experience in farming, nor did those appointed by the JCA to manage the colony. By 1895, after a series of crop failures and natural disasters, many of the settlers had abandoned their homes and gone elsewhere.

Perhaps they gave up hope too soon. Within a year the fortunes of the settlement changed. Several bountiful harvests, higher prices for their crops and the return of good weather made Hirsch attractive to new immigrants. By 1899 a number of new settlers had arrived, among them — via British Columbia — Sim Alfred Goldston, an English Jew, who set up the first Jewish school in western Canada with both regular and religious education. By the turn of the century, Hirsch was a

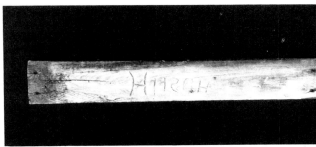

Upper: Pamphlet issued by the Jewish Colonization Association in the 1910s: "Important questions and right answers for those that aspire to settle on the land in Canada."

Lower: Hirsch Colony signpost.

Upper: Rabbi Marcus Berner farmed at the Hirsch Colony from 1899 to 1931.

Lower: Polish and Russian Social Democrats and members of the Bund, honouring the victims of the October 1905 pogrom in Vilna, Poland.

thriving community — it would survive another fifty years — with a synagogue, two Jewish schools and Saskatchewan's first Jewish burial ground.

Despite their achievements, the relationship between the Hirsch colonists and the JCA was anything but smooth. With some justification the settlers complained that the affairs of the colony could not be run from Montreal, as the JCA managers insisted. Decisions affecting the colony, they argued, could not be made by people who knew nothing about the conditions of life in western Canada. Furthermore, funds promised by the JCA were rarely forthcoming. Despite the attempts of various influential Jews to mediate the dispute, relations between the JCA and its various settlements would remain rocky.

By the turn of the century the flow of Russian Jewish immigrants had become a flood, and to these were added thousands of others. Lithuanian, Galician and Polish Jews were arriving at Canadian ports in increasing numbers. Romanian Jews were pouring out of their country as the pressure on their communities became more severe, with new restrictions preventing Jews from holding jobs, being educated or even owning land.

To highlight their tribulations — as well as to escape the consequences — in 1899 a large number of Romanian Jews began walking across Europe towards the Atlantic ports. The *fusgeyer*, or wayfarers, became a *cause célèbre* as country after country urged them to go elsewhere. When thousands of Romanian Jews descended on England, British Jewish leaders urged the JCA to resettle them overseas. Since the United States had introduced a more restrictive immigration policy, Canada seemed to be their only hope.

And Canada seemed initially receptive. A new government under Wilfrid Laurier had been elected in 1896 and an aggressive immigration policy had been launched. The Minister of Interior, Clifford Sifton, was determined to populate the west and to attract as many European agricultural immigrants as he could — but only as long as they were not Jewish. As he told the prime minister, "experience

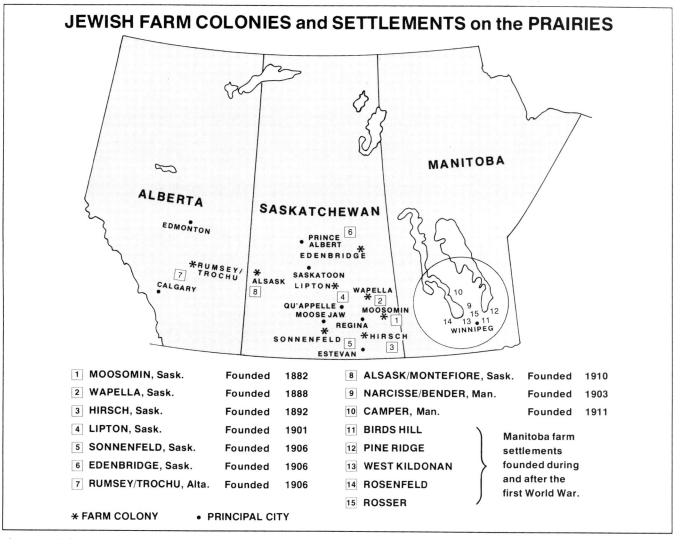

JEWISH FARM COLONIES and SETTLEMENTS on the PRAIRIES

1	MOOSOMIN, Sask.	Founded	1882		8	ALSASK/MONTEFIORE, Sask.	Founded	1910
2	WAPELLA, Sask.	Founded	1888		9	NARCISSE/BENDER, Man.	Founded	1903
3	HIRSCH, Sask.	Founded	1892		10	CAMPER, Man.	Founded	1911
4	LIPTON, Sask.	Founded	1901		11	BIRDS HILL		
5	SONNENFELD, Sask.	Founded	1906		12	PINE RIDGE		
6	EDENBRIDGE, Sask.	Founded	1906		13	WEST KILDONAN		
7	RUMSEY/TROCHU, Alta.	Founded	1906		14	ROSENFELD		
					15	ROSSER		

Manitoba farm settlements founded during and after the first World War.

＊ FARM COLONY   ● PRINCIPAL CITY

shows…[that] Jewish people do not become agriculturalists." Yet Laurier, in a private meeting in London, had assured Herman Landau that Canada would indeed welcome Jewish settlers.

To many European Jewish leaders, Canada with its vast empty plains seemed to be the answer to Europe's "Jewish problem." Where else could the homeless, penurious Jews of Eastern Europe find such an idyllic setting? The climate was much like that they left behind, the land seemed productive, the opportunities appeared endless and, most important, the government of Canada gave every sign

Lipton, Saskatchewan,
homesteaders, *c.* 1890.

of welcoming them. Canada was anxious for immigrants; Eastern European Jews were anxious to immigrate. What could have been better?

Such were the thoughts of prominent European Jewish financiers as they desperately sought a home for the hundreds of thousands of Jews pouring out of Russia, Romania, Galicia and Poland, many of whom were victims not only of pogroms but also of poverty and hunger. With the United States closing its gates, only Canada seemed to hold out the promise of a life without hunger, fear and oppression. Led by Israel Zangwill, a number of Jewish financiers from Britain, France and Germany created the Jewish Territorial Organization. Their proposal to the Canadian government in the early years of the twentieth century was to purchase a large area of land in western Canada and to settle it with as many Eastern European Jews as it could accommodate. The organization would cover all the costs of transportation and settlement, and would underwrite the building of a railroad to the settlements, as well as schools, roads and farms.

It would be a multi-million-dollar project, the likes of which the Canadian government had never seen. Here was an opportunity to settle a large expanse of the prairies at minimal cost to the government. It was an intriguing proposition, but it presented one problem: all the immigrants would be Jews. No government official was prepared to recommend approval of the scheme, but how could they say no without offending the Jewish bankers, whose goodwill they wished to retain? In the end they did not say no; they did not say anything. They simply allowed negotiations with the organization to drag on for years until the project died away, the victim of Ottawa's bigotry and inertia.

Meanwhile, immigration officials — particularly Sifton — were aghast at the prime minister's offer to allow Jewish refugees into the country and ordered it rescinded. But before they could countermand it, Canada's chief immigration officer in London, W.R.T. Preston, told JCA authorities that Canada would willingly accept "able-bodied and physically and morally suitable immigrants…[so long as they do not] infiltrate into the towns and swell the already overgrown population of Canadian cities." This was precisely the sentiment of the YMHBS, which pleaded with JCA officials not to send any more Romanian immigrants to Montreal — in 1899 and 1900 over four thousand had landed — but to send them to western Canada instead.

Taking advantage of Laurier and Preston's invitation, the JCA agreed to underwrite all of the transportation and settlement costs of four hundred Romanian refugees. In return, the Canadian government agreed to provide the land to create a colony, but insisted that it must choose both the land and the immigrants. In selecting the former, it could not have acted more irresponsibly. The person assigned to choosing a site was D.H. Macdonald, a local businessman in Fort Qu'Appelle, Saskatchewan. Either dishonest or incompetent — or perhaps both — he selected probably the worst possible location, an area in the Qu'Appelle Valley some forty-five miles northeast of Regina, and twenty-five miles from the closest railway, in a region noted for its poor land and early frosts.

Despite the generous funding provided by the JCA, local officials did not build any shelters for the new immigrants, nor did they provide them with any seed, tools or equipment. Instead the green settlers were taken in hand by Indians from a nearby reservation and taught how to build homes and plough the land. Without this help, the Jewish settlement of Lipton would have been stillborn.

And at the beginning many thought it should have been. The land was unsuitable for wheat, the supervisors and land inspectors could not converse with the immigrants who spoke no English, and both local officials and residents were anti-semitic and wanted nothing to do with the new settlement.

Over the next few years, though more than half the original settlers left, their place was taken by new recruits from Romania and Russia. And when the JCA realized how destructive was the leadership provided by the government's appointees, it severed the relationship,

Isaak Kruger's land grant, Lipton, 1908.

Upper left: Toba Cohen, Lipton, 1916.

Upper right: First Jewish religious services held in the Lipton Colony, 1906.

Lower: Wedding ceremony in Lipton Colony, 1916.

appointed a new administrator and reorganized the colony on a more productive basis.

By 1904 there were upwards of 375 Jewish settlers and more than 19,500 acres under cultivation. Before long a synagogue was erected, teachers were hired, a cemetery was consecrated and three public schools were built, Herzl, Yeshurun and Tiferes Israel — or Typhus Israel, as it was later known to its numerous non-Jewish students.

Lipton was the last settlement founded by the JCA in Canada. Given the difficult birth and terrible growing pains of Hirsch and Lipton, the JCA thought it more beneficial to support individual farmers rather than entire settlements. And indeed, most Jewish settlers in Canada took up land on their own, without JCA assistance, like other immigrants to this country. Whenever federal officials opened up new land for homesteading, groups of young Jews applied and formed their own communities.

Perhaps the best example of this type of settlement was Sonnenfeld. In 1905, a few graduates of a JCA agricultural school in Galicia arrived in western Canada. Most worked at Hirsch, but within a year three of them, Israel Hoffer, Philip Berger and Majer Feldman, applied for homesteads in an area fifty miles west of Estevan. They first named the colony New Herman, likely for an early settler whose legs had been amputated after an accident, but then chose to honour the director of the JCA, Sigismund Sonnenfeld, by naming it after him.

It is hard to imagine a more forbidding site for a farm settlement. There were no roads and the closest railway stop was in Estevan.

The land was rocky, there was little drinking water and the climate was brutal. Yet by 1909, Sonnenfeld was a thriving community of some fifty-five Jews on twenty-five farms. Though there were never more than 150 people in the settlement, Sonnenfeld had a synagogue, two public schools and even a Jewish Farmers' Co-operative Credit Union.

In the first decade of this century, a number of other Jewish settlements came into being. In 1903, a group of Russian immigrants founded a new colony just north of Winnipeg, named Bender Hamlet, in honour of its first settler, Winnipeg land speculator Jacob Bender. This was the only attempt to create in Canada a Jewish settlement modelled on the Eastern European village. Each settler received 160

Left: Children dancing on grounds of Tiferes Israel school in Lipton, 1916.

Upper right: Inside Tiferes Israel school, 1915.

Lower right: Tiferes Israel school and synagogue, 1915.

Isaac Blatt and his sons Henry and Jack stocking wheat sheaves in Sonnenfeld, Saskatchewan.

acres of land, but lived five miles away, in the village. The land was swampy and rocky, and farming was exceedingly difficult, yet up to forty families settled there and did not do badly, especially after the arrival of the railway in 1914. Other Jewish settlements were founded in Camper, Manitoba — also known as New Hirsch — and at Rumsey-Trochu, Alberta and Alsask-Montefiore, Saskatchewan.

Perhaps the most intriguing of these settlements was founded in 1906. A group of about twenty Lithuanian Jews who had migrated to South Africa were attracted by the Canadian government's offer of 160 acres of land to any immigrant willing to settle on the prairies. Without Jewish organizational support, certainly without the support

of the JCA, the group headed for northern Saskatchewan, where they set up their homes along the Carrot River.

The Lithuanians, including the Vickar brothers Sam, David and Louis, were soon joined by refugees from the sweatshops of London who arrived brimming with radical ideas. These settlers, including Mike and Dave Usiskin, Alex Springman and others, had been attracted by an advertisement by the Carrot River homesteaders in the London Jewish press. To them, working the land with their own hands was a liberating experience. They were secular Jews, passionate Yiddishists and socialists who insisted on a Jewish name for the colony. They suggested Jew Town and then Israel Villa. But both were rejected by federal authorities as too ethnic. Finally when the creative settlers came up with the euphonious and seemingly meaningless name of Edenbridge, triumphant officials quickly accepted it. But the Jewish farmers had the last laugh. Little did the officials know that Edenbridge stood for "Yidden Bridge," or "Bridge of the Jews," commemorating the narrow steel span over the Carrot River in the middle of the settlement.

So dense was the brush around Edenbridge that it was reported that one early settler got lost on his own homestead. Nevertheless, the settlement was vibrant and relatively successful. It attracted an unusual group of settlers — people who were prepared to work all

Left: Jewish settlers arriving in Sonnenfeld Colony, 1928.

Upper right: Esther and Louis Singer, Sonnenfeld, *c.* 1910.

Lower right: Removing stones from farmland, Sonnenfeld.

Upper left: Levitt homestead, Camper, Manitoba, 1915.

Upper right: Sholom Friedel Levitt, Narcisse Colony, 1920.

Lower: Gertie Rodin, Bender Hamlet, *c.* 1916.

day, and debate and study all night. With its drama society, large library, debating club and community centre it became, in the words of one of the historians of the community, "in microcosm, a total Jewish community usually found only in large urban centres." It was not unusual for the colony to host a visiting rabbi one night and a prominent left-wing radical the next. Though at its peak it never surpassed one hundred families, Edenbridge produced mayors, reeves, a member of the legislature, justices of the peace, and an impressive array of writers, merchants and teachers.

But farming was not the only vocation for Jews west of Winnipeg. Perhaps it was not even the major one. Many of the Jewish immigrants who came to the area tried to make a living as pedlars, a business that required enormous energy and dedication, but limited investment and experience. Throughout the 1880s and 1890s Jewish "backpackers" could be found on every trail and in every farm community in the west. Because they spoke a variety of languages, they had no problem communicating with the settlers, most of whom were also newcomers from Eastern Europe. Even with a horse and wagon, the work was backbreaking and the rewards were minimal. Hard-pressed farmers simply did not have the cash to pay for the goods the pedlars offered. Often bartering was the only form of payment possible.

Though most historians agree that the widely spread-out towns and villages of the prairies desperately needed the services of the

Picnic at Edenbridge Colony.

ubiquitous pedlar, he was considered a pariah. Many small-town newspapers of the period carried the most vituperative anti-semitic attacks on his morals and alleged dishonesty. One paper urged its readers "to give pedlars the cold shake...[because] they had no business reputation to sustain...[and were] more likely to skin you than not." Even the usually supportive *Manitoba Free Press* complained that "Canadians never heard of peddling until the Jews came." A Winnipeg member of Parliament, Joseph Martin, on various occasions spoke out in the House against the depredation of the "Jew pedlar."

As soon as they had enough money, many pedlars opened up general stores. Like the pedlar, the Jewish country storekeeper became an institution, though one much less pilloried. As the chronicler of Manitoba Jewry, Arthur Chiel, points out: "As country merchants they were more than mere storekeepers. They served as interpreters, counsellors and trusted friends and their stores became informal gathering places — institutions of friendship." There was scarcely a town, village, hamlet, crossroad or railway stop where there was not a Jewish storekeeper who sold everything the settler needed, from seed to yard tools, from medicines to fuel. In return he

Leonoff Boot and Shoe, Winnipeg, *c.* 1920.

usually took whatever crop, livestock or dairy products the farmer had to exchange. The Jewish country store served as a centre for the exchange of not only goods but gossip, news and information. Most storekeepers sent their children to nearby urban centres for an education — and to maintain their Jewishness — but rarely did a child return to take over the business. The Jewish country store proved to be a one-generation phenomenon, but an important one in the development of western Canada.

Those who settled in the west between 1880 and 1914 were truly remarkable men and women. Many of the Jewish settlers were driven by the "back to the land" movement that had swept through European Jewish communities in the 1870s and 1880s. Forbidden to farm in their homelands, they deliberately set out to prove their emancipation in their new countries. Some went to Palestine to fulfil their Zionist dream, but most came to North America. In Canada these courageous settlers were among the first to establish agricultural communities, well ahead of the Ukrainians, Poles, Doukhobors, Russians and others, and preceded only by British, Mennonite and Icelandic immigrants.

For most settlers, life on the farm proved untenable. Year after year, farmers saw their hopes destroyed by blistering heat, devastating hailstorms, hordes of grasshoppers or, most often, drought. An entire year's work and profit could be lost in one short, sudden storm. The backbreaking task of clearing land, removing rocks and stumps and draining swamps, all the while withstanding armies of bloodthirsty insects; the days spent walking to and from the closest railway station or town for necessary supplies; the miles to hospitals and medical care — each of these alone was probably enough reason to leave.

Yet many stayed and flourished. As in the urban centres, there were charity teas sponsored by the women, lectures on a variety of Jewish topics by visiting experts, and in some places a Yiddish acting troupe. They learned to build homes and barns with plaster made

Mrs. Israel Hoffer feeding chickens, Sonnenfeld, 1926.

from manure, straw and water, which they mixed with their feet. They made their own candles and soap; shoes were stitched together from tanned cowhide, clothes from used flour sacks.

Most of these chores, as well as raising and feeding children, working in the fields, feeding and caring for the livestock, bringing in wood and water and keeping the family together, were done by women. Often a man was away from the farm for several days or weeks, and his wife had to do all of his usual chores as well as her own. To her as much as to her husband or father should go the credit for whatever successes the settlers achieved.

Those intrepid Jews who ventured into the Canadian interior at the turn of the century were a unique group. Some headed west because they had no choice; others were driven by a dream, by a mission to settle the land. In the end many failed, but their courage, dedication and sacrifice were an inspiration to the generation following them.

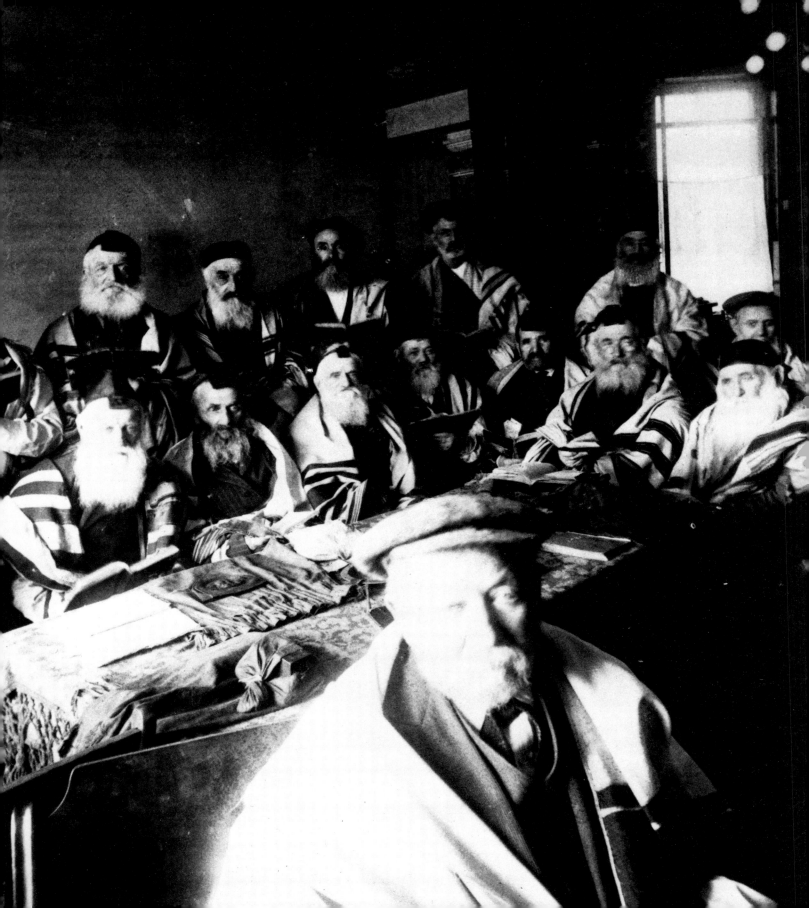

CHAPTER SIX

CREATING A COMMUNITY

1 8 8 0 - 1 9 1 4

As the number of Jews in the country increased, so did the opposition to their presence. For Canadian Jews, no period was more dramatic than the thirty-four years between 1880 and 1914. In 1880 there were a handful of Jewish communities in a few parts of the country; by 1914 communities of Jews could be found in cities, small towns and villages from coast to coast. From maybe a half-dozen synagogues in 1880, there were well over one hundred by 1914. Most important, the face of Canadian Jewry had changed. By 1914 it was not the Anglicized, comfortable, integrated community it had been thirty years before. Rather, the majority of Canada's Jewry were now Yiddish-speaking, Orthodox, penurious immigrants.

At the beginning of this period, Jews were of little concern or relevance for most Canadians. Indeed, except for their religion, Jews were thought to be no different from anyone else. They faced few restrictions. They could live anywhere, run for any political position and apply for any job. When Henry Nathan was elected to Parliament in Victoria in 1871, his Jewish origins never came up in the campaign. Nor was his faith a problem for Newman Leopold Steiner, who for five consecutive terms from 1880 to 1885 was elected an alderman in

Morning service in the chapel of the Winnipeg Jewish Old Folks Home, *c.* 1920.

Sigismund Mohr.

Toronto. Dr. Hiram Vineberg was appointed a board of health officer in Manitoba only a few years after his arrival in Canada, while in Quebec Jules Heilbronner, an Alsatian Jew, became editor of a French-language newspaper, *La Presse*, something no Jew has done since.

Their religion did not impede scores of Jewish merchants and businessmen from making their mark. Jesse Joseph was made president of the Montreal Gas Company in 1887. At about the same time, Sigismund Mohr, a German Jew, and a pioneer in the development of hydro-electric power in Canada, was head of both the Quebec Electric Company and the City Telegraph Company. Indeed many Canadians saw Jewish business activity as beneficial to society as a whole. The newspapers of the 1870s and 1880s often carried stories complimenting Jews for their "astuteness" and "business creativity." "If only more of our citizens were like the Jews," lamented a Montreal newspaper, "we would be a far more industrious and progressive nation."

Certainly the Canadian press made much of the selection of Rabbi Abraham de Sola as the first foreigner to deliver the invocation at the opening of the United States House of Representatives, in 1872. He might be a Jew, but he was a Canadian, crowed one Montreal paper. And indeed, Canadian politicians and journalists took pride in the accomplishments of the country's tiny Jewish population. In commending the loyalty and bravery of a local boy, Lawrence Miller, who had volunteered to help put down the Riel Rebellion in 1885, Toronto papers all commented on his "Hebrew" background.

But beneath the surface, pressures were building and events were conspiring that would give rise to a vile anti-Jewish campaign. It was nothing like the anti-semitism of Eastern Europe, of course; there would be no pogroms, in fact, there would be hardly any violence at all. Nor would the Jews be the only group vilified; far worse was in store for Chinese, Japanese and others as Canadians reacted to an immigration policy they found too liberal and worried about the future of their country.

A significant number of intellectuals and government officials did not approve of the substantial Jewish immigration into Canada, but no one worried more about the future face of the country, and no one made anti-semitism more respectable, than English Canada's leading thinker, Goldwin Smith. Born in England and raised in a wealthy family, Smith travelled the route of most scions of the British establishment: schooling at Eton and Oxford, and then a career in politics, education and journalism. A prolific scholar, he eventually reached the pinnacle of his profession on being named to the Regius Chair in modern history at Oxford.

For many that honour would have been sufficient, but not for Smith. Restless and unhappy, Smith decided to break entirely with the Old World, and in 1866 he accepted a position at Cornell University in upstate New York as its first professor of English history. Five years later he moved to Toronto, married a wealthy widow of the old Family Compact and settled into her home, the famous Grange — now part of the Art Gallery of Ontario, which stands on property donated to the city of Toronto by Smith.

Goldwin Smith.

For the next three decades, Smith lectured and wrote extensively, and he was soon recognized as the intellectual leader of his new homeland. There was scarcely any academic, social or political activity in which he did not play a role or about which he did not have something to say. He was a leader of the nationalist Canada First Party, was the first president of the National Club, and helped found several important journals.

Though Smith wrote on many topics, the Jew was one of his favourites. His books, reviews, articles and letters are replete with condemnation of the Jews. They are, he wrote, a "parasite race" whose "tribal religion was based on exclusiveness." They are "dangerous" to any country that allowed them to enter and "needed to be watched very closely." Nor could they become good citizens, he warned, because they form a "closed group...a tribe scattered yet united, sojourning in all communities, blending with none and forming a nation within a nation." The two "greatest calamities that have ever befallen mankind," he wrote, were "the transportation of the Negro to this hemisphere and the dispersion of the Jews."

At a time when Cossacks were running amok among Russian Jews killing, maiming and raping thousands, and forcing hundreds of thousands more to flee for their lives, Smith cautioned his countrymen against providing sanctuary. Thus in 1891, when he heard that the premier of Manitoba was in Europe attempting to attract immigrants — including Jews — Smith was beside himself. He immediately wrote to the *Winnipeg Tribune* that it would be disastrous to allow Jews into the Canadian west. They have no "agricultural aptitude," he charged, and they "feed like parasites on the product of native labour." Unfortunately, the *Tribune* and several other western papers took their cue from him. Thundered the *Tribune*: "If there is anything this country does not want it is parasites."

Smith's influence was profound. He was no crank or fanatic, and he had no shortage of platforms for his bilious message. Not only did many newspapers, academics and politicians begin to react favourably to his ideas, but word of his activities even reached prospective Jewish immigrants in Europe. As early as 1884, the London *Jewish Chronicle* warned its readers to stay away from Canada since there seemed to be much anti-semitism "even among the natives of the New World."

Smith's voice was not, of course, the only one raised against the Jew in English Canada. In 1901, the principal of Toronto's St. Michael's College, the Reverend Dr. Teefy, vigorously denounced the Jew for his "covetousness, his anti-Christian spirit [and] his fondness for pleasure." For the Jews struggling to survive on isolated homesteads in western Canada or in sweatshops in Montreal, Teefy's words must have sounded quite bizarre.

More grievous was Smith's impact on events that took place long after he died. Among those he spoke or wrote to on the subject of Jews was the young William Lyon Mackenzie King, whose anti-semitism was one of the major factors in the dreadful tragedy of the 1930s and 1940s, when Canada closed her doors to desperate Jewish refugees fleeing Nazi death camps.

Another important figure who was profoundly affected by Smith was a young French-Canadian member of Parliament, Henri Bourassa, to whom Smith was the "most illustrious of English writers" and the "most profound Liberal thinker of the day." Choosing to ignore Smith's well-known animus towards French Canadians, Bourassa became his most important Canadian convert. The newspaper he founded, *Le Devoir*, would over the next fifty years be one of the most vocal opponents of Jewish immigration to Canada, and a constant thorn in the side of Quebec Jewry.

There are some academics who argue that Smith was not an anti-semite, that he did not dislike Jews or their religion. They accurately point out that he contributed to the building of the Holy Blossom Synagogue and attended its opening ceremony. All he wanted, they argue, was for Jews to become proper Canadians — that is, to be completely assimilated with the Christian majority at the expense of their rituals, their way of life, their traditions and their culture, in other words, to cease being Jews in anything but name.

As the nation's most widely published intellectual, he always found an attentive audience, but not all English Canadians agreed with his views. George Grant, the principal of Queen's University, took Smith to task for his nativist attack on the Jews. It was wrong-headed, Grant wrote in 1894, for Smith to demand that Jews should "cease being Jews." Rather, Smith and others like him should respect the Jews for their distinctiveness and their traditions. Respecting differences, Grant said, not religious persecution, would make Canada a healthier nation.

Although Goldwin Smith's ideas had a strong impact in Quebec — his anti-Catholicism notwithstanding — anti-Jewish feeling was already well rooted there. By the 1870s, an ultramontane view had taken hold in Quebec. Its supporters believed that the Vatican had the absolute right to intervene in the secular world and that only a society based on the teachings of the church was a healthy one. If Quebec was to be a French-Canadian province guided solely by the church, then any non-Catholic who attempted to play a role in the public life of the province was dangerous. And most dangerous of all, according to church leaders, was the Jew. Thus Catholic newspapers in Quebec began to vigorously denounce Jews. Edited by ultramontane priests, over the next fifty years *La Vérité*, *La Semaine religieuse*, and *L'Action sociale catholique*, among others, carried the unmistakable message that Jews were the enemy of the church.

Throughout the late nineteenth century, many of French Canada's prominent intellectuals associated Jews with the forces of modernity and revolution, both of which they feared were threats to the church and the French-Canadian way of life. Though only a small number of Jews had made their way into Quebec, by the 1890s there existed in the province a strong anti-Jewish ground swell. And as more Jewish immigrants arrived, tensions grew apace. Promulgated by clerical leaders such as the ultra-nationalist Jules-Paul Tardivel, scurrilous anti-semitic literature was being disseminated throughout Quebec.

The movement received an important boost through the writings of the notorious French anti-semite Edouard Drumont, whose ideas found fertile soil in Quebec. Drumont's *La France Juive*, perhaps the most insidious anti-Jewish book published in the nineteenth century, was stocked in most libraries and bookstores in Quebec and received favourable reviews. Drumont's description of Jews as despoilers of society, as ritual murderers, as allies of the devil and as enemies of honest work found a ready echo in a number of Quebec newspapers and journals.

The Dreyfus affair, in which a Jewish-French military officer was unjustly convicted of treason, created almost as profound a sensation in Quebec as it did in France. French-Canadian newspapers had a field day; most naturally sided with the church and the anti-Dreyfusards. Jews, as well as others supporting Alfred Dreyfus, were denounced by clerical leaders as plotters trying to undermine the Catholic church and its values. So much anti-Jewish feeling was created that the handful of Jews in Quebec felt it necessary to join together to create defence organizations. Out of these meetings emerged the first Anglo-Jewish newspaper in Canada, the *Jewish Times*. In its first issue it warned: "The anti-semitic movement in Europe is not without an echo in this country. It is to be found daily in those newspapers which take their Old World inspiration largely from those organs of opinion which are inimical to the Jewish People. This unjust and dangerous influence must be met and combatted in the proper manner...guarding...against the spread of moral poison which is not only a danger to us Jews but also dangerous...to them who absorb it."

In 1898 the Montreal Chamber of Commerce for the first time refused membership to an applicant simply because he was a Jew. At the same time, an anti-semitic organization, the Union of Franco-Canadians, comprising up to twenty thousand members, was founded by L.G. Robillard, who was denounced by the *Jewish Times* as the "Haman of Canada." Inspired by Robillard's group, a large meeting of young Catholics in 1906 passed a resolution supporting the creation of a province-wide anti-Jewish organization.

Another aspect of life in Quebec that outraged the Jewish community was the reluctance of the province to grant any money to Jewish charitable organizations, because, in the words of a member of the Quebec legislature, "all Jews are rich, and if there are any poor Jews, they too would soon be rich." Meanwhile the church and press had launched a crusade to bar the famous actress Sarah Bernhardt from Quebec, since as a Jew she represented "moral corruption against Christian society." Her appearances in the province were highly charged affairs; she was pelted by young stalwarts of the faith with eggs, tomatoes and other such missiles.

Evidence of anti-Jewish feeling was appearing everywhere. The Three Rivers city council expropriated the old Jewish cemetery "for health reasons" and removed the handful of bodies to a less prominent location. City councillors in Montreal tried on various occasions — and through various subterfuges — to disenfranchise Jewish voters. And according to the Jewish press, there were countless physical attacks on Jews — beards pulled, children beaten on the way to school, store windows broken, synagogues defaced — with no police intervention. If there was intervention, complained the Jewish newspapers, it was usually the victims who were arrested.

Perhaps the most flagrant anti-Jewish incident occurred in March of 1910. Joseph Edouard Plamondon, a journalist, notary and well-known anti-semite, was invited to address a meeting of the *Association canadienne de la jeunesse catholique* in Quebec City. Quoting extensively from Drumont and misquoting even more extensively from the Talmud, Plamondon proved to the satisfaction of his eager audience that Jews were ritual murderers, usurers and enemies of the church. Following the speech, his excited listeners marched out into the street where they damaged Jewish stores. When Plamondon's speech was published the next day, enraged crowds vandalized Jewish businesses and assaulted individual Jews. Two of those whose businesses were damaged launched a civil action against Plamondon in the Quebec courts. The leading Jewish lawyer of the time, Sam Jacobs, later a member of Parliament, undertook to argue the case.

The trial did not begin until 1913 and it unfortunately coincided with the furor raised throughout the world over a trumped-up case in czarist Russia in which a Jew, Mendel Beilis, was accused of ritual murder. While Jacobs and a host of witnesses — including rabbis — argued that Plamondon's charges were false, vicious and inflammatory, various Catholic clergy and journalists came forward as "expert" witnesses in support of the ritual murder charge against the Jews. On a technicality the suit against Plamondon was dismissed, the judge deciding that while indeed the Jewish race had been slandered, the two plaintiffs had not specifically been. Later that year, the decision was overturned by the Quebec Court of Appeal, which noted that since there were only seventy-five Jewish families in a total population in Quebec City of some eighty thousand, the plaintiffs were enough of a "restrictive collectivity" to bring suit against Plamondon.

Not all French-Canadian leaders were contemptuous of the Jews. In 1897, when the Central Conference of American Rabbis convened in Montreal, the province's lieutenant-governor, J.A. Chapleau, and representatives of the Quebec and federal governments spoke glowingly of the contributions made by Jews to public life in Quebec. And some clerics and journalists were openly critical of the ultramontane campaign against the Jews. Most important, the anti-Jewish attitude of the church and the French press did not stop the flow of Jews into Quebec.

Outside Quebec, Jews seemed little affected by the growth of anti-semitism. Though some clubs and organizations were closing their membership to Jews there were still few restrictions. Indeed when the Duke and Duchess of Cornwall — later King George V and Queen Mary — visited Vancouver in 1901, a young Jewish girl, Norma Hamburger, was selected to present the duchess with flowers.

For the most part, Canada's Jews were too busy to pay much attention to the outbursts of a Goldwin Smith or a Henri Bourassa. They were just trying to survive, to find homes and jobs and to build new lives, and they were too concerned with their own community problems to pay much heed to the cranks around them. Their agenda was to create a vital Jewish community; for this they needed more synagogues, Jewish schools, teachers and rabbis. They worried about the poor and the sick and who would provide for them; they worried about the survival of the Yiddish language, and of their culture and traditions. Compared with these anxieties, the jottings of a handful of intellectuals were of little concern.

For the leadership of Montreal Jewry, May 28, 1902 was like old times again. For some time the city's Jewish establishment had been on the defensive. The pressure had begun in the 1880s with the arrival

Moses Bilsky (seated) with his daughter Lillian Freiman (seated), her husband A.J. Freiman and their children, Ottawa, *c.* 1914.

of large contingents of desperate Yiddish-speaking immigrants who needed food, clothes, homes and jobs, and had increased throughout the nineties as thousands more landed in even worse condition. Then the vicious assaults by nativist newspapers and church leaders had begun. But all this was forgotten as Montreal's leading citizens gathered on that sunny May morning to dedicate a brand new building on Bleury Street that housed the Baron de Hirsch Institute.

Invitations to the opening were few and highly coveted. The Governor General himself, Lord Minto, was to be present, along with federal and provincial politicians, the mayor of Montreal, the principal of McGill University, the French consul and the cream of Montreal society. It was a gala event, the community's first in many years. No one noticed — perhaps because no one cared — that missing were representatives of the group the institute was to serve, the recently arrived Jewish immigrants.

The immigrants noticed, however. Though they appreciated the efforts of the city's affluent Jews on their behalf, they were deeply resentful of their patronizing attitude. Following the ceremony, a small group met with the leaders of the Baron de Hirsch Institute. They warned that they were no longer prepared to be treated simply as "objects of philanthropy." They wanted control of their own lives and a role in the decision-making bodies of the Jewish community. It was, remembered one of the participants at the meeting, for all intents and purposes a "declaration of war" between the uptown establishment and the downtown newcomers, a war that had been in the making since the mass immigration had begun, a war for which no one was to blame.

The leadership of Canada's Jewish community had been very receptive and generous to the new Yiddish-speaking immigrants. It was obvious that they took seriously one of Judaism's holiest precepts, that of *tsedaka*, of helping those less fortunate, of providing assistance to those in need. Philanthropy and charity were distinct hallmarks of Canadian Jewry from its earliest origins. Through the Baron de Hirsch Institute, the YMHBS and a host of other organizations, Canadian Jews upheld this fundamental tenet of their religion.

Certainly they were far more forthcoming — with both money and effort — than their American co-religionists, who were frightened by and often hostile to the arrival of so many Jews who spoke a different language, maintained different customs, and had very different views on a variety of religious and social issues. Canadian Jews in the latter part of the nineteenth century were far closer in background to the immigrants than were American Jews. Unlike the United States, where the *Yahudim*, German-Jewish establishment families, still dominated Jewish life, in Canada the original founding families had been supplanted to some extent by the mid-century arrival of English, Lithuanian and Polish Jews, many of whom were sympathetic to the new immigrants. Established Canadian Jews lobbied extensively for the admission of the new immigrants and strained the resources of the community to the breaking point to support them. Yet they, too, were anxious to preserve their hegemony over Jewish life in Canada, and were wary of any movement towards self-expression by the immigrant masses.

The most important members of the Jewish establishment were the settlers who had landed in Canada in the 1860s and 1870s and taken up residence in rural areas along the St. Lawrence, in towns such as Cornwall, Kingston, Lancaster and Maberly. These families, the Jacobses, Cohens, Vinebergs, Kellerts, Friedmans and others, had eventually moved to Montreal to take over the community's leadership. Thus, for example, William Jacobs — father of Samuel Jacobs, a future member of Parliament and president of the Canadian Jewish Congress — settled in Lancaster in 1864. Five years later the dynamic Lazarus Cohen, father of another future president of the Congress, Lyon Cohen, settled nearby. Another pioneer who moved into the area was Moses Bilsky, the first Jew to settle in Ottawa and the city's premier Jewish leader for years.

Lazarus Cohen emigrated to Canada from Poland in 1869 and became a leader of Montreal's Jewish community.

Left: Reverend Jacob Mirsky and four of his children, Ottawa, 1898. (Ottawa Jewish Historical Society 1-079)

Right: Byward Market, Ottawa, early 1900s. (Ottawa Jewish Historical Society 2-018)

Bilsky's rise to prominence was a fascinating journey. Born in Lithuania, he arrived in Canada as a child in 1845. After some years in New York, the adventurous Bilsky decided to make his fortune in the Cariboo. But like many in the gold rush of the 1860s, he failed. Rather than remaining in the Jewish community of Victoria, he headed off on horseback to San Francisco, some 1,500 treacherous miles away. He did not stay there for very long either. The tall, broad-shouldered Bilsky was immediately recruited to do some prospecting in Central America, but on his arrival in Panama he discovered he had been hoodwinked: his employers were not looking for miners; they wanted mercenaries to launch an assault against a neighbouring state. Bilsky stowed away on the next boat to California, enlisted in the Union army and found himself putting down a riot in San Francisco following the assassination of Abraham Lincoln.

Bilsky seems to have eventually tired of his escapades; he headed back to Canada, where he set up a business in the lumbering town of Mattawa some 150 miles northwest of Ottawa. In a few years, his fortune made, he settled in Ottawa, opened a successful jewellery store, married, and set about helping create and nurture the Ottawa Jewish community. Though he had eleven children of his own to care for—plus four of his late sister's—he never turned away a needy family. As his daughter Lillian Freiman recalled in later years, she would often come home from school to find that her room had been given to some newly arrived immigrants, or that some of her sweaters had disappeared to help another newcomer through the frigid Ottawa winter. Bilsky's legendary generosity made him an institution in the Canadian Jewish society of the period, but he was by no means unique. Most of the "old familes" were almost as munificent and unstinting in their efforts on behalf of the immigrants.

Toronto's Jewish community was also changing as a new generation of leadership replaced the original settlers. The most influential of the new group was Edmund Scheuer, an Alsatian who had originally settled in Hamilton. He concentrated much of his enormous energy on the Holy Blossom Synagogue and led the movement to turn it into a full-blown Reform congregation. Joining the Samuel family in their metals business were two English brothers, Alfred and Frank Benjamin, who also became active in most of the community's charitable organizations. Throughout the 1860s and 1870s, Jews from Lithuania and Galicia took up residence in Toronto and began filling the growing community's leadership positions.

Up to the great migration at the end of the nineteenth century, the Jews of Ontario and Quebec were comfortable, well integrated and totally English Canadian in their culture, attitude and language. Holy Blossom even introduced a special service for the Thanksgiving holiday. Indeed the great Yiddish scholar, Alexander Harkavi, who spent some years in Montreal in the 1880s, complained that Canadian Jews refused to speak Yiddish no matter how bad their English was. "They were ashamed lest they be recognized as Jews," he lamented.

The mass migration between the 1880s and 1914 drastically changed the face of Jewish Canada. The community became a significant minority in the country rather than a negligible one, increasing from around 2,500 in 1882 to well over 100,000 by 1914. In that year, in the country's three largest cities, Toronto,

Upper: Bessie Morris (left) who emigrated from Russia to live with the Carlofsky family in Ottawa, shown with the Carlofsky children, *c.* 1917. (Ottawa Jewish Historical Society 1-075)

Lower: Mr. and Mrs. Abraham Lithwick in front of their Byward Market store, Ottawa. (Ottawa Jewish Historical Society 2-036)

Upper: St. Lawrence Boulevard, the Main, Montreal, *c.* 1915.

Lower: "To Let" signs from Rubin's Stationery, on St. Lawrence Boulevard in Montreal.

Montreal and Winnipeg, Jews constituted more than six per cent of the population and were the largest immigrant communities in each. Ottawa's Jewish population had skyrocketed from 20 to 3,000; Vancouver's from a few dozen to over 1,000. Other cities and towns had experienced similar growth.

More important than the growth in numbers, however, was the change in composition. By 1914 the acculturated Anglo-Jewish community had all but disappeared; gone was their serene, comfortable, stable world. In its place had emerged the new world of Canadian Jewry, the seething, crowded, chaotic, noisy, Yiddish world of the Eastern European newcomers. Leadership still remained in the hands of the old guard; their wealth, influence, contacts and ability to speak English assured that. But they were losing their control over the Jewish community.

If the two groups were in different spheres spiritually and ideologically, they were also in distinct spheres physically. The immigrant's world was the crowded housing and crammed neighbourhoods of St. John's Ward in central Toronto, along the Main (St. Lawrence Boulevard) in Montreal, and north of the CPR tracks in Winnipeg. It was a milieu of congested streets, noisy markets, cramped workplaces; of ragpickers and junk dealers; of pushcarts and pedlars; of lines of young and old waiting at street corners before dawn every morning to be picked up by employers who wanted a cheap day's work. Two or three families often shared the same flat, ten or twelve people the same small house; all competing for space with sewing machines and other tools required for piecework done at home. A babel of languages: Yiddish above all, but also Polish, Lithuanian, Russian, Ukrainian, Romanian — everything, it seemed, but English and French — assaulted the ears.

Such a world was totally alien to the established Jewish residents of Montreal and Toronto, who were much disturbed by the behaviour and appearance of the immigrants. They were "too conspicuous," complained the rabbi of Toronto's Holy Blossom. How could they successfully integrate into Canadian society, he worried. From the point of view of the established community, the new arrivals were not moving quickly enough to rid themselves of their old European habits. As for their language, to the ears of many of the establishment, Yiddish was sheer "jargon," its harsh, guttural sounds "grating." The newspaper of the wealthy, the *Jewish Times*, pleaded with the immigrants not to use their language in public. Yet despite their concerns, the Jewish establishment created a plethora of organizations to provide both economic assistance and material and moral support.

The most important of these was, of course, the Baron de Hirsch Institute. Not only did it cover the costs of sending newcomers to western Canada, but it provided immigrants in Montreal with housing, loans, jobs and education. In its spanking new building, the institute housed a library and meeting places where immigrants could learn English and other useful skills, and where they could meet and discuss their concerns. Under the inspired leadership of men such as Lyon Cohen and Sam Jacobs, the institute became the model for philanthropic and immigrant-aid organizations for the next generation.

Perhaps the most remarkable aspect of Jewish philanthropy in this period was the role played by women. Barred by custom — and occasionally even by law — from taking a more active part in the political and economic spheres of society, many women found an outlet in philanthropic work. Indeed most of the early benevolent societies in the Jewish community were funded by women. The Ladies' Montefiore Hebrew Benevolent Society, founded in 1878, was one of the first philanthropic organizations in Toronto. By the beginning of the new century, much of the immigrant-aid work was being done by an increasing number of women's groups; Montreal had its Ladies' Aid Society, Ladies' Hebrew Benevolent Society and Young Ladies' Work Society, among others; in Toronto, joining the Montefiore women, were the Austrian Ladies' Aid Society, the Polish

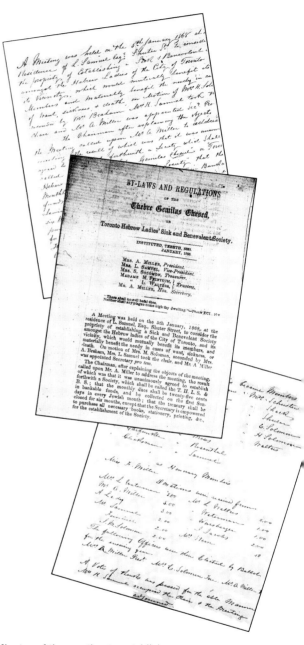

Minutes of the meeting to establish the Toronto Hebrew Ladies' Sick and Benevolent Society in Toronto, 1868.

Upper left: Camilla Levy, one of the founders of the Deborah Ladies' Aid Society in Hamilton.

Upper right: President and officers of the National Council of Jewish Women, Toronto, 1928.

Lower: Toronto Hebrew Ladies' Aid Society minute book, written in Yiddish, 1903. (Toronto Jewish Congress/CJC Ont. Region Archives)

Ladies' Aid Society, the Ezras Noshim Society, and the two most successful, the National Council of Jewish Women (NCJW) and the Toronto Hebrew Ladies' Aid Society.

Perhaps no women's organization has been more active — and more creative — over the past century than the NCJW. Founded in the United States in the 1890s, it arrived in Toronto in 1897. Appealing largely to women of the established Jewish community, its efforts were concentrated on helping newcomers to Toronto to integrate, find jobs and be educated. It was not until after the First World War that the organization expanded its membership across the country.

At the turn of the century the Toronto Hebrew Ladies' Aid dominated the other women's groups. Its mandate was to provide assistance to anyone who asked; the applicant was not compelled to prove need in any way. No investigation was held; no corroborating evidence was asked for. The society's determination to maintain the dignity of the poor was exceptional among charities of the period.

In many ways the Jewish women of Canada were far ahead of their male counterparts in the field of philanthropy, and they were the real pioneers in this area among Canadian women. As early as 1878, the energetic women of Hamilton had founded the Deborah Ladies' Aid Society. Over the next twenty-five years, women's organizations to help the immigrant poor were founded in Winnipeg, Calgary, Ottawa, Vancouver — indeed, in every city and town with more than

Left: Hayter Street, the Ward, 1911.

Right: Map published by the Bureau of Municipal Research in Toronto, 1918, indicating conditions in the Ward such as lack of water and building defects.

a handful of Jews. All of these operated on the same principles. Membership was restricted to women, each of whom was required to pay monthly dues ranging from five cents to one dollar. Each society had its own constitution, its own sphere of interest and its own fundraising mechanisms, usually via teas, door-to-door canvassing, dances, concerts and picnics. Each society also had committees responsible for distributing relief and working with the needy.

The assistance provided by the Jewish organizations was essential to community life for newly arrived immigrants. Most came penniless and without skills. For those who did not go out west to farm, only two types of jobs were available, factory work or peddling, and neither was very remunerative.

By European standards, the Main in Montreal, the Ward in Toronto and Selkirk Avenue in Winnipeg's north end were not true

Children in the Ward, 1911.

ghettos; people were free to leave and live elsewhere, or so the newcomers were told. But the growing hostility to the immigrants encouraged them to live in a few specific areas. Most were happy to. There they were among friends, relatives and townsfolk from their homelands. The food, the smells, the language were familiar. The ghettos of the New World cushioned the shock of arrival in an alien society and allowed newcomers time to recuperate from the trauma of immigration.

These ghettos, for the Jews as for other immigrant groups, provided a breathing space before they and their families were

Canadianized. Here the immigrant found a historical continuity to his life, a sense of fellowship, a sense of status. Here in the corner stores, the synagogue, the market, the front yard, kin and friends from home towns in the old country gathered to pass on advice, to gossip or to make collective decisions on whom to send for from their village. As well, they debated the politics of both their new and old homes, talked about working conditions and organized unions. For the immigrant, the ghetto became his anchor in the New World.

The Jewish establishment discovered to its dismay that it was impossible to impose any order on ghetto life. Just blocks away from their homes was a Jewish world they scarcely recognized and assuredly did not like. They failed to recognize that a community was taking shape before their very eyes, a community made up of Jews from various countries, cities, towns and *shtetls* of Eastern Europe, a community riddled with conflicting ideas, concerns and ideologies. There were Zionists and anti-Zionists, socialists, anarchists, Yiddishists, secular and Orthodox, each with their own agenda, each with their own plan for the survival of the Jewish people in Canada. The arguments, the noise and the dissension were often too much for the uptown Jews. How would it look, they wondered, to their Canadian hosts? They feared that the orderly, sedate Jewish society they had worked so hard to create was suddenly bursting apart.

Yet even to the Jewish leadership, it was clear that in the Yiddish-speaking neighbourhoods of Winnipeg, Toronto and Montreal there was a vitality, a uniqueness, which was both frightening and inspiring; frightening because with so many conflicting voices, it seemed as though the community would destroy itself; inspiring because of the creativity and energy being generated there. As the famed journalist Reuben Brainin wrote of Jewish life in Canada in 1914: "It is now the high season of our organizational life; steaming and boiling, smoke and gunpowder; assemblies, concerts, lectures of all sorts, banquets, resolutions, conferences, balls, tag days, suggestions, collections, protests…arguments, intrigues, circulars, handbills…dissension."

Upper: Agnes Street in the Ward, 1910.

Lower: Kensington Avenue, Toronto, on market day, 1924.

This generation of immigrants would produce the synagogues, societies, schools, newspapers, theatres, unions and benevolent organizations that would become the foundation of Jewish life in Canada in the twentieth century, just as these products of the ghettos would come to dominate Canadian Jewish society.

The earliest waves of the Eastern European immigrants were deeply concerned with creating a proper religious life. Holy Blossom and the Spanish and Portuguese synagogues were not for them, nor were the slightly less fancy Goel Tzedec in Toronto and Shaar Hashomayim in Montreal. Almost upon their arrival, tiny new synagogues called *shtiblach* sprang up; they were in virtually every detail Eastern European transplants. Each ethnic group, each group of men from the same home town, wanted its own prayer hall to ensure that its unique customs would not be forgotten. By 1914 dozens of *shtiblach* in Montreal, Toronto and Winnipeg were catering to their own communities. There were Romanian, Polish, Hungarian, Ukrainian, Russian and Moldavian synagogues. Eastern European Jews who had spent some time in Britain opened up their own "Men of England" synagogue. There were synagogues for the men of Minsk, Lagov, Apt, Kiev, Ostrowiecz and a veritable atlas of Jewish settlements in Poland or Russia. In 1912 Winnipeg alone had three full-time rabbis and twelve synagogues, including one just for Zionists.

The synagogues were not simply places to pray. They were social halls, schools and cultural centres. They united the religious and social life of the neighbourhood and were part of the immigrant's psychological map, his safety net, his security blanket. When all else failed, he knew he would find understanding — if not succour — among his fellow congregants. And outside the synagogue, congregants could mingle, argue or flirt with the neighbourhood girls.

Almost as important as the synagogue — and to the secular, more important — were the burgeoning fraternal and mutual benefit soci-

Hebrew Aid and Immigrant Society picnic, Vancouver, 1910.

eties. Based on the deeply rooted Jewish tradition of communal self-help, these organizations were integral to an immigrant community. The immigrant could not count on government help; none was forth-coming. Worse, the government was aggressively deporting those who were destitute and had no means of support. Nor could he or she rely on the limited resources of the established Jewish community. Despite the valiant efforts of the Baron de Hirsch Institute and the various women's charities, they could not possibly deal with all the needs of such a large immigrant population. In any case, most newcomers wished at all costs to avoid the stigma of relying on charity.

Everyone could belong to the mutual benefit society; all the dues collected were put in a common pool from which anyone could draw when the need arose. And while most immigrants were young and healthy, the system worked. The members of these societies did not understand actuarial tables. They did not have to so long as Eastern Europe kept depositing her young Jews on Canada's shore. The society provided insurance, loans to buy homes or businesses, burial plots and funeral benefits; many even hired doctors specifically to service the society's members. Since Jewish doctors did not have ad-mitting privileges to most hospitals, some societies endowed beds in various hospitals to assure their members of a place when illness struck. Most societies were made up of men and women from the same town or region in the old country. These *landsmanshaftn* were key to integrating the newcomer into Canadian society. An old-timer would take a greenhorn under his wing and find him a home, a job or even a suitable spouse. And the societies' premises were a place to relax, to play cards, to meet girls. It was another cushioning layer for the immigrant on his path to accommodating himself to his new environment.

Though largely isolated from the host society, most ghetto dwellers hungered for news and information both about life in their new country and about the communities they had left behind

Zionist Athletic Club, East Side Champions, Winnipeg, 1903.

The Canadian Jewish Times

Vol. XV.   MONTREAL, TAMUZ 20th, 5672, JULY 5th 1912   No 30

HIS NAME SHALL NEVER DIE IN OUR HEARTS AND IN THE HEARTS OF OUR CHILDREN

Eighth Anniversary of the death of Dr. Theodor Herzl.

Canadian Jewish Times, 1912,
published on the 8th anniversary of
the death of Dr. Theodor Herzl.

in Europe. To satisfy this need, the Yiddish newspaper became a staple for every immigrant family, many of whom spoke no English. There were papers from New York, Warsaw and Berlin, but most popular were those produced at home. Montreal's Anglophone Jewish community already had a paper, the *Jewish Times*, established in 1897 by Lyon Cohen and Samuel Jacobs and edited by a non-Jew, Carrol Ryan. It spoke for and to the Montreal Jewish establishment.

It was not until 1907 that the first regular Yiddish daily papers began publishing — the *Kanader Adler* (*Canadian Eagle*) in Montreal and the *Kanader Yid* (*Canadian Israelite*) in Winnipeg. Four years later the *Zhurnal* (*Journal*) began in Toronto. These were not merely newspapers; for the newcomer they were an introduction to the New World; they were forums of debate, vehicles for self-expression. Stories from other Yiddish newspapers all over the world, or translated from the English press, were reprinted. Some of the world's leading Yiddish journalists — Reuben Brainin, Israel Medres, Abraham Rhinewine, Mark Selchen and Leon Chazanovitch — wrote for these Canadian papers. The papers serialized the latest novels and had extensive literary and cultural coverage. They were, for all intents and purposes, the university of the Jewish common man and woman. They were read and reread, savoured and passed around; they provided the ammunition for debate and discussion, reflecting as they did the cacophony of voices and views of the period. In the words of the founder of the *Adler*, Hirsch Wolofsky: "Like other American Yiddish periodicals, the *Adler* rose to the challenge of transforming the last migrants from Russia…into progressive citizens of the New World. This became its specific *raison d'être*."

Another phenomenon of the immigrant neighbourhoods was the Jewish bookstores. These did more than sell books and newspapers. They were meeting halls, gathering places where newcomers, students, union organizers and others could browse through newspapers and books, drink soda water, meet friends and argue. Dworkin's in Toronto and Hershman's in Montreal were the most renowned of these establishments. As David Rome has described them: "The bookstores in the ghetto were an intimate stage…The bookseller was not just working for a living. He was propagating his philosophy by distributing pamphlets and papers close to his own views…The bookstore crystallized the cultural and political interests of the immigrant society." As well, they often served as lending libraries for those who could not afford to buy books. For many, these stores were the first introduction to the wonderful world of Yiddish literature, as well as to the variety of ideologies being debated over seltzer and tea.

From the bookstores the newcomer graduated to the libraries, the most important, of course, being the Jewish Public Library in Montreal, founded in 1914 by Reuben Brainin and the well-known Hebraist Yehuda Kaufmann. The library was the community's cultural centre. Around its tables, workers, intellectuals, pedlars, even the occasional boss sat and read and debated — often late into the night, until they were forced out by an overworked library staff. The library offered courses on a vast array of topics, sponsored lectures and brought in authors from all over the Yiddish world.

Another institution was the Jewish travel agent. More than just a ticket seller, he acted as lawyer, accountant, marriage broker, employment bureau and political-influence pedlar. His store was the centre of much traffic as workers came in to put weekly deposits on passages for a wife, child, mother, brother or sister left behind. While there, they arranged for the agent to deal with the police or city hall over their business licences or their housing problems.

The ghettos also spawned a vibrant Yiddish theatre. By the early 1900s, there were three Yiddish theatrical groups in Montreal, most of whose productions took place, paradoxically, in the theatre of the Monument National, a building put up by the ultra-nationalist St-Jean-Baptiste Society as a monument to the French-Canadian nation. In fact, the building became a home to the stars of the Yiddish stage in New York and elsewhere who regularly performed with the Montreal

Upper: Hyman's Book and Art Shop, Toronto, 1925. (Toronto Jewish Congress/CJC Ont. Region Archives 1171)

Lower: Yehuda Kaufmann.

125

Cast at the Queens Theatre in Winnipeg performing a benefit for the orphanage, 1918.

acting troupe. Often the plays were written and produced by local playwrights. Winnipeg also produced a variety of theatre groups. The Queens Theatre, at one time a church, became Winnipeg Jewry's Monument National. As early as 1904, Winnipeg had its own Jewish opera company and a Yiddish dramatic club. Toronto Jewry also had its own theatre, the Lyric, another renovated church.

In the words of historian Stephen Speisman, the Yiddish theatre was "a place where [the immigrant] could laugh uproariously after a day in the factory, where he could rise out of the indignity of his existence as a ragpicker to heights unattainable outside the fantasy of the stage, where the catharsis of weeping simultaneously over one's own lot and over the tragedy of the fictional character was to be had for ten cents." Meanwhile the *Jewish Times* lamented that the creation of a Yiddish theatre marked "a revival of the ghetto instinct."

Though most children attended public schools, it was their Jewish education that their parents worried about. If their traditions and culture were to survive, if Yiddish was to stand a chance against the compelling pull of English, then the children of the community would have to be educated properly. In the Jewish neighbourhoods of most Canadian cities, the Jewish school system seemed as if it had been transplanted from an East European *shtetl*. Following a full day in a public school, instruction was given in *chedarim*, or one-room schools. Teachers were mostly failed shopkeepers or men too old or too ill to work in factories. Occasionally these men went door to door to peddle their teaching skills. It was not until various groups began building community-supported schools called Talmud Torahs that a real educational system began to develop.

As on most subjects, the Jewish community was divided over schooling. Some wanted only religious schools; others wanted secular ones. Some thought the language of instruction should be Hebrew; others preferred Yiddish. Some wished the schools to be thoroughly Zionist; others demanded they be socialist. In the end, they all won. As a result of the competing pressures, a variety of night schools was founded, each with its own ideological or religious underpinning.

Montreal's first Talmud Torah came into being in 1896. By the First World War the city had five Jewish schools, ranging from the religious to the secular, including two that were socialist — one Zionist and one non-Zionist. Toronto had two Orthodox Talmud Torahs — one Hebrew, the other Yiddish. Its Jewish National Radical School was Yiddish, secular and socialist. According to an American Jewish newspaper, the best Hebrew school in Canada — and one of the best three in North America — was Winnipeg's Hebrew Free School. In addition, the city boasted a Labour Zionist school, the Peretz School, and a non-Zionist socialist school, the Folks Shule. It also had a dynamic spiritual leader in Rabbi Israel Isaac Kahanovich,

Upper: Jack (Cohn) Berliner Touring Troupe.

Lower: Poster for a production at the Queens Theatre.

Upper: Toronto Jewish Old Folks
Home. (Toronto Jewish Congress/CJC Ont.
Region Archives 253)

Lower: S. Hart Green.

a Lithuanian immigrant, who arrived in 1907 and for the next thirty-eight years was the dominant force in the city's religious and educational life. Kahanovich was instrumental in creating most of the city's Jewish institutions. More than anyone else, he was responsible for the almost legendary dynamism of Winnipeg's Jewish life.

As early as 1901 the Jews of Saint John, New Brunswick — all three hundred of them — built a Talmud Torah. Schools sprang up in Glace Bay, Fort William, Calgary, London, Hamilton and dozens of other locales, including the tiny farm settlements in the west, which then fought among themselves for qualified teachers.

How much learning went on in these schools is moot. But at least each community had indicated its commitment to providing a Jewish background for its young.

Though the established Jewish community, outnumbered and out-organized, looked with deep concern on the activities of the new immigrants, they nonetheless dug deep into their pockets to sustain the newcomers. In the first two decades of this century, Montreal Jewry, as historian Gerald Tulchinsky points out, built and provided the operating budgets for the Baron de Hirsch Institute, a clinic, a sanitorium, two orphanages, an old-age home, an athletic and cultural club, a reform school and a host of other organizations that dealt with the needs and problems of the immigrant community. This generosity was duplicated by the Jews of Toronto and Winnipeg. As a Toronto paper enviously noted in 1910: "There are no more philanthropic people than our Jews. Would that more of our citizens were like them." Similarly the *Winnipeg Free Press* editorialized in 1912: "It is the proud boast of the Jewish people that they do not leave their poor to the mercy of strangers."

But Jewish philanthropy extended far beyond their own poor. As early as the first years of this century the Jewish community contributed handsomely to non-Jewish institutions. In 1908, when the Winnipeg General Hospital was in desperate financial straits, a meeting was held among Jewish leaders and a considerable amount of money was raised. Montreal Jewry were in the forefront of much of the city's charitable work. Despite the enormous amounts they donated to their own community, they also contributed much to the larger community. The lieutenant-governor of Quebec pointedly praised Montreal's Jewry for its generosity.

But it was not only money that established Jews were giving to Canadian society; it was also time and effort. During the years before 1914, Samuel Rosenthal in Ottawa, Nathan Freed and Jacob Miller in Cornwall, Moses Finkelstein and Abraham Scoliter in Winnipeg, Samuel Shultz in Vancouver, Abraham Blumenthal and Louis Rubinstein in Montreal, Sam Minden in Webwood, Ontario, and Louis Singer in Toronto were all elected aldermen. In Kenora, Ontario, Simon Cobrin was elected mayor. Montefiore Joseph of Quebec and Simon Leiser of Victoria were chosen as presidents of their respective boards of trade. And in 1914 Samuel Shultz was appointed Canada's first Jewish judge. Even more important, perhaps, a young Jewish lawyer whose family had settled in New Brunswick some fifty years before, S. Hart Green, was elected to the Manitoba legislature, the first Jew to sit in a provincial assembly since Confederation. And in 1916 Peter Bercovitch took a seat in the Quebec legislature, the first Jew elected since Ezekiel Hart.

The new Jewish immigrants were also beginning to make their mark, and none with more flair than the Rubinstein family of Montreal. Long before he was elected alderman, Louis, the son of Polish immigrants, was Canada's premier figure skater. Indeed in 1890 he won the world's championship in Russia. For more than ten years he was Canada's best. When he retired, his younger brother Moses took over as Canada's champion. Not to be outdone, their sister Rachel also won a brace of titles. The daughter of Lithuanian Jews who had arrived in Montreal in the 1880s, Pauline Lightstone (known professionally as Donalda) was rapidly becoming one of the world's leading opera singers. Israel Rubinowitz, whose parents had settled in Vancouver in 1892,

AN APPEAL

To the Electors of

St. Louis Division

PETER BERCOVITCH, K.C.
Liberal Candidate

Election Day, Monday, May 22, 1916

Peter Bercovitch's election pamphlet, 1916.

Pauline Lightstone (Madame Donalda).

was Canada's first Jewish Rhodes scholar. Of the five high school graduates in the Yukon in 1904, three were Jewish and all were accepted by the University of Toronto. Marcus Sperber, himself an immigrant, graduated first in his class in law from McGill in 1900. Ironically, while Max Lesses, a young Jew, was graduating with the gold medal in medicine from Queen's University, the university was lobbying for legislation that would make it totally "Christian in character" and allow it to bar Jews. After much debate in Parliament, the bill was amended so that Queen's would be "Christian in character" only in regard to its administration and teaching staff. In effect, Jews could be accepted as students but not as faculty or administrators.

In Montreal the influx of so many Jewish immigrants brought to a head the long-simmering dispute over education in Quebec. Under the laws of the province, all educational facilities were either Catholic or Protestant. For purposes of education, Jews had no rights; during school hours Jewish children were expected to become Catholic or Protestant. The Anglo-Jewish establishment simply opted to send their children to English-speaking Protestant schools. In return they paid the school-tax portion of their property taxes to the Protestant school board. As long as the Jewish population was tiny and the community prosperous, it was no problem for the Protestant board to accept the few dozen Jewish children and happily benefit from the taxes.

But by the early 1900s, the Protestants were growing increasingly uncomfortable with this arrangement. The few dozen Jewish children had grown to over one thousand; they now constituted over seventeen per cent of the student body. Because their parents were mainly poor tenants who did not pay school taxes, no extra funding was forthcoming. In addition, English-speaking Protestants in Montreal were on the defensive. The city had a Francophone majority, and even among the Anglophone population Irish Catholics predominated. With the number of Jewish immigrants increasing every time a boat docked in the harbour or a train arrived from Halifax, it seemed that English-speaking Protestants were rapidly losing their influence. Something had to be done — quickly. The unwitting target was Jacob Pinsler, a studious fifteen-year-old immigrant who graduated first in his class and was therefore entitled to a scholarship to attend high school.

When Pinsler arrived at his new school, he was denied the scholarship on the grounds that his father was a tenant and did not pay taxes to the Protestant school board. His family sued and the case was taken over by Maxwell Goldstein, a McGill law graduate, and Sam Jacobs. Despite their efforts, the court ruled in favour of the school board. In effect, it said, Jews in Quebec were second-class citizens who had no right — unless they owned property — to send their children to school. Goldstein's argument that this contravened the famous acts of the 1830s giving Jews full rights and freedoms as citizens of Quebec was disregarded.

Though the situation was rectified within a few months by an act of the legislature that guaranteed all Jewish children admission into the Protestant school system, the issue was hardly settled. Indeed it got worse as more and more Jewish students enrolled. By 1914 Jews made up over forty per cent of the system; by 1916 there were over 10,000 Jews in Protestant schools among a total enrolment of around 22,000. Yet, while Jewish children were legally considered Protestants for purposes of education, their parents were still Jews and, as such, were barred from becoming teachers or members of the board. Even though many schools now had a Jewish majority — indeed some were almost entirely Jewish — Jews were specifically forbidden from playing any role in the system. It was, thundered the *Jewish Times*, clearly a case of "taxation without representation." Various bills introduced into the legislature to broaden Jewish educational rights were defeated. Protestant school authorities, supported by Catholic colleagues who were worried about the implications for their own schools, were concerned that they would lose control if Jews were given representation. Jews were here at "our sufferance" remarked a leading Protestant cleric, and they "must be reminded of their place."

It was not the children of the wealthy Jews the board objected to; it was the children of the poor. And it was precisely these children that the Jewish establishment also worried about. If they could not attend Protestant schools, who would provide their education? Jewish leaders realized only too well that it would be their responsibility. They feared that in the end they would have to create and fund a separate educational system for the Jewish community.

The uptown Jews were determined that this must not happen. Not only would the expense be beyond their means, but the principle of separate parochial education was too horrifying to accept. As their spokesman Peter Bercovitch put it: "[It would be] wrong and destructive…to send our children [to schools] with a Jewish atmosphere…We have no desire to create a Jewish state within the province of Quebec…We want our children to be citizens of the province and of Canada…Schools [should be] the melting pot where they will get their education and the ideals of this province."

The immigrant community had a far different view. In 1912 some of them called a "people's conference" on the school question, and resolved to end the Protestant education of Jewish children and to set up a separate school board for Jewish children where Yiddish and perhaps Hebrew would have the same status as English and French. Their spokesmen made it clear that nothing less than an autonomous Jewish school system could ensure the survival of the Jewish people in Canada. How long, they wondered, could Jewish children remain Jewish if they were educated in schools controlled by a Protestant board and taught by Protestant teachers and forced to take Christian religious education?

Their concerns were given a fillip by a strike of some five hundred Jewish children at the Aberdeen school, who put down their pens and books to protest overtly anti-semitic comments by a teacher.

Though the students eventually went back to school, nerves had been rubbed raw. Both the Protestant and Jewish communities were up in arms over the problem. According to the superintendent of schools, the Protestant schools were just that: schools for teaching Protestant children the basis of their Christian heritage. Jews could attend these schools, but they must understand the ground rules. Jewish leaders, on the other hand, simply wanted equality and representation. If the schools could not be non-denominational as they were elsewhere in Canada, then at least the board should allow Jewish representatives and teachers to enter the system. The public school system was not only a problem for Montreal's Jews, but in other parts of the country as well. Schools were regularly being picketed by children for their insistence on providing Christian religious instruction in schools that were predominantly Jewish. In Toronto, Lansdowne school was shut down by the students after they were ordered to sing Christmas carols. At King Edward school, several blocks away, and in five other schools, Jewish students walked out over the school's refusal to hang up a Jewish flag alongside the flags of other nationalities in classrooms. Despite an act in 1930 that struck a compromise between the needs of the Jewish community and the fears of the Protestants, the problem would fester for years.

What was perhaps most worrisome to the established Jewish community was that not only was a new society taking shape in the immigrant neighbourhoods but a new class was being forged— a class with strange and exotic ideas brought over from the old country as part of its cultural baggage. The Jews who arrived after the dreadful pogrom in Kishinev in 1903 and the catastrophic failure of the revolution against the czar in 1905 were more likely to be politically radical than those who had preceded them to Canada. Many were members or supporters of the Bund, a secular left-wing movement committed to Jewish autonomy. They were imbued with the notion that socialism, with its promise of a fair and just society,

Founders and directors of the Workmen's Circle Centre, Toronto. (Toronto Jewish Congress/CJC Ont. Region Archives 3054)

and not Zionism was the only answer to their problems. These immigrants drifted naturally into trade unions, protest movements and organizations such as the Arbeiter Ring (Workmen's Circle). Ostensibly a mutual benefit society for the Jewish working class, the Arbeiter Ring was much more. An American organization imported holus-bolus into Canada, it saw itself as part of a movement to bring the oppression of workers to an end and to overthrow the capitalist system. It provided the worker with an explanation for his suffering, and a remedy for it. Socialism, trade unions and a new economic system, the immigrant was told by the various lecturers sponsored by the organization, were the only solution.

Other immigrants, influenced by such thinkers as Ber Borochov and A.D. Gordon, were equally convinced that Zionism, the creation of a Jewish state, was the only practical solution to the "Jewish problem." Many of these who were socialists as well drifted into such organizations as the Labour Zionists to do battle not only with the uptown plutocrats but with their non-Zionist, working-class colleagues in the Arbeiter Ring. The conflict over a Jewish homeland would be a hallmark of Jewish life in Canada for years to come. The noisy, dramatic but usually non-violent battles would split families, destroy relationships and undermine working-class unity for fifty years.

CUTTING MEN'S CLOTHING.

One of the interesting sights in connection with manufacturing is shown in this picture. It represents a section in our cutting room. Fifty-two men are employed in this division. The cloth shown in the picture is first put through a shrinking machine, and is then spread layer upon layer on tables 58 feet in length, until there are about 30 thicknesses. Then a marker goes over the material with patterns, marking it out to the best advantage, so as to have as little waste as possible. Notice table in foreground. It is now ready for the cutters, who use electric cutting machines, that are so perfected as to cut rapidly and more satisfactorily than it could be done by hand. The different pieces are then assembled and sent to our tailor shops to be made up into men's and boys' suits and overcoats.

This picture is merely a slight demonstration why we can offer such splendid values in clothing.

THE T. EATON CO. LIMITED

TORONTO   CANADA

Front and back of a stereograph produced by the T. Eaton Company.

What united all immigrants, however, was a common feeling of exploitation — particularly in the workplace. Most worked for the burgeoning garment industry, which by 1900 had become largely Jewish. For most Jewish entrepreneurs of an earlier period, it had been perhaps the easiest industry to gain entry into. Capital requirements were minimal — a sewing machine or two, some bolts of cloth and a commitment to work — and competition was cut-throat. Everybody thought he could make a fortune, but many manufacturers were out of business in a year or two. Those who survived did so by keeping their costs — especially for labour — to an absolute minimum.

By the early 1900s, some of the most successful firms in the country were Jewish-owned. Many of these entrepreneurs had started off as storekeepers selling clothing and dry goods. Frustrated by the erratic delivery of supplies, they had branched off into manufacturing, hiring some unemployed tailors or housewives to supplement their inventory. Solomon Levinson, for example, opened up a clothing store in Montreal in 1874. Unhappy with the quality of the goods he had to sell, he began to contract out work to neighbourhood women. Soon he hired skilled tailors, pattern-makers and cutters. By 1900, S. Levinson and Son was Canada's largest men's clothing company. Similarly, in Winnipeg,

Moses Hadas' store eventually became the Western Shirt and Overall Company, and Ben Jacob's became Jacob and Crawley; these were then two of the most important clothing empires in Canada. Not far behind were the firms of the "Lancaster bunch," those families including Lazarus and Lyon Cohen, Harris Kellert, Noah and David Friedman and Harris Vineberg, who had originally opened up stores in the area around Lancaster, Ontario in the 1860s and 1870s. With their modern factories, distribution networks, wholesale operations and quality products, they dominated the garment industry in Montreal in this period. But for the most part the industry consisted largely of small firms operating in lofts, kitchens or living rooms, employing a handful of men, women and even children, and doing contract work for larger companies.

Whether it was piecework at home or a job in a factory, the working conditions were horrific — so bad, in fact, that the government set up various commissions of enquiry. They found that the factories were unventilated — searing hot in the summer, frigid in the winter; hours were long — some workers worked twelve hours a day, seven days a week. Eighty-hour work weeks for women and children were not uncommon. A Toronto paper reported in 1908 that in one house in the Ward there was "a room in the basement about 15 foot square, [in which] a family of 6 or 7 persons were engaged at 11 o'clock at night working on ready-made garments, while in the same room used for sleeping, cooking and eating as well as working, a young girl was lying in bed sick."

Conditions in Montreal were even worse. Immigrants had to compete for jobs with French Canadians fleeing the exhausted farmlands of rural Quebec. Wages were lower and hours of work longer than anywhere else in the country, and illness and hunger the workers' steady companions. During the economic downturn of 1908, various Jewish organizations came together to found a "people's kitchen" to feed the poor. Within a month it was feeding thousands.

First Pioneers, Toronto Cloakmakers' Union, 1911. (Toronto Jewish Congress/CJC Ont. Region Archives 13)

When the Jewish bakers in the city applied to their international union in the United States for life insurance, almost half were rejected because they had tuberculosis.

For the immigrant there was little choice but to work in the garment industry; often these were the only jobs available, the only jobs for which they had any training. In the old country, each town or village had had its tailors and seamstresses; they and their apprentices supplied the manpower to keep the machines along the Main or in the Ward running. Also, in spite of its harsh conditions, the industry held out some hope of upward mobility. Many of the "bosses" had once been lowly workers themselves.

More important, for the Jewish immigrant the garment industry was home. Both his bosses and his fellow workers were Jewish. Everyone spoke Yiddish, and if he was religious, he would probably not have to work on the Sabbath — though he would have to come in on Saturday night or Sunday to make up for the time missed. A father was less reluctant to allow his daughter to work at a factory if there were friends and relatives to look after her. The opportunities for Jewish women were acutely limited in Canadian society at this time, but their income was essential for the economic well-being of their families. By 1911, sixty per cent of those employed in the industry in Toronto were young, unmarried women.

Although married women were expected to stay home and look after their families, often they, too, were not exempt from having

George Mandel's membership certificate in the Jewish National Workers' Alliance of America, 1921.

to contribute to the families' earnings. So close to total destitution were immigrant families that wives and mothers — to say nothing of grandmothers — were forced into doing piece-work at home or part-time work in factories or taking in boarders. In Europe it was part of the Jewish tradition that a woman worked to provide an income so that her husband could feel free to immerse himself in the study of the Talmud. Sending women out to work in North America was not as much of a cultural shock as some historians claim.

What was shocking, however, was the type of work they did. Slaving over a sewing machine, stitching linings for ten hours a day; subject to fines for arriving late, leaving early or not meeting quotas; charged rent for the chairs they sat on and the machines they used; victims of sexual harassment — these women were among Canada's most exploited workers. It is no wonder that many were as militant as the men in their shops. Moreover, although no strike would have been possible without their support, they were allowed to play only a minimal role in the Jewish trade unions.

Outside the workplace, Jewish women in Montreal and Toronto led what were probably the first consumer boycotts in the country. Upset by the high price of meat and bread, as early as 1908 the women organized the Jewish community not to buy these foods until the prices came down. In Montreal in 1910, immigrant Jewish women organized a mass meeting of about a thousand people to protest the price of bread. Some agreed to bake bread themselves and set up a co-operative bakery. During Toronto's notorious 1917 "Bread Strike," vigilante groups of women actually stormed into restaurants and groceries to remove bread that had been bought from the offending bakeries. In both cities the prices came down.

By 1914 immigrant women were beginning to rebel against the limitations of their domestic situation. They were expected to marry and have children, but, for many, marriage and motherhood were no longer enough, especially for those who had some schooling. They demanded a more important place in Jewish society; they wanted

Camp Yungvelt, sponsored by the Arbeiter Ring.

recognition, not only of their grievances but of their contributions. And these were indeed enormous. The ladies' auxiliaries of various synagogues, *landsmanshaftn* and unions energized the community. They were the first to set up the organizations to visit and help the ill, which eventually grew into clinics, hospitals, orphanages, old-age homes and a host of other institutions.

It would take time but over the next generation or two such women as Lillian Freiman, the founder of Hadassah in Canada, Becky Buhay, a leading radical trade unionist, and others would emerge from the shadows and take their places in the forefront of the community.

It was clear early on that for most Jewish immigrants — both male and female — Canada was not the promised land. The sweatshops and their one-room flats were rapidly becoming the cemeteries in

Workers leaving the headquarters of the Dressmakers Joint Council, Industrial Union of Needle Trades Workers, Toronto, 1932.

which their dreams about the *goldene medina*, the Golden Land, were laid to rest. The tyranny of the Cossacks had been replaced by the tyranny of the bosses; they had fought the former and were now prepared to fight the latter. Fired by socialism or Zionism, or by their memories of oppression in the homeland, these newcomers were not going to accept their lot passively. Even the non-political, the timid, the religiously observant were radicalized by their working experiences. It was these men and women who gave birth to the Jewish labour movement.

Often they found their strongest opposition in the fellow Jews who owned the shops. Most of the "bosses" had at one time been workers and immigrants themselves. They knew what it was like to be poor, to be an alien in a strange land. Yet they made it on their

General Strike Committee, International Ladies Garment Workers' Union, Toronto, 1919.

own through hard work, thrift and — though they would never admit it — some luck. And if they had made it on their own, why couldn't others? They were thus determined to thwart the immigrants' unions, whatever the cost. They had no choice — or so they thought. Any increase in labour costs, any improvement to working conditions, any decrease in working hours, might ruin their companies. Though some, like Lyon Cohen, truly sympathized with the plight of the workers, most fought the unions tooth and nail.

Yet despite the class differences and bitter industrial conflicts, there was still a bond between the boss and his workers. They met at synagogues, at *landsmanshaftn* meetings or at communal events. The owner often lent his worker money to bring over relatives from Europe or to support his family. At the same time, however, he was determined to keep the union out of his factory and to keep wage rates low, while the worker was equally determined to shut down the shop unless his boss was more forthcoming.

Some of Canada's most bitter strikes occurred in these Jewish factories. In 1900 the United Garment Workers' Union went out on strike against Mark Workman, whose firm was notorious for its harsh treatment of immigrant workers. Without missing a beat, Workman simply replaced the striking workers with scab labour and continued production. In 1907 the union tried again, this time attempting to shut down S. Levinson and Son and several other firms. This strike failed as well; newly arrived immigrants rushed into the breach to take the jobs of the strikers. In 1908, Noah Friedman's company successfully put down another strike. Not until 1912 did the workers score a major victory.

This strike, in Montreal's men's clothing industry, was a turning point for the city's Jewish unions. Until then the workers had achieved none of their goals: union recognition, higher wages, better working conditions, shorter hours, sanitary and safety standards, an end to the piece-work and contracting-out systems and equal pay for men and women. It was a long and virulent strike lasting more than seven weeks, but this time the workers remained united. Rather than striking one company, they struck almost the entire industry. Except in the smallest firms, tailors, pressers, cutters and pattern-makers all walked out. There was some violence as "goons" hired by the companies beat up strikers. The manufacturers even tried importing strikebreakers from Toronto and New York. But the workers would not break. Supported by the downtown community, massive parades and demonstrations were held in front of the factories. Strike funds were set up; tag days held; workers in other industries contributed part of their pay to support the strikers. Eventually a compromise was reached. Though the union did not win its major demands — there would be no union recognition, for example — it won enough concessions to claim a major moral victory.

Jewish garment workers elsewhere in the country would have been happy to achieve even the limited success of the Montreal workers. When Hamilton and Winnipeg workers went out on strike to gain union recognition and better working conditions, they were smashed. In Winnipeg, Ben Jacob, who led the manufacturers' counter-attack, was particularly harsh with his workers. Nor were the far more numerous Toronto workers any more successful. There were a number of acrimonious strikes against Jewish employers — one lasting for more than a year — with little to show for them. Despite the pro-worker position of the Yiddish press, most of the fraternal and other neighbourhood organizations and even the synagogues, the owners were too well entrenched to give in. There were always desperately poor and hungry workers available to take the place of those on strike.

Perhaps the most important — and the least successful — strike occurred in Toronto, where conditions of "home work" were especially brutal. In a series done for a local newspaper, a young University of Toronto student by the name of Mackenzie King alerted the public to the horrific plight of workers. As he wrote in his diary following a particularly dreadful experience in a sweatshop: "What a day I have had and how I have witnessed the oppression of man under his fellows. What a story of Hell..." To improve these conditions, Toronto workers banded together into trade unions. Taking their cue from the successful strike of the International Ladies Garment Workers' Union in New York in 1910, Toronto cloak-makers affiliated their union with the ILGWU in 1911 and chose as their major target the T. Eaton Company.

They could not have chosen worse. Not only was Eaton's the country's leading retailer but its twelve-storey manufacturing complex in the heart of the Ward was the city's largest employer. Though most of its employees were Jewish — all factory workers, there would be almost no Jewish salespeople at Eaton's for another thirty years — there was also a substantial number of other ethnic minorities. Eaton's employed about 1,200 Jews and fully seventy-five per cent of the city's Jewish cloak-makers worked there. From all the evidence it appears that the company was not a bad place to work; certainly it compared favourably with sweatshops elsewhere in the city or in Montreal or New York. But the recently formed ILGWU was itching for a fight and unwittingly Eaton's provided the pretext.

In February of 1912, the company ordered a change in production quotas without notifying the workers. Immediately some 65 union members walked out in protest and were summarily fired. Though only a small percentage of the company's workers were union members, almost all walked out in support of the 65. Approximately 1,300 workers were locked out by the firm and told not to come back.

The strike lasted eighteen agonizing weeks. The union tried every tactic it could think of to force the company to negotiate. There were huge demonstrations, a twenty-four-hour picket line, a parade of the strikers' children through downtown Toronto, even a boycott of the famous Eaton's mail-order catalogue — thousands were returned by sympathetic recipients. But all in vain. The company was determined not to give in. It felt that it had been fair to its employees and had done more for them than any other manufacturer in the country. Its wages were higher, its working conditions healthier and its hours of work shorter. Indeed John Craig Eaton, the son of the company's founder, considered the strike an insult to his family and he was determined to use whatever methods were necessary to crush it. Boatloads of strikebreakers were imported from England — one hundred young women from Yorkshire alone — and others were hired from the United States. Police were brought in to break through the picket lines and intimidate strikers.

Eventually the strike collapsed. The workers just did not have the financial resources to stay out any longer. It was a wiser but poorer group of workers who began looking for other jobs, with little to show for their long months on the picket line. The Jewish trade unions had suffered a demoralizing setback from which they would not recover for some time. To this day there is no union at Eaton's.

As a result of the strike and the economic depression in the country in the years before the First World War, a number of Toronto's unemployed Jewish workers began setting up their own tiny shops to manufacture items such as suspenders, buttonholes, sleeves and collars. From these lofts and basements would emerge the Spadina *shmata* trade, the hundreds of small garment manufacturing companies that would revolutionize the manufacturing and wholesale clothing industry in Canada. In the end the strikers could claim a victory. The tiny needle-trade shops and the larger ones that succeeded them eventually broke the almost total monopoly of the Eaton company in the manufacturing of ladies' garments.

By the middle of 1914 and the onset of the war the era of mass migration was over. More Jews arrived in Canada in the year before the outbreak of war than in any other year in Canadian history, but these 20,000 or so were submerged among 400,000 other immigrants who landed in Canadian ports during that same period. To the present time neither number has ever been matched.

And as these Jewish newcomers streamed out of Halifax for Montreal, Toronto, Winnipeg, Vancouver and places in between, little did they realize that the Europe left behind would never be the same. Four years of bloody war would see to that. Nor did they realize that the Canada they were now entering was a far different country than it had been 15 years before. The arrival of some three million immigrants, including over 100,000 Jews, had seen to that.

CHAPTER SEVEN

ERA OF ORGANIZATION

1914 - 1930

If there was a common thread to Jewish life in Canada in the years between 1914 and 1930, it was the growth of organizational life. Organizations sprouted up everywhere and everyone joined. There were societies for cultural, political, charitable and social activities. The Yiddish press had a field day trying to keep track of all the activities and meetings — and not only in the major population centres. Everywhere they went, Eastern European Jews took with them their need to coalesce. Cape Breton Island, Timmins, Regina, it made no difference. Wherever Jews settled, connections were made, groups organized, and cultural and charitable activities begun.

For European Jewry, the end of the nineteenth century, marked by pogroms in the East, by a growing anti-semitism symbolized by the Dreyfus affair in the West, and by economic dislocation everywhere, was a watershed. Fundamental decisions had to be made that would forever affect the life of their community. Many chose to move to other, more hospitable European countries; others to emigrate across the seas to the "Golden Continent." Some chose — perhaps they really had no choice — to stay.

But even for them, life would never be the same. New ideas and new movements were percolating their way through European

Left: Group of war orphans in Revno, Ukraine, 1921, before leaving for Canada. (Ottawa Jewish Historical Society 4-018)

Right: Hebrew Immigrant Aid Society, Warsaw, Poland, 1921.

Courtyard of the Hebrew Immigrant Aid Society, Warsaw, Poland, 1921.

Jewry. Socialism, anarchism, Hasidism, Zionism and a host of other ideologies competed for support among the Jewish masses. There was a revival of Jewish consciousness, of the feeling that Jews must try to take control of their own lives. The period sparked a renaissance of Jewish culture, of Yiddish literature, of the Hebrew language and of the growing idea of Jewish self-government and self-determination.

Many of those arriving in Canada in these years carried these ideas with them as part of their baggage. It was they who brought forth the Jewish labour movement and, more significantly, Zionism. Like their brethren in Europe, they, too, were caught up in the nationalist revival sweeping the Jewish world. For them—even though they had come to Canada, not Palestine—Zionism was ultimately the only answer to their problems.

In few places in the world was Zionism as popular with the Jewish masses as in Canada. Perhaps their zeal was inspired by the harsh conditions they confronted here. Could primitive Palestine be any worse than a desolate shack on a wind-swept prairie, or a fetid sweatshop in a Toronto factory, or an unheated room in a Montreal tenement? But immigrants to the United States faced similarly harsh conditions and they were far less enthusiastic about the Zionist cause. There was clearly something in Canada that provided the nutrients for a flourishing Zionism.

For one thing, a number of non-Jewish Canadian Zionists were loudly trumpeting their support for a Jewish homeland in Palestine. Henry Wentworth Monk, an eccentric but respected businessman, spent much of his time and money crusading for a Jewish homeland. In the 1870s and 1880s — long before Theodor Herzl, the Austrian founder of Zionism, even thought of a Jewish state — Monk took up a campaign in Canada and England to raise funds to buy land in Palestine for European Jews. In 1881 Monk even proposed setting up a Jewish National Fund. He issued manifestos, wrote long articles, spoke to assorted meetings and lobbied extensively in England and Canada to realize his dream. Nor was Monk alone. There were a number of others, mostly clergymen but also some politicians and journalists, who took up the Zionist cause in those years. Indeed, when the Zionist Federation was formed in Canada, there was scarcely a convention that was not attended by a number of leading Canadian Christians, and there were always effusive greetings from cabinet ministers, mayors, lieutenant-governors and other officials.

Organized Zionism first came to Canada in the personage of Alexander Harkavi, a Russian-born Yiddish journalist. With a small number of his followers he founded the Lovers of Zion (Hovevei Zion) Society in Montreal in 1887. Within a few months there were branches in Toronto and Winnipeg. Perhaps the effort was premature, for the organization collapsed a short time later when Harkavi left the country. Its place was taken in 1892 by the Return to Zion (Shovei Zion) organization, whose most influential member, the philanthropist Lazarus Cohen, optimistically went to Palestine to purchase land for Canadian settlers. Within a year or two several Montreal Jewish families actually made *aliyah*, literally, a going up to the Holy Land — certainly the first Jews in Canadian history to do

Zionist membership card.

Clarence de Sola.

so — and took up residence in Palestine. Unfortunately the hostility of the Turkish government, which ruled Palestine, soon forced them to return, and the Shovei Zion organization fell apart.

It was not until 1897, when Theodor Herzl succeeded in calling the first World Zionist Congress in Basel, Switzerland, that modern Zionism was finally on a sound footing. Two years later, the Canadian Federation of Zionist Societies opened its office in Montreal. It consisted chiefly of one society, the Agudath Zion, made up almost entirely of members of Montreal's uptown synagogues. Though the organization was ostensibly headed by Dr. David Alexander Hart, a descendant of the Three Rivers family, leadership actually rested in the hands of Clarence de Sola, son of the late rabbi of the Spanish and Portuguese Synagogue and a wealthy businessman. There were other groupings outside of Montreal, in Toronto, Winnipeg, Quebec City, London, Ottawa and Kingston, but only the Agudath Zion and possibly the Winnipeg Zionist Society could be considered anything more than *ad hoc* organizations. Not surprisingly, Montreal Jewry would dominate the Federation — as they would Canadian Zionism — for the next half century. The city's community was better organized, better connected and wealthier; above all it had Clarence de Sola, whose organizational talents, financial resources and energy would be the movement's greatest assets in its early years.

Yet it is equally true that the most fervent Zionists were centred in Winnipeg. It was they who continually demanded that Zionism be taken literally and that Canadian Jews settle in Palestine. While the Federation was prepared to buy land in Palestine for the settlement of European Jews, Winnipeg Zionists insisted that the land be reserved for immigrants from Canada. When their recommendations were sidetracked by de Sola, a group of Winnipeg Zionists tried to buy land in Palestine for themselves, but their efforts proved unsuccessful.

Under the leadership of de Sola, who was president of the Federation from 1900 through the First World War, the movement expanded rapidly. Soon branches were opened up in many of the

Canadian Zionist Convention,
Ottawa, July 1912.

country's cities and towns. The Federation was important to Canadian Jewry in ways other than simply as a Zionist organization. It was also Canada's first national Jewish society. Its annual conventions — the first was held in Montreal in 1900 — were the only opportunities for Jews across the country to meet and discuss common problems, many of which had little to do with Zionism. They served as forums for communities, large and small, to learn about each other's existence. Relations formed there would be key elements in the various other activities of Canadian Jewry in these years.

Largely because of de Sola, the Federation took hold of significant segments of Canadian Jewry. He had an enormous correspondence with individual Jews from Glace Bay to Victoria and travelled extensively to meet them. He gave the organization credibility and his establishment origins attracted the support not only of middle-class Jews, but also of non-Jews. His major failure was with the immigrant community. He did not pretend to understand them, and, in any case, they had so little money that he did not see them as important contributors to the Zionist cause. As he saw it, the purpose

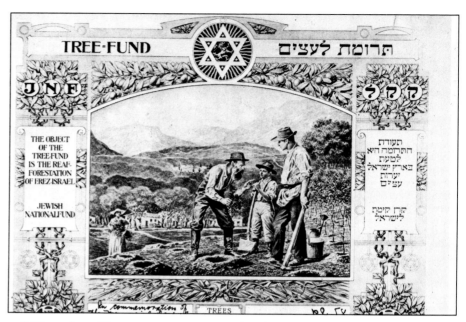

Left: Jewish National Fund Golden Book of Inscriptions, acknowledging donations.

Right: Certificate received by donors to the Jewish National Fund's campaign to plant trees in Israel, 1923.

of Canadian Zionism was to raise funds, not consciousness; that he would leave to others.

Still, no one could question de Sola's commitment to the movement. Largely through his efforts, there were more than 5,000 Federation members across Canada. From Halifax to Hirsch, from Windsor to Wapella, from Fort William to Fredericton, de Sola had succeeded in planting the Zionist seed: Yarmouth, St. Catharines, Brandon, there was scarcely a good-sized town in Canada without a Zionist society. And what Jew was not impressed when in 1913, at the Federation's convention in Ottawa, acting prime minister George Perley urged the delegates to continue the fight for a Jewish homeland in Palestine, which he described as "a just cause."

The major thrust of the movement in Canada was fundraising. In 1903 the Jewish National Fund, the fabled Keren Kayemeth, was founded and thousands of little blue tin boxes called *pushkes* were sent across the country to be filled with pennies, nickels and dimes. It was through the *pushkes* at schools, synagogues, neighbourhood stores or community halls that most Canadian Jews first came into contact with Zionism and the idea of a Jewish homeland. The achievements of the

Poalei Zion Group, Toronto 1913.
(Toronto Jewish Congress/CJC Ont. Region Archives 2913)

Zionists in fundraising were phenomenal, given the small number of Jews in the country and their relative poverty. Through the Jewish National Fund and a variety of other means, by 1924 over a million dollars had been raised — perhaps the highest per capita contribution of any Jewish community in the world.

There were Zionist organizations to suit everyone. The religious had their own society, the Mizrachi; some *landsmanshaftn* started their own Zionist groups, as did some student groups. There were clubs for Yiddish speakers, for workers and for bosses. Even the Reform movement, whose American leaders thundered against the heresy of Zionism — its leader, Rabbi Isaac Mayer Wise, chose a Montreal platform to denounce Zionism as a "momentary inebriation of morbid minds" — provided much-needed support to the movement in Canada.

Perhaps no group had more Zionist societies than Canada's Jewish women. Shut out of most of the male-dominated movement's organizations, Jewish women across the country set up their own clubs. In Toronto the B'not Zion (Daughters of Zion) was founded in 1900. A year later Montreal women formed the Young Ladies' Progres-

Left: Mrs. Willinsky, an organizer of the original Hadassah Chapter in Toronto and one of the first members of the Council of Jewish Women.

Right: First group of Pioneer Women, 1920.

sive Zionist Society. Soon there were B'not Zion branches across the country. These were later joined by the Herzl Ladies' Society, the Young Ladies' Zionist Society, the Queen Esther Cadets, the Nordau Girls Group, the Palestinian Sewing Circle and a host of other groups. Most of these were cultural and fundraising organizations, but their leaders soon became active in Zionist politics and many served on the executive of the Federation of Zionist Societies. In 1917, the first chapters of the Hadassah, the Women's Zionist Organization founded in the United States by Henrietta Szold, had appeared in Canada. Under the leadership of Lillian Freiman, Hadassah was the major fundraiser for the movement's activities in Canada and Palestine. Much later the Labour Zionist women founded their own organization, the Pioneer Women, as did women affiliated with the Mizrachi.

The most important organization within the Zionist movement — the one that held out the greatest attraction to the large numbers of new immigrants in the country — was the Labour Zionist (Poalei Zion) Movement. It saw the national struggle of Jews as part of a larger class struggle and found much support in the nascent Jewish labour movement, in turn providing that movement with much of its early leadership. Poalei Zion activists carried Zionism into the streets and factories. Brought to Canada by the more politicized immigrants following the failure of the Russian Revolution of 1905, the movement did not limit itself to the struggle for a Jewish homeland. Early Poalei Zion members were in the forefront of the battle to spread Yiddish culture, to open a separate Jewish school system and to create trade unions. It was both a political party and a fraternal organization whose goal was the reconstruction of the Jewish people. And its leaders, particularly Hananiah Meir Caiserman, a young Romanian immigrant who arrived in Montreal in 1910, spent as much time organizing unions as they did working on behalf of a Jewish homeland in Palestine.

The activities of the Poalei Zion were of great significance for Canadian Jewry. They showed that it was possible to be both a socialist and a Zionist, to fight for social justice for the Jew as a worker and as a citizen of the world, to enter into conflict with some elements of the community over labour matters yet unite with them on the question of Jewish survival. For the most part, the Poalei Zion was an urban movement, based in the working-class neighbourhoods of Toronto, Winnipeg, Montreal and, to a lesser extent, Hamilton; middle-class Jews and those living in small cities and towns were not attracted to the ideological nature of the Poalei Zion. Nor for that matter were de Sola and his Federation partners. Angered by the Poalei Zion's anti-religious attitude, its socialism, its union activities and its special fundraising campaigns on behalf of workers in Palestine, the Federation was reluctant to recognize it as a legitimate Zionist organization. Certainly de Sola and his friends were not happy when unions affiliated with the Poalei Zion led a series of massive strikes in Montreal's garment district against employers who were generous donors to the Zionist campaigns.

Despite these schisms, prewar Zionism thrived in Canada. Zionist leaders in Europe regularly praised de Sola for his remarkable

Upper: Hananiah Meir Caiserman, general secretary of the Canadian Jewish Congress from 1919-1950.

Lower: Zion Benevolent Association, Toronto, 1923. (Toronto Jewish Congress/CJC Ont. Region Archives 1911)

Upper: Montreal Committee for the Jewish Legion of Palestine, 1917.

Lower: Recruitment sign for the Jewish Battalion, Winnipeg, 1917.

achievements. It was a wonder to them that such a relatively small number of Jews, most of them immigrants, spread across three thousand miles of rugged country, could create one of the strongest Zionist movements in the world.

The outbreak of war in 1914 further split Canadian Jewry. Few in the country were as avidly pro-war as the established Jewish community. In their hearts and minds, they were Anglophile to the core. Canada might be their home, but Britain was their model, and when she asked for help no group responded more enthusiastically than Canada's Jewish leadership. Prominent Jews like Mortimer Davis of the Imperial Tobacco Company even promised to raise and fund their own battalions. More recent immigrants were less supportive. They had nothing against Britain itself, but in this war the British were allied with the devil incarnate, czarist Russia. How could Canada side with the despotic Romanovs? How could Jews be expected to fight for a regime guilty of the most heinous crimes against their people? The czar had driven them out and now he expected them to return to fight for his cause.

Furthermore, Germany and Austria had been more tolerant than czarist Russia. Vienna was the birthplace of modern Zionism; Berlin, with its Jewish bankers, politicians and intellectuals, represented the pinnacle of Jewish success. Compared with the cruelties visited upon the Jews by the Russians, the Germans paled. Perhaps it would be better, the immigrants reasoned, for Germany to succeed in her battle with the hated czar; it might save Eastern European Jewry from the wretched excesses of the Russians.

There were now deep divisions within the Jewish community, and as the war progressed they grew more profound. No one person could speak on its behalf; no one leader could purport to represent its interests. For that reason, various groups and individuals began lobbying for a Congress, a Parliament of Canada's Jewry, where decisions could be made, viewpoints could be debated, agendas could be set, and, above all, the community could be united again.

Jewish Reinforcement Draft
Company, Montreal, 1917.

Most vociferous in their calls for a Congress were the immigrant communities. They felt that for too long power had been in the hands of the uptown community in Montreal, and of the upper and middle classes in Toronto and Winnipeg. Eastern Europeans now made up a majority of the Canadian Jews. It was time their numbers were translated into power.

This idea was anathema to the established residents. It was their money, their efforts, their links to the non-Jewish community, their institutions, such as the Baron de Hirsch Institute, which had allowed the immigrant community to survive. Their leadership had rescued it from the brink of disaster many times since the onset of mass immigration. And in any case, what kind of Congress would it be if most of its members could barely speak English, and had little education and even less money? Would the government and other Canadians take the community seriously? Did Canadian Jewry really want to be represented by militant Yiddish-speaking socialists?

Their misgivings notwithstanding, even within the establishment there was a growing sense that a more representative body was needed. The war was posing new problems such as the relief of

Reuben Brainin (right) with Hirsch Cohen (middle) and Mordechai Ginsburg.

Jews in the war zones and the fate of Palestine. Since the Turks had allied themselves with the Germans, Palestine would become war booty. Canadian Jewry must have a united voice when it fell to the British, as it no doubt would. Also, because of the government's desire to mobilize all communities, was wartime not the appropriate moment to make claims on it for a variety of grievances? Furthermore, in other countries with sizeable Jewish populations there were similar movements to create representative bodies. As the leading exponent of what became the Canadian Jewish Congress, H. M. Caiserman, put it: "The Canadian Jewish Congress was not a locally isolated movement. Its origin was to be found in the sudden revival and simultaneous organization of the Jewish masses in every part of the world."

It was also fortunate for Canadian Jews that Reuben Brainin decided to spend a few years in Canada. A dynamic, eloquent, passionate Jew, Brainin arrived in Montreal in 1912 to edit the *Adler*. In the four years he spent in the city before leaving for New York he became the major spokesman for the Congress idea among the country's Yiddish-speaking population. He was their ideologue, their conduit to the uptown community, with which he had much in common. He used the pages of the *Adler* as a propaganda vehicle until he was fired for criticisms of the city's Jewish establishment.

The first tentative steps towards a Congress were taken by a Poalei Zion branch in Montreal with the founding of the Canadian Jewish Alliance in 1915. Thirteen organizations attended the founding meeting, the purpose of which was to create an umbrella organization of Canadian Jewry to co-ordinate aid to European Jewry and to speak for Canadian Jewry on all issues. Brainin agreed to become the Alliance's president, though most of the organizational work would be undertaken by active Labour Zionists.

Within months there were organizational meetings in Winnipeg and Toronto to affiliate with the Alliance. Promises of support also came from Jewish communities across the country.

Above all, most Canadian Jews pressed for the creation of a relief fund to help their families, friends and *landsleit*, the townspeo-
ple, caught in the war zones.

Strongly opposed to the Alliance were the wealthier Jews and
the Federation of Zionist Societies. The latter was naturally reluctant
to support the creation of a rival national organization which would
challenge its primacy. Nor did the established community support the
concept of a separate fund for European Jewry. It would be better,
they argued, to support the Canadian government's own "Patriotic
Fund," even though not a penny of this money would go to Jews in
war-torn Europe.

As a counter to the Alliance, the Zionist Federation founded the
Canadian Jewish Conference, but it found few supporters in the wider
Jewish community, which rejected its elitism. The Federation did not
support a Congress elected by popular franchise; rather it wanted
a conference of notables selected by various Jewish organizations.
Moreover, the major concern of most of the country's Jews was to
send help to their co-religionists overseas — a concern fully shared
by the Alliance. Indeed many Jewish organizations were launch-
ing fundraising campaigns on their own. In Winnipeg, the Western
Canada Relief Alliance collected thousands of dollars — including
$2,500 from the Winnipeg city council — and sent it to the Joint
Distribution Committee in New York for immediate transmission
to Europe.

The bickering between the two elements of Canadian Jewry
continued until 1917. By then events were moving inexorably to
strengthen the position of the Alliance. In that year American
Jewish leaders agreed to create their own Congress, and in June,
elections were held across the country to select representatives. In
the same year, while the British army was driving the Turks out
of Palestine, British Foreign Secretary Arthur Balfour was toying
with the idea of gaining support for the British war effort from
world Jewry — and from the United States — by supporting the

Parade in front of the Talmud
Torah, Winnipeg, in honour of
Clarence de Sola's visit, *c.* 1918.

Left: Balfour Day parade, Ottawa, May 1917. (Ottawa Jewish Historical Society 1-174)

Right: Regina parade in support of the Balfour Declaration, 1918.

concept of a Jewish homeland. He travelled to North America to meet with representatives of the American Jewish community and with President Woodrow Wilson and senior American officials. In a stopover in Canada to brief Canadian leaders, he made time to confer with Clarence de Sola, who impressed on him the need for a Jewish state in Palestine.

On November 2, 1917, Balfour issued his famous declaration committing his government to support a Jewish homeland in Palestine. It was a glorious moment for world Jewry and no one felt more euphoric than Clarence de Sola, who took some credit for influencing Balfour. There were huge rallies in Canada in support of the Balfour Declaration—close to seven thousand attended a massive demonstration in Montreal, while over six thousand gathered in Winnipeg to hear Manitoba's lieutenant-governor pay tribute to the Zionist cause.

The wedges that had driven the community apart seemed to dissipate in the glow of the Balfour Declaration. New young leaders were coming to the fore in the Federation to challenge de Sola's leadership and to try to find common ground with the

immigrant leaders in the Alliance. A. J. Freiman, a wealthy Ottawa businessman, Moses Finkelstein, a Winnipeg lawyer, and Louis Fitch and Michael Garber of Montreal were rapidly gaining control of the Federation and were far more sympathetic to the Congress idea. They were particularly impressed when two conferences sponsored by the Alliance in Winnipeg and Toronto attracted hundreds of delegates from across western Canada and Ontario who unanimously supported the call for a Canadian Jewish Congress.

By the end of 1917, much of the Zionist opposition to a Congress had been eroded. It was clear that most Canadian Jews did not share de Sola's views that the major concern should be the creation of a homeland in Palestine: though most Jews shared that dream, they were more concerned with helping their stricken brethren overseas. A Congress of Canadian Jewry, they felt, would be the most appropriate vehicle to deal with the plight of European Jewry as well as with the question of a Jewish state.

Perhaps the clearest indication that the fragmented community was edging closer together was the election to Parliament of Sam Jacobs in the Montreal riding of Cartier in 1917. Though Jacobs

Upper left: Roumanian Hebrew Benevolent Society demonstration, Toronto, c. 1917.

Upper right: A.J. Freiman.

Lower: Samuel William Jacobs.

List of delegates sent by the Welcome Club for Jewish Working Girls to the founding meeting of the Canadian Jewish Congress.

was an uptown Jew—he was Canadian-born, wealthy and spoke not a word of Yiddish—he won over the downtown community. He supported the call for a Congress, declared himself an ardent champion of a Jewish homeland in Palestine, and promised to work within his party to widen the immigration gates and to open up communal leadership to the newcomers. Though the Liberals were badly defeated throughout the country, Jacobs won a smashing victory—getting ten times as many votes as his nearest competitor. He was the first Jew to take a seat in Parliament since Henry Nathan some forty-five years earlier.

In 1918, the American Jewish Congress convened for the first time. In attendance were five observers from Canada, including J.A. Cherniack from Winnipeg and Peter Bercovitch and Hirsch Wolofsky of Montreal. On their return to Canada they set in motion the machinery to convene a Canadian Congress. A preparatory committee under H.M. Caiserman was struck. The Zionist Federation agreed to join with those calling for a congress, and in January of 1919 the Montreal Conference for the Jewish Congress met, ironically, at the bastion of uptown Montreal, the Baron de Hirsch Institute, to iron out final arrangements. To ease the concerns of the established community, Lyon Cohen was asked to become president of the Conference, with Caiserman taking on the duties of general secretary.

On March 2 and 3, 1919, about twenty-five thousand Jews went to polling booths, set up in synagogues and community offices across the country, to vote for delegates to the Congress. These were perhaps the most hotly contested elections in Canadian Jewish history. Everybody, it seemed, wished to attend the historic event. Blocs were formed, coalitions put together and deals made among the various parties and organizations to make certain their candidates were selected.

The vast majority of Canadian Jews took part in the election. Indeed Caiserman claimed that almost every adult Jew in the country voted. Two weeks later—on March 16—209 Canadian Jews gathered in the Monument National Theatre in Montreal to take part in the founding of the Canadian Jewish Congress.

Except for the fact that very few women were present, it was perhaps the most representative body of Canadian Jews ever to meet under one roof. There were delegates from the Zionist Federation, from the Poalei Zion, from the Mizrachi; from the non-Zionist Arbeiter Ring, from a variety of labour unions, mutual benefit societies and charitable organizations. There were delegates from every part of the country — from Englehart, Ontario; Kamsack, Saskatchewan; Sibbald, Alberta; Campbellton, New Brunswick; La Macaza, Quebec; as well as from the major population centres. Many prominent Jews who had not been selected as delegates came as observers.

More than 2,500 non-participants came to watch Canadian Jewish history being made. They were not disappointed. Bands played; school children sang; visiting dignitaries from the United States and Europe spoke; various rabbis blessed the assembly; and a series of non-Jewish speakers, including the Solicitor General of Canada, brought greetings from their respective governments, churches and organizations. The Montreal city council even invited the delegates to a reception at city hall and provided streetcars bedecked with Jewish and Canadian flags to convey them there. Much to the joy of the delegates, they found a huge Jewish flag over the mayor's chair.

By acclamation the delegates elected Lyon Cohen as their president. Though Cohen was a charter member of Montreal's uptown community, his philanthropy and honesty and his commitment to Zionism and to Canadian Jewry made him popular in the newcomer community as well. He was, according to Caiserman, the "perfect choice...[his] unfailing good humour, his deep desire for fair play, his toleration and respect for the view of others, as well as his intelligent grasp of vital aspects of every problem presented, made him an ideal chairman for a gathering composed of such a mixed element as the Congress." To balance the ticket, Caiserman himself, as leader of the Labour Zionists, was chosen general secretary.

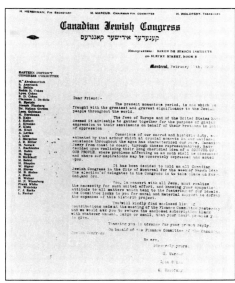

Upper: Cover of the *Canadian Jewish Chronicle* for the first Plenary Assembly of the Canadian Jewish Congress, 1919.

Lower: The letter announcing the first Plenary Assembly.

Lyon Cohen.

For three days the delegates discussed a broad range of topics, though immigration and Palestine were the prime issues. It was evident from the beginning that the Labour Zionists had done their homework. They came to the Congress with a better political machine than anyone else, and their resolutions usually passed. Thus the Congress called for the creation of a permanent representative body for Canadian Jewry to be elected by the community on a universal suffrage system. Resolutions were also passed supporting a World Jewish Congress that would have separate representation at the peace negotiations in Versailles. The Balfour Declaration was applauded and the Congress voted unanimously to support the creation of a Jewish homeland in Palestine, though a few Bundist delegates abstained. The Congress also demanded that Canada maintain an open-door immigration policy and decided to create a bureau to assist Jewish immigrants. Thus was born the Jewish Immigrant Aid Society (JIAS). Finally the delegates passed resolutions expressing their loyalty to Canada — "a loyalty which takes second place to no other people in this grand country of ours," said Lyon Cohen — and thanking the Canadian government for its support and for its contribution to the war.

With the singing of the Canadian national anthem, the Jewish national anthem and — symbolically — the Socialist anthem, the Congress adjourned on March 18. It would not reconvene for another fifteen years.

Nevertheless it had done its work well. There was now a sense of unity and purpose the community had heretofore lacked. Delegates went back to their homes, factories, stores or farms confident that Canadian Jewry finally had a voice and a common agenda and that the government would finally have to take the Jews seriously.

The community could proudly point to its own contribution to the war effort. Canadian Jews fought in every branch of the Canadian armed forces and a significant number won decorations and citations for bravery under fire. It is estimated that more than five thousand

Jews served with the Canadian expeditionary forces and another three hundred or so volunteered to fight in the Jewish Legion of the British army. Louis Rosenberg, the statistician of Canadian Jewry for over fifty years, estimated that close to thirty-eight per cent of all Jewish males of military age served in the armed forces, a ratio much higher than the national average. The percentage of Jews winning medals for distinguished military service was also higher than the overall rate for Canadian soldiers. Three Jews, Maurice Alexander, L. Lerner and H.H. Lightstone, even achieved the rank of lieutenant-colonel, while almost one hundred others served as majors, captains or lieutenants. Considering that the majority of Canadian Jews were former subjects of the murderous czarist regime, and that many others were Orthodox and could not carry out their religious and dietary laws in the armed forces, the number of Jewish enlistments was impressive. In fact, no one knows for certain how many actually enlisted, because many chose to hide their origins, so fearful were they of drawing attention to their Jewishness. Indeed, when Rabbi Herman Abramowitz, the distinguished spiritual leader of Montreal's Shaar Hashomayim Synagogue, was appointed honorary chaplain to Canada's Jewish troops, his first act was to denounce this practice. In a widely distributed letter, "Captain" Abramowitz lamented that "a great many Jewish soldiers...have enrolled under assumed names [and under assumed religions]...attempting to conceal their Jewish identity." He pleaded with Jewish servicemen to come forward and proudly proclaim their identity since their enlistment "greatly rebounds to the credit of the Jewish people." Some, though not necessarily all, followed the rabbi's advice.

But if the community thought its war efforts and the creation of the Congress would make the government more amenable to its grievances, it was sorely mistaken. While the government would continue to pay lip service to the creation of a Jewish homeland in Palestine, since it cost them little — "of all the results of the [war]," said the leader of the Conservative Party in 1925, Arthur Meighen,

Upper: Saskatchewan and Alberta Conference for the Relief of War Orphans, 1918. "Jews! Save our future generation!" reads the Yiddish text of the banner.

Lower: Coupon from a fundraising fair for Jewish War Relief, 1922.

"none is more important and more fertile in human history than the reconquest of Palestine and the rededication of that country to the Jewish People" — on an issue far more nettlesome it was less forthcoming.

For the better part of the war years there had been little immigration into Canada. Now, with the war over and large sections of Europe ravaged, Canadian Jews were anxiously awaiting the chance to welcome their relatives and friends. The situation in Europe was horrific. Starvation was rampant, destruction widespread, and the continent's economy was in tatters. Now more than ever the immigration doors needed to be opened as widely as possible.

Instead, they began closing. Like the United States, Canada was caught up in a "Red scare" following the Russian Revolution of 1917, and was reluctant to accept any immigrants lest they bring with them their alien ideologies. Red-baiting and nativism rapidly swept over the North American continent. In any case, with the postwar recession in full swing, Canada was not about to reopen its doors too quickly. Almost as soon as the war was over, the government introduced a series of restrictive measures to stem the flow of immigrants. Most drastically affected were the Jews.

For Canadian officials Jewish immigrants had been a great disappointment. Despite government policy that immigrants should head to the interior, to the farms, forests and mines of western and northern Canada, the bulk of Jewish immigrants had settled in the ghettos of Toronto, Montreal and, to a lesser extent, Winnipeg. The successes of individual Jews on the farmlands and in the small towns of rural Canada made little impression on immigration officials. They looked only at the numbers, and saw that most Jewish newcomers were settling in the crowded cities of the east.

As a result, a series of orders-in-council were introduced in the 1920s that made it more difficult for immigrants — especially Jews — to enter Canada. For the first time, no matter what their citizenship or country of origin, all Jews were classed as a "special permit" group.

While their fellow Poles or Romanians could still enter fairly easily, Jews from these same countries were assigned a special status which all but closed Canada's doors to them. In effect, the era of mass migration of Jews was over.

Naturally the Jewish community was up in arms over these overtly discriminatory practices. Had the community not proved its loyalty during the war? Had it not contributed immensely to Canadian society? Was it not law-abiding and industrious? These arguments achieved little: the rising tide of nativism and racism in North America was unyielding. Leading educators, politicians and journalists, supported by farm and labour groups, formed a powerful anti-immigration lobby during the 1920s. The immigrant, they argued before an increasingly receptive Canadian society, was just not assimilating. Canada was becoming "balkanized" with so many ethnic groups speaking their own languages, maintaining their own ways of life and resisting all efforts to bring them into the mainstream. As the premier of British Columbia put it in 1923: "We are anxious to keep this a British country. We want it British and nothing else."

As nativism spread and the economic situation deteriorated, the flood of immigrants slowed to a trickle. The Jewish community was frantic. Loved ones left behind, they feared, would never be allowed to enter. The postwar collapse of the economies of most European countries and the bloody pogroms in the Ukraine and elsewhere made the lot of Eastern European Jews even more precarious.

The Canadian Jewish Congress did what it could. It sent petitions, organized demonstrations and lobbied members of Parliament. But aside from relenting on the issue of family reunification, immigration officials would not budge. In any case, the Congress was not the proper organization to deal with the problem. Following its founding convention, the Congress became inactive; after the heady experience of meeting together and setting up a national organization, it appeared that Canadian Jews simply lost interest

Tribute to Lillian Freiman, founder of Hadassah-Wizo of Canada, who helped found the Great War Veterans' Association and aided in the rescue of Jewish war orphans from the Ukraine.

Upper: First group of Ukrainian Jewish war orphans to be granted permission to enter Canada, 1921.

Lower: Donation receipt from the Jewish War Orphans Committee of Canada to establish a kitchen for orphans in Elizavetgrad, Russia.

in it. Perhaps they were too taken up with their own day-to-day existence to concern themselves with broader issues. The problem of restricted immigration was better dealt with by the Jewish Immigrant Aid Society.

Throughout the 1920s, JIAS was the most active Jewish communal organization. It was a JIAS official who first met the immigrant when he arrived, who took him by the hand and led him through officialdom's inhospitable processes. It was JIAS that made certain the immigrants arrived at their destination and provided them with loans, housing and schooling to prepare them for their new life in Canada. Not only did it support immigrants already in Canada, but it spent much of its time trying to force immigration permits out of an increasingly hostile immigration department. There were some small successes. Largely through the influence of A.J. Freiman and the work of his wife Lillian, $100,000 was raised to bring in 150 Jewish war orphans in 1920. Three years later, through lobbying by Sam Jacobs and others, a permit was given to allow 5,000 Jewish refugees from Russia into the country, but only 3,300 gained entry; before the movement was complete the government pulled the plug, largely because of the intercession of the new assistant deputy minister of immigration, Frederick Charles Blair, who would prove to be the Jewish community's nemesis.

Perhaps as important as JIAS in introducing newcomers to their life in Canada was the Jewish labour movement. In the 1920s and 1930s, it was at the peak of its power and influence, deriving much of its strength from the geographic concentration of the Jewish working class. In the few square blocks surrounding the Main in Montreal, Spadina Avenue in Toronto and the north side of the CPR tracks in Winnipeg lived the vast bulk of the Jewish workers. This dense concentration provided the basis for the emergence of a mass Jewish trade union movement. A culturally and socially homogeneous mass, those people had gone through a common historical experience — immigration, proletarianization,

Picnic of the Jewish Labour
Cultural Association, Winnipeg,
1924.

exploitation — in a short period of time and were therefore primed for a common reaction.

The Jewish labour movement in Canada was made up of unions in the needle trades, the various fraternal organizations associated with them, and the Jewish sections of such left-wing political parties as the Socialist Party of Canada, the Communist Party and the CCF. Though it exhibited the characteristics of other ethnic labour organizations, in a very real sense the Jewish labour movement was unique. No other ethnic group dominated a single industry the way the Jews dominated the garment industry, and none expended as much energy and funds on behalf of progressive candidates and causes. This gave the Jewish labour movement economic and political clout far beyond what its relatively small membership warranted.

Upper: Nodelman sisters in front of their father's Toronto store and "kibbutzarnia," a meeting place for Jewish labour activists.

Lower: Jewish Workers' Cultural Centre mandolin orchestra, Toronto, 1932.

Some Jewish immigrants came to Canada as convinced socialists, and had even served an apprenticeship in the revolutionary movements of czarist Russia. But for most, the Jewish labour movement provided an introduction to socialism. To the forlorn, exploited Jew steeped in the Old Testament, it held out great appeal; it had, in the words of one participant, the prophetic ring of the coming of the Messiah. Although within its fold the Jewish labour movement contained a host of competing ideologies — anarchism, Communism, Labour Zionism, Bundism and secularism among others — its underlying central ideology was nonetheless fundamentally socialist.

The Jewish labour movement also provided a new home — and perhaps even a new spiritual temple — to those alienated from traditional Judaism. Indeed, for most urban Jews it constituted their first real introduction to Canadian life. Educational and cultural programs were an essential part of the movement's activities, and the allied fraternal organizations provided immigrant workers with a familiar milieu while they were overcoming the trauma of dealing with alien institutions, a new language and a vastly different way of life. Much time and money was devoted to providing rank-and-file members with English lessons, lectures, plays and reading material.

Because of their historic experience, Jews have tended to be sensitive to oppression and to threats to religious and political freedom. Thus the Jewish labour movement rejected the straightforward trade unionism of other Canadian unions. In its stead it substituted a concern for social justice — not only for its own members but for all workers, and, indeed, for all Canadians. Jewish unions were in the forefront of most of the progressive movements in Canada after the First World War. And unlike other unions, Jewish unions held intellectuals in high esteem, not only as advisers and teachers but also as purveyors of new social ideas.

Predictably there was much ideological turbulence within the movement. It was a major battleground in the bitter conflict between the socialists and the Communists which raged with such fury in the years following the creation of the Soviet Union in 1917. The socialists were entrenched in such unions as the International Ladies Garment Workers, the Amalgamated Clothing Workers, the Millinery Workers and several others. They had their own fraternal organizations — the Arbeiter Ring for the non-Zionists and the Poalei Zion for the Zionists — and their own newspapers and periodicals, the most influential of which was the *Forward* from New York.

The Communists had significant numbers in some of these unions but their strength was concentrated in the Trade Union Unity League and, later, in the Workers' Unity League. They also dominated the United Garment Workers and, for a time, the Fur and Leather Workers. The United Jewish People's Order (UJPO) was their fraternal organization, and their major newspapers were the *Freiheit* from New York and the *Kamf* (later to be called the *Vochenblatt*) in Canada.

The unrelenting and rancorous war between these two factions dominated the movement for much of its short history and weakened it immeasurably. Many of the major protagonists later ruefully conceded that the incredible amount of energy and time spent infighting could better have been used against Jewish labour's real enemies.

The Jewish labour movement was unique in another way as well: it was a one-generation phenomenon. Rarely was the Jewish factory worker either the parent or the child of a worker. Workers scrimped, saved and sacrificed to make certain their children would never work in a factory, and the movement's educational activities were so successful that they undermined it. Many immigrants grew confident enough to strike out on their own and become successful merchants, manufacturers and professionals. And if they did not, their children would. The social mobility and the deproletarianization of the Jewish worker were astonishingly rapid.

Yet in its short history, the Jewish labour movement contributed much to the quality of life not just of Jewish workers but of all Canadian workers. It pioneered industrial unionism, new collective-

Upper: Activists in the Young Communist League and Freiheit Club, Toronto, 1926.

Lower: Arbeiter Ring school, Winnipeg, c. 1928.

Graduation certificate, Toronto Hebrew Free School. (Toronto Jewish Congress/CJC Ont. Region Archives 55)

bargaining techniques and industry-wide general strikes. For a time it stimulated and underwrote much of the cultural and humanitarian activity of organized labour in Canada. It also lobbied energetically, and often alone, for enlightened human rights and progressive social legislation. Long before it became fashionable, the Jewish labour movement took the lead in demanding a less restrictive immigration policy. It educated and acted as a social escalator for thousands of new immigrants, and played a key role in the growth and development of the CCF and the Communist Party. It was without doubt the conscience of the Canadian labour movement.

The movement thrived despite the fact that it was centred in perhaps the most competitive industry in the country. There was always stiff competition among the manufacturers in Toronto, Montreal and Winnipeg to produce the least costly garments, and unions in these cities were constantly at odds with one another over the questions of wages and lost jobs. Certainly the employers in the industry were among the most anti-union in the country. Militant workers were blacklisted; no employer in Canada would hire them. Nor were the bosses loath to use police to break strikes. In one instance in Toronto, a young woman striker was arrested for throwing a snowball on a picket line, and sentenced to a month in jail and deported back to Poland on her release. At the same time an owner who attacked a worker with a steel bar was acquitted because he was "defending private property." On many occasions police escorted strikebreakers through picket lines and arrested strikers who stood in their way. Since many immigrants knew that an arrest might lead to deportation, paths usually opened quickly through the picket lines.

During the 1920s, conditions of work in the industry had changed very little. The problems of an earlier period persisted — low wages, long hours, speed-ups and unsanitary working conditions; tuberculosis was widely known as "the tailor's disease." As one Montreal worker described it: "There was no such thing as a cloakroom. Your clothes, you had to shake them out so that those

Fur factory, Winnipeg, 1922.

cockroaches weren't on your coat, or you wrapped them up in a box right near your work. And your sandwiches, you ate them right there…There was no such thing as rest period of course. Your lunch you ate at your work and you worked as you ate." Despite the efforts of the nascent unions, most workers were still paid starvation wages. In 1921, for example, the average male garment worker in Toronto earned $1,050 a year, the average female only $670. Social workers of the time estimated that a family needed to earn at least $1,655 in order to survive.

Chaim Freiden, scrap metal collector, Moose Jaw, Saskatchewan, 1913.

The most tragic figures in the Jewish community were the ragpickers, of whom there were six hundred in Toronto alone in 1914. Many were elderly and widely respected in the old country as scholars, but could get no other job because as observant Jews they would not work on the Sabbath. These venerable men, some of whom were ordained rabbis, spent their days picking their way through filthy, smelly rags, in which they occasionally found dead animals and aborted fetuses. So dreadful were their working conditions that some formed a ragpickers' union and even conducted a successful strike.

Though the Jewish labour movement played little role in the famous Winnipeg General Strike of 1919, when the city was isolated from the rest of the world for forty-five days by the walkout of some thirty thousand workers including those in the railway, telephone and postal systems, individual Jews did play a prominent role — at least in the eyes of the government. Of the five "foreigners" arrested by the Royal North West Mounted Police at the end of the strike, three were Jews, Samuel Blumenberg, Michael Charitinoff and Moses Almazov. Eventually they were let go, but all three "voluntarily"

Toronto ragpicker, 1911.

left Canada a short time later. Though many of the city's Jewish community opposed the strike, secret police memoranda to the federal government made it appear that the community was almost entirely radical and could not be trusted. Indeed, some time later the commissioner of the Manitoba Provincial Police claimed that Jews were actively engaged in an international conspiracy to destroy western civilization.

The strike did act as the inspiration for the Jewish left to become more involved in politics. As a direct result of the class and ethnic

Winnipeg General Strike, June 21, 1919.

divisions generated by the strike, Jewish working-class candidates began contesting — and winning — various elections. A British Jew, John Blumberg, a motorman with Winnipeg's street railway company, was elected as an alderman for the city's north end and was re-elected for the next thirty-five years. More important, another British immigrant, Abraham Albert Heaps, an upholsterer with the CPR and a labour alderman in the city council who was acquitted of seditious conspiracy charges for his role in the strike, was elected to the federal Parliament as one of its first labour members. He would serve with distinction until 1940. Other Jews supported by the labour movement, such as Rose Elkin, William Tobias and Marcus

176

Hyman, won elections to the legislature, school board and city council. But Winnipeg was the exception. Though the Jewish labour movement in Montreal and Toronto supported a variety of left-wing and progressive candidates, few Jews were elected there.

Some Jews believed that the terrible conditions of the Canadian worker could not be changed without a complete overhaul of the existing social and economic structure. To them the solution was simple: Communism.

Certainly the Russian Revolution had struck a strong responsive chord among some Canadian Jews. Many Russian Jews had been in the forefront of the revolution, and it had ended for once and for all the detested czarist government with its dreaded pogroms. Attracted by the Soviet example, numbers of Jewish workers deserted the Poalei Zion and the Arbeiter Ring to join the plethora of Communist-dominated organizations and unions that sprang up in the 1920s. This struggle between Jewish Communists and non-Communists for leadership of the Jewish working class was a hallmark of the immigrant community in the inter-war period.

By the 1920s, a new Jewish leadership had arrived in Canada. The established English-speaking leadership had been gently pushed aside and replaced by militants from the upstart immigrant community. How could it have been otherwise? The immigrant community was so dynamic, its agitation so unceasing, that no amount of pressure could stem its creative energies. It soon breached the ghetto walls and inundated the old-time community, some of whom adopted its principles and became its leaders. Many of the immigrants, or their children, broke free from their neighbourhoods — but not their origins — and became leaders in the uptown communities. Although the Jewish community was still divided along class lines, its leadership had passed to a new generation.

A.A. Heaps, 1924.

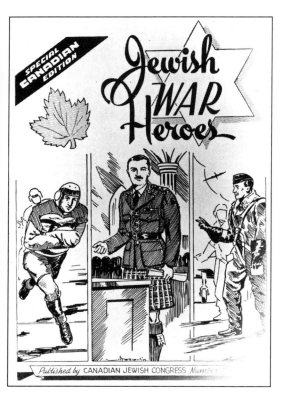

CHAPTER EIGHT

THE DARK YEARS

1930-1945

In June of 1934 one of the most bizarre strikes in Canadian history occurred, and for the Jewish community the most telling. Samuel Rabinovich, a young medical student who had graduated first in his class at the University of Montreal, was offered an internship at Notre Dame Hospital. On the day he was to begin work all fourteen of his fellow interns walked out, refusing to work with a Jew. They picketed the hospital and refused to accept even emergency cases — their newly sworn Hippocratic oath notwithstanding. They were soon joined by fellow interns from five surrounding Catholic hospitals, as well as by the clergy of neighbouring parishes.

It was a sensational story and the French-language press gave it front-page coverage. The interns were all interviewed and their story was told sympathetically. They all said that they did not wish to spend a full year working with a Jew — who could blame them, asked Quebec's leading French-language newspaper, *Le Devoir* — and that they were concerned that Catholic patients would find it "repugnant" to be treated, or even touched, by a Jewish physician. To the support of the indignant interns came such organizations as the St-Jean-Baptiste Society, various county councils and co-operatives and

Left: In 1944, the Canadian Jewish Congress published a series of comic books for children telling the stories of Jewish soldiers during the Second World War. These comics were intended to increase awareness of the contributions made by Canadian Jews to the war effort.

Right: Toronto's Swastika Club terrorized a Jewish baseball team, leading to the Christie Pits riot, August 1933.

179

Demonstration sparked by the Christie Pits riot.

prominent members of the Catholic clergy. Within a few days the hapless Dr. Rabinovich submitted his resignation. Jews, a Quebec paper gloated, had now learned their place, and "it is not in Quebec."

Nor, it seemed, was it in Saskatchewan. At about the same time Rabinovich was losing his job, the Regina General Hospital refused to hire two Jewish doctors as radiologists. As the hospital's superintendent explained to the press, a Jewish appointment would be "unacceptable" to the staff and the public at large.

The infamous Montreal interns' strike was one of literally hundreds of anti-semitic incidents that tainted Canadian society in the years between the wars. In August of 1933 Toronto experienced the notorious Christie Pits riot, when large numbers of youths who were members and supporters of a local Swastika Club fought with a Jewish baseball team and its supporters in a battle that poured out onto surrounding streets and lasted most of the night. There was also violence in the streets of Winnipeg and Vancouver as anti-Jewish gangs and Jews confronted one another.

These were, of course, isolated incidents. Canada was not Eastern Europe. Though there was some harassment and certainly some vandalism against synagogues and Jewish schools and businesses, there were few violent outbursts. Yet it is evident that the Canada of the 1920s and 1930s was a country permeated with anti-semitism. As a committee of the Canadian Jewish Congress reported in 1937: "During the past few years we have witnessed an amazing growth of anti-semitism. Manifestations of an intensified anti-Jewish sentiment have been springing up everywhere...Jews have been barred from hotels, beaches, golf courses and parks...[There are] many signs posted in front of parks and beaches to the effect that Gentiles only are admitted...[There has been] a startling increase in the number of individuals and companies who refuse to rent living quarters to Jews...; [there is] a spreading policy of not employing Jews; the boycott of all Jewish firms; the sporadic attempts by various organizations to involve Jews in disturbances and violence..."

Examples of anti-semitic signs that appeared in Ontario during the 1930s. The sign on the right reads "Only Gentile Business Solicited."

A year later the Canadian Jewish Congress commissioned a study of the status of the Jew in English Canada. What it discovered was so profoundly unsettling — though hardly surprising to Canadian Jewry — that the report was never released. For Jews, it reported, quotas and restrictions had become a way of life. According to the study, few of the country's teachers and none of its school principals were Jewish. Banks, insurance companies and large industrial and commercial interests, it charged, also excluded Jews from employment. Department stores did not hire Jews as salespeople; Jewish doctors could not get hospital appointments. There were no Jewish judges, and Jewish lawyers were excluded from most firms. Not only did universities and professional schools devise quotas against Jewish students, they did not hire Jewish faculty — Canadian universities were almost totally *Judenrein*, at least in their academic staff. Few civil servants were Jews, and the exceptions were rarely promoted. The report added that it was almost impossible for Jewish nurses, architects and engineers to find jobs in their fields. Some only succeeded when they adopted Christian surnames — at least until they were unmasked.

If a Jew found it difficult to find a job or receive an education, it was perhaps even more difficult to find a suitable place to live or to vacation. Increasingly, restrictive covenants were put on various properties preventing them from being sold to Jews. Signs were springing up at beaches and resorts throughout the nation informing the Jew that he was not welcome. A Laurentian hotel warned: "No Jews or Dogs allowed." A Toronto beach posted a "No Jews Allowed" sign. A tourist camp in Gimli, Manitoba, put up signs warning Jews to keep away. Throughout Ontario's Muskoka area various hotels issued warnings that Jews should keep out.

So threatening did the situation appear that a Jewish member of the Ontario legislature warned his co-religionists: "Unless something is done quickly the Jewish people may well meet the same fate in Canada that the Jews are meeting in Germany...No fire is so easily kindled as anti-semitism. The fire is dormant in Canada, it has not yet blazed up, but the spark is there. Germany is not the only place with prejudice. Look at Quebec."

And indeed it was in Quebec that the Jew seemed most threatened. While in English Canada there were no powerful institutions or movements advocating anti-semitic action, in Quebec both the Roman Catholic church and its lay allies in the French-Canadian nationalist movement were aggressively anti-Jewish. As Maurice Eisendrath, the rabbi of Holy Blossom, put it: "In Quebec anti-semitism is a way of life. In the rest of Canada it is more an afterthought. Here it is much more subtle. There it is widespread and demonic."

To the French-Canadian nationalists of this period, the Jews — indeed all foreigners — were a threat. Surrounded by the pervasive, all-encompassing North American way of life, and dominated in their own country by an apparently narrow-minded English-speaking majority, French Canadians had always felt threatened. Their way of life, traditions, language, culture and religion were, at least in their eyes, constantly under attack — and never more so than between the wars. Anything that tended to undermine the influence of the church was anathema. The most dangerous threats were modernism and materialism, and their purveyor, the Jew. It was he who personified the danger; he was, in the words of one Catholic scholar, the worldwide carrier of the bacteria of secularism, materialism, Communism and internationalism. He was perceived to be the propagator of the American way of life and the major source of social disruption and moral decay.

In the writings and speeches of many leading church and nationalist figures in Quebec, the Jew was commonly depicted as a parasite, a germ spreading an insidious disease that was undermining the national health. The remedy for disease was eradication and quarantine, and the elite of Quebec society worked ardently to bar all Jews from entering Canada and to ostracize those already here. They led anti-immigration crusades and lobbied strenuously to keep Jews out, while maintaining a boycott campaign against Jewish merchants. "If we do not buy from them," thundered *Action catholique*, an official church journal, "then they will leave." From this sprang the notorious *Achat chez nous* movement, sponsored by leading church officials, urging French Canadians to buy from their co-religionists and to stay away from Jewish storekeepers, who, according to *Le Devoir*, "have cheating and corruption in their bloodstream." Though the boycott originally began as a nationalistic strategy for the economic advancement of French Canadians, it soon became aggressively anti-semitic. As one senior clergyman told his fellow priests, "It is to free us from Jews and usurers."

The movement had the support of the church, most of the press and local merchants. As the anti-semitic restaurant association journal warned, "Do you want to be poisoned? Buy your food from Jews." Also actively pushing the boycott was the massive ultra-nationalist St-Jean-Baptiste Society, many of whose rallies throughout the province ended with the parting vow repeated by all those present: "I promise that under no circumstances shall I ever buy from a Jew."

The swastika, used as a symbol of anti-semitism in Quebec in the 1930s.

The spiritual head of this movement was the leading French-Canadian intellectual of the time, Father Lionel Groulx. In many ways, what Goldwin Smith was to English Canada in the nineteenth century, Groulx was to French Canada in the twentieth. A prolific writer and powerful orator, possessed of a brilliant mind, Groulx was the undisputed leader of the new generation of French-Canadian nationalists. Like Smith he influenced a great many of his fellow Québécois, many of whom would become leaders in their society: its priests, politicians, teachers and journalists. And like Smith he wrote contemptuously of the Jews.

Probably the issue that best illustrated the precarious position of Jews in Quebec was the school question. The Protestant school board continued to resent the intrusion of Jewish students into its system. There was a constant struggle between the board and the Jewish community over representation, religious education, the curriculum, anti-semitic teachers and the right of the board to bar Jewish students from attending schools. It took a series of court battles and various pieces of legislation before the matter was settled in the 1920s, and even then neither side was satisfied with the conclusion.

Caught between the upper and nether millstone of Protestant inflexibility and Catholic hostility, the Jewish community looked for succour from the provincial government. In 1930 a Jewish Schools Commission Bill was introduced into the Quebec Assembly. Its purpose was to establish a committee which would deal with the Protestant and Catholic school boards with regard to the education of Jewish children. It did not allow for the rights of Jewish parents to vote for school board members or to run for election. But despite the severely limited rights it gave to the Jews, the bill was fiercely denounced by church and nationalist leaders who feared that it raised the spectre of a secular school system that would imperil Catholic Quebec and the church. So fierce was the anti-Jewish campaign launched by these forces that the provincial government repealed the bill — a "victory over the foes of Christianity," crowed *Action catholique*.

What is most surprising about this concentrated campaign is its irrationality. The Jewish community in Quebec was tiny, both politically and economically impotent. It made up just over one per cent of the province's population, and in only one county, Montréal–Gésu, did Jews make up more than one one-thousandth of the residents. Most Jews were recent immigrants and—like most French Canadians—ill-educated, poor, powerless and oppressed.

But in Quebec the "Jewish problem" was part of the national question. Caught between the English hammer and the French anvil, the Jew was the target of abuse from both sides—especially from the French Canadians since the Jew was perceived as an ally of the English. He lived in their sections of Montreal, read their newspapers, went to their schools and spoke their language. As well, Jews were concentrated in some of the traditional economic activities of French Canadians, as shopkeepers, petty traders and unskilled workers. They competed for the same jobs, often when few of those jobs were available.

Despite their virulent activities, Quebec's anti-semites scored few victories. There were few outright acts of violence against Jews—indeed, few acts of any kind. Church leaders denounced the Jews, newspapers painted the most lurid pictures of Jewish excesses, politicians called for their isolation—all to little effect.

Across the country, such organizations as the Social Credit Party, the Native Sons of Canada, the Orange Order and the Canadian Corps were rife with anti-Jewish feeling. Throughout the 1930s, outbursts against Jews became more frequent on the editorial pages of some of the nation's newspapers, as well as from some Protestant pulpits. Preachers at Toronto's huge Knox Presbyterian Church, which was located in the heart of the Jewish district on Spadina Avenue, would regularly warn the congregation of the "invidious Jew"; their sermons were often flatteringly reported in the city's press, particularly in the Toronto *Telegram*, a paper not over-friendly to the Jewish people.

Souvenir edition of the *Kanader Adler*, celebrating the coronation of the new king, 1937.

What were the causes of Canadian anti-semitism? To some extent the massive propaganda of the Nazis had its impact. Some people were taken in by it, and by such American hate-mongers as auto-maker Henry Ford, Father Coughlan, Gerald L.K. Smith and others. Also, the thirties were a time of economic depression and the search for scapegoats invariably ended at a Jewish doorstep. The prominence of Jewish names in the left-wing movement also convinced many gullible or malevolent Canadians that most Jews were Communists.

In addition, many Canadians were reacting to three decades of almost unlimited immigration. The rapid rise of nativism in the 1920s came out of a concern over the type of Canada these millions of largely uneducated, illiterate aliens would produce. For many, the Jew symbolized a feared "mongrelization" of the country. Much of the anti-semitism in Quebec and in fundamentalist areas of western Canada originated from religious teachings. Jews, churchgoers were told, had killed Christ, had refused to repent or convert to Christianity, and were therefore damned. Also, some non-Jewish immigrants — particularly from Eastern Europe — had brought over anti-semitism as part of their baggage. Generations of an anti-Jewish tradition could not be forgotten overnight.

Many Canadians — especially the elite, the country's opinion-makers, its politicians, academics, writers, businessmen and journalists — continued to believe that the Jew did not fit into their concept of Canada. Theirs was to be a country of homesteaders and farmers, and few Canadians felt that Jews could make successful agriculturalists, in spite of their success at making the deserts of Palestine bloom. Those immigrants who did not farm were expected to go into the woods, mines, smelters, canneries and textile mills or to join construction gangs in the north. The Jews were seen as city people, pedlars and shopkeepers in a country that wanted loggers and miners. They were seen as a people with brains in a country that preferred brawn, as a people with strong minds in a country that wanted strong backs.

Still, there were many prominent Canadians who stood shoulder to shoulder with the Jewish community in its battle. The elderly Henri Bourassa recanted his earlier anti-semitism and denounced the outrages of some of his fellow Québécois. The Montreal French-language newspaper *Le Canada* opened up its pages to refutations of the anti-Jewish canards in the nationalist press. Various clerics, politicians and journalists in English-speaking Canada were also active in support of the Jewish community. Unfortunately, there were not enough of them. In dealing with the widespread xenophobic attitudes of the period, Jews were largely on their own.

Within the community itself, there was no organization capable of coping with the problem. The Congress was inert, the Zionists were more concerned about the fate of Palestine, and other Jewish organizations were too weak, too insular or too parochial. Never had the community felt so isolated, so vulnerable, so weak; never had there been a greater need for unity.

The rise to power of Adolf Hitler in Germany made little impact in Canada. Though the press regularly carried stories about his excesses and the mistreatment of Jews, Canadians were too busy trying to cope with the Depression to worry about the activities of the funny-looking cartoon character who had taken over a country thousands of miles away. The Jewish community felt virtually alone in its concern.

But what could it do? How could it mobilize public opinion? Canadian Jews were too far from the seats of political and economic power to make any impact. They had little influence in Ottawa; when they spoke, few listened. Instead they exercised the "politics of the street." Perhaps parades, demonstrations, mass meetings, even strikes might alert the people to the dangers of Nazism.

First off the mark was the Winnipeg Jewish community. In the spring of 1933, to protest Hitler's accession to power, the community organized a massive protest march through downtown Winnipeg. A few days later, 1,500 turned out in Vancouver to protest the events in

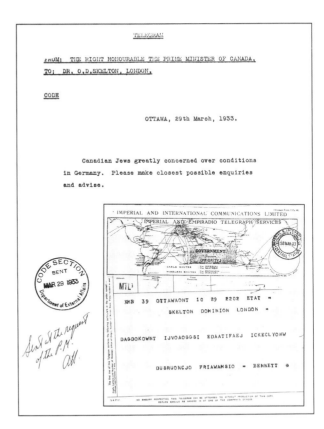

Telegram (and coded transmission) sent to London by the prime minister of Canada in response to Jewish lobbying, 1933.

The *Jewish Post* exposes "new aspects of the Jewish situation under the Hitler regime," Winnipeg, 1933.

Germany. In Toronto, Jewish factory owners and storekeepers closed down their businesses so they and their workers could join in a massive march to the legislature. Thousands attended a rally in Montreal to denounce the anti-Jewish activities of the Nazis. Not surprisingly, a large counter-demonstration was held in that city a week later by French-Canadian nationalists protesting the Jewish rally.

But more than demonstrations and parades was necessary. The Jewish press and various organizations began calling for the revitalization of the Congress, which had lain dormant since 1919. These calls were especially vociferous in the west, where the Jewish community felt most isolated. In May of 1933, some Jewish societies in Winnipeg met to form a Western Canadian Jewish Congress Committee. They invited delegates from all over the west to attend an emergency meeting. The response was overwhelming. Hundreds of delegates arrived and unanimously agreed to re-establish a Congress which could deal with the problems of Canadian anti-semitism and the plight of European Jewry.

Toronto and Montreal were slower to respond. There the established community, "the Yahudim," as Caiserman pejoratively called them, were reluctant to convene a congress they knew would be dominated by immigrant "hotheads." Westerners kept applying pressure. As the secretary of the Western Canadian Jewish Congress Committee, M.A. Gray, warned Caiserman: "I am afraid that the West will be compelled to shoulder the entire responsibility of organizing Canada, as we feel that we cannot remain dormant in the face of the present events affecting the Jewish people in Canada and the world over."

Caiserman had of course been propagating the Congress idea for some time. Through his speeches and articles he had done more than anyone else to try to keep it alive. From his small office in the Baron de Hirsch Institute, he carried on a correspondence from coast to coast proposing a revival of the Congress. Finally in June 1933 he arranged a meeting in Toronto of delegates from across the country who were favourable to the suggestion. There Caiserman himself was appointed the secretary of a committee to convene the next Congress convention. In December a call went out from the leaders of Canadian Jewry — Lyon Cohen, Sam Jacobs, A.J. Freiman, Moses Finkelstein, Caiserman and others — for all Canadian Jews to send their representatives to Toronto on January 27, 1934, for the second convention of the Canadian Jewish Congress.

The selection of delegates in the first week of that month brought out the real splits in the community. The Zionists still had their own internal divisions among the Labour Zionists, the Mizrachi and the middle-of-the-road societies. To these had been added the Revisionists, the militant followers of Vladimir (Ze'ev) Jabotinsky, who called for a Jewish homeland in the biblical land of Israel, including those areas the British had unilaterally lopped off Palestine to form Trans-Jordan. The Jewish left had spawned a variety of Communist, anarchist, socialist and anti-Zionist organizations that were determined to undermine the Labour Zionists and the more established organizations. As well, many wealthier Jews were opposed to the whole enterprise. They were fearful of a democratically elected constituent assembly, preferring the model of the American Jewish Committee, where power was centred in the hands of a small number of establishment leaders.

The elections of delegates were occasionally rowdy affairs. As one Winnipeg participant described it: "Passion had been roused to the extent of having occasioned at least at one meeting a near riot with blows, black eyes and spilling of blood...[No] less than 3,800 people came to cast their ballot travelling long distances, coming from all parts of the city, despite the twenty-five below zero weather and an icy, piercing wind that blew through the day. Streams of people of all ages, classes and description, waited in line..." More often the elections were orderly, though bitterly fought. The stakes were high and every faction and society wished to have its opinions made known.

Upper: Morris Abraham Gray.
Lower: Moses Finkelstein.

Second Plenary session of the Canadian Jewish Congress, Toronto, 1934.

The second meeting of the Canadian Jewish Congress opened on a blustery, wintry January morning in the Crystal Ballroom of Toronto's King Edward Hotel. The sombre delegates listened to a series of addresses from Jacobs, Caiserman and others detailing the tenuous lot of European Jews and the sad state of affairs in Canada. Missing was the celebratory, joyful mood that had accompanied the first meeting some fifteen years before. The state of world and Canadian Jewry had changed drastically — and not for the better.

Though there was a variety of contradictory points of view on what should be done, the delegates agreed that the only way a national Jewish organization could succeed was if it had relatively autonomous regional executives centred in Montreal, Toronto and Winnipeg. As for the national executive, Sam Jacobs was elected president and Caiserman once again took the key position of general secretary. The agenda hammered out at the two-day plenary session was simple: keep the pressure on the government to allow more Jewish immigration; mount campaigns to fight the Nazis abroad and the anti-semite at home; urge the British to open up Palestine to Jewish settlers; and find ways to fund the various cultural, religious and educational activities of Canadian Jewry. It was an agenda that would change little over the next decade.

Sadly, for the next few years the Congress achieved little. Jacobs was too busy in Parliament to spend much time on Congress activities; though passionate and committed, Caiserman was a hopeless administrator. The uptown community in Montreal would still have little to do with an organization it felt was too far left, too Zionist and too much the mouthpiece of the immigrant community. The Congress was shunned by the monied Reform community, who denounced the organization for its "militant Zionism." Thus from the outset the Congress was strapped for funds. For the next few years, Caiserman spent most of his time trying to raise a few thousand dollars to keep it functioning. At times, he could not even afford to pay the organization's secretary her weekly salary of eight dollars. It was not until 1938, when the wealthy Samuel Bronfman turned his attention to the Congress, that it became a real force in the Jewish community.

One project the Congress undertook was to co-ordinate a boycott of German products in Canada. Though many Jewish storekeepers and manufacturers co-operated, there was little support outside the community. Indeed, while the Congress was desperately pleading with Canadians to boycott German imports, Mackenzie King was writing Nazi leader Herman Goering in 1937 to try to arrange "improved commercial relations" and "increased trade" between the two countries. Predictably, little came of the boycott campaign.

But while the national organization dithered, the regional executives flourished. In both western Canada and Ontario, most of the wealthy Jewish establishment took an active interest in Congress. The small-town Jewish communities in the two regions, fearful of their isolation, looked to the regional executives for succour and support. Both regions played vital roles in lobbying provincial and municipal governments, in sponsoring anti-Nazi activities and in pushing for the admission of Jewish refugees.

By the mid-1930s a series of Fascist organizations had taken root in Canada. Failed journalist Adrien Arcand organized the largest of these, the Order of Goglus, in Quebec. As well, he edited a number of weekly newspapers whose sole purpose was to spread lies about

Stamp distributed by the Jewish Anti-Fascist League of Winnipeg, 1938.

Upper: Nazi uniforms to be used in Canada, 1930s.

Lower: Anti-semitic literature in Canada, 1930s.

Jews. Financed by wealthy supporters, at one time Arcand claimed a following of over fifty thousand in Quebec alone. But their activities, while bothersome and painful to the Jews, were not taken seriously by most Québécois.

In western Canada an English immigrant, William Whittaker, created an organization modelled on the Nazi storm-troopers. Wearing khaki shirts, brown breeches and riding boots, Whittaker's Brownshirts paraded through Jewish areas of Winnipeg and launched a virulently anti-semitic periodical, the *Canadian Nationalist*. In Ontario local anti-semites organized Swastika Clubs — gangs of youths wearing swastika badges who intimidated Jews on beaches and in public parks. None of these groups amounted to much, though they did hold a national Fascist convention in Toronto's Massey Hall in July of 1938, which was attended by hundreds of delegates and several hundred curious observers.

The Jewish community vainly attempted to have legislation passed against these hate groups, but they were successful only in Manitoba, where provincial MP Marcus Hyman successfully introduced the nation's first group libel law, the Manitoba Defamation Act, which allowed any member of an identifiable religious or racial group to apply for an injunction against any publisher of hate material. Otherwise the community concentrated on forming coalitions with church and other groups to contain the Fascists. Large rallies addressed by leading clergymen, politicians and journalists were the community's most effective public relations weapons.

Though the years between 1930 and 1945 were indeed dark and brutal ones for Canadian Jewry, they were also a period of vitality, experimentation, passion and creativity. While everyone was concerned with the spread of anti-semitism and the persecution in Europe, Canadian Jews were busy building their own communal structures. Despite the rigours of the Depression — or, more accurately perhaps, because of them — a host of new charitable organizations were created. *Landsmanshaftn* increased their activity to deal with the enormous

problems of indigent Jews. The Zionists, though splintered internally, mobilized to fight the British government's efforts to restrict Jewish immigration into Palestine. Synagogues and schools were built; a Workmen's Circle school was started in Calgary, a Hebrew day school in Edmonton, a left-wing Labour Zionist school in Toronto, a new Talmud Torah in Montreal; a new Orthodox congregation in Toronto, the Shaarei Shomayim, bought a new building and the Holy Blossom moved into a magnificent temple on the northern outskirts of Toronto. In Montreal a new Young Men's Hebrew Association building and old folks' home were completed and the Jewish General Hospital was founded. Yiddish newspapers expanded their circulation, and new Anglo-Jewish periodicals were published to meet the needs of a growing English-speaking readership. Winnipeg alone had two, the *Jewish Post* and the *Western Jewish News*. From Cape Breton to Vancouver, every Jewish community, every Jewish organization, expanded its scope of activity.

Though immigration was at a standstill, the community nevertheless had to house, feed and support the handful of refugees who

Upper left and right: Graduates and graduation certificate, Winnipeg's Yiddishe Folks Shule, 1939.

Lower: Marcus Hyman, *c.* 1932.

א זעהר אינטערעסאנטע לעקציע
פון
עמא
גאלדמאן
איבער דער טעמא
"די יוגנט אין קאמף"
"THE YOUTH IN REVOLT"
וועט פאָרקומען
זונטיק, 14טען אפריל
אװנט 8.30
אין לייבאָר ליסעאום
346 ספעדיינע עוועניו
פאָרלירט ניט די געלעגענהייט צו הערן עמא גאלדמאן
איבער דיזער טעמא פאר איר אפשיד פון קאנאדא
אראנושירט פון בר. 339 ארבעטער רינג

Poster announcing a lecture by Emma Goldman at the Labour Lyceum, Toronto, 1937, organized by the Workmen's Circle. (Toronto Jewish Congress/CJC Ont. Region Archives 4980)

had managed to break through the barriers. Every arrival was a major event; no expense was spared to make the newcomers welcome. Through JIAS the community made certain that no immigrant went on welfare. After all, the federal bureaucracy seemed determined to deport every foreign-born indigent in the country. And if that indigent was Jewish, so much the better—at least in the opinion of officials in the Immigration Department.

Active as well were the Jewish trade unions, even though the Depression had devastated the garment industry. Bankruptcies, unemployment, miserable working conditions, low wages—always the hallmark of the industry—were exacerbated by the world economic collapse. Wage rates fell by up to forty per cent; jobs by fifty per cent. Many of those who held jobs were forced into part-time work: most union members averaged about two days' work a week in this period. Worst hit were women workers; because many women were protected by minimum wage laws, owners simply let their women go and replaced them with men, who had no such legal protection.

Many women did not accept their dismissals passively. While the Jewish unions themselves were bastions of male supremacy, Jewish women proved to be every bit as militant as their male counterparts. As historian Ruth Frager's study of Canadian Jewish working women makes clear, their contributions were fundamental to the success of the Jewish labour movement.

And, surprisingly, there were some successes. During the 1930s there was more union militancy in the garment industry than in any other sector of the Canadian economy. At a time when few workers were willing to jeopardize their jobs by striking, Jewish garment workers were mounting their largest and most successful strikes. This dynamism was partly the result of the formation of the Communist-led Industrial Union of Needle Trades Workers (IUNTW), whose leaders included some of the most colourful radicals of the time, including J.B. Salsberg, Joshua Gershman and Becky Buhay.

Determined to break the ILGWU hegemony over the industry, they launched a massive organizing campaign and sponsored some of the largest strikes, including a general strike in Montreal in 1930.

The socialists and Labour Zionists in the ILGWU, firm in the conviction that the Communists had to be undermined, took their union into the most militant phase of its history. Led by Bernard Shane in Montreal, Sam Kraisman in Toronto and Sam Herbst in Winnipeg, they mounted a series of strikes in those cities. Their strategy was simple. Workers would walk out in April or August, at the height of the production season. Any shop that could not manufacture in those months could forget about the rest of the year. Most settled on the union's terms.

In order to avoid the Jewish unions, some companies even attempted to move away from their workers. In one memorable incident a leading firm, Superior Cloak, having just signed its first agreement with the union, disappeared one night from its Spadina area location and reappeared the following morning in Guelph, Ontario, some forty miles away. Machinery, patterns, files and furniture had been secretly trucked in overnight. When workers discovered their workplace had vanished, they simply hired a fleet of trucks and began picketing outside the new plant. When newly hired local workers refused to cross the picket line, a chastened Superior returned to Toronto. A few firms attempted the same ploy, with equally unsuccessful results.

Other unions were busy as well. Toronto's Jewish Bakers' Union organized most of the city's Jewish bakeries. The fur workers were less successful, as the conflict between the Communists and the socialists in their union grew so heated that the union split. So active were the Jewish trade unionists in this period, whether they were organizing or feuding, that a prominent Toronto rabbi ruefully remarked that there was more "Jewish hustle and bustle" taking place at the new Labour Lyceum building on Spadina than in any synagogue or community hall in the country.

Upper: Three union activists, Toronto, 1945. Left to right: Jenny Zalick, Annie Eisner and Annie Dolgoy.

Lower: Joshua Gershman (second from left) working as a fur dresser and dryer, Winnipeg, 1922.

Toronto May Day parade, 1935. With signs in foreground are Jewish labour activists J.B. Salsberg, Max Dolgoy, Alec Richman and Jack Hilf.

As the situation of European Jewry further deteriorated, and as the Canadian government proved even more unyielding on the refugee question, the Jewish labour movement turned its energy towards helping fellow Jews and away from its union activities. For a short time, the internal divisions were papered over as Bundists, Labour Zionists and Communists joined forces with their bosses to fight antisemitism and to lobby for Jewish refugees. Antagonism in the union hall and the workplace was forgotten — or at least temporarily put aside — to battle a common enemy.

Despite the harshness of the period, in some areas of society, Jews were scoring astonishing successes. For example, the Bronfmans had turned the family's small liquor concern in the west into Canada's most successful distiller of alcoholic beverages. In Quebec City, Maurice Pollack's tiny store had blossomed into the area's largest retail outlet. In Ottawa, A.J. Freiman had built his retail furniture business into the city's most prosperous department store. Hundreds of other Jewish businessmen were opening or expanding their stores and factories. But the community's most striking advances were in the area of politics.

Throughout most of the 1930s, there were three Jewish members of Parliament, Sam Jacobs from Montreal, A.A. Heaps from Winnipeg and Sam Factor from Toronto. Admittedly all three sat for constituencies with large Jewish populations, but they received significant non-Jewish support as well. At the provincial level, Peter Bercovitch, Joseph Cohen and Maurice Hartt sat in the Quebec legislature, as did (for a short time) Louis Fitch, an active Zionist.

A dynamic young lawyer, David Croll, the mayor of Windsor, won election to the Ontario legislature in 1934 and became Canada's first Jewish cabinet minister as the Minister of Labour and Welfare in the new Liberal government of Premier Mitchell Hepburn. He was joined on the government benches by two other Jewish members, John Glass and E.F. Singer. In Manitoba Marcus Hyman sat in the provincial assembly, as did Congress activist M.A. Gray, elected in

Fanny Rosenfeld.

1941. Across the country, significant numbers of Jews were elected to city councils and school boards, even in areas where there was a tiny Jewish population.

Though many Jews took great satisfaction from the political achievements of their fellows, most derived far greater satisfaction from the accomplishments of Canadian Jewish athletes, whose exploits brightened the dark days of the inter-war period. Who in the community — indeed, who in Canada — did not take pride in the remarkable feats of Fanny Rosenfeld of Toronto? Known affectionately as "Bobby," Rosenfeld was the country's premier woman athlete of the period. In the 1928 Olympics in Amsterdam, she won a pair of medals including a gold. She set records in at least six different track-and-field events and was among the best women tennis players in the country. She also led her basketball, baseball and hockey teams to championships. Rosenfeld was deservedly chosen in 1950 as Canada's Female Athlete of the Half-Century.

Boxer Sammy Luftspring, a Canadian champ who was favoured for an Olympic medal, defiantly refused to attend the 1936 Olympics because they were held in Nazi Germany. Instead, with some other Canadian Jewish athletes, he went to Spain to participate in a counter-Olympics. Both he and another Toronto fighter, Ben Yackubowitz — known as "Baby Yack" — were among the most popular boxers in Canada.

In hockey, Alex Levinsky, a grandson of a founder of the Goel Tzedec Synagogue in Toronto, was a star forward for the Toronto Maple Leafs. Cecil Hart, a scion of the great Quebec Jewish family, was instrumental in the creation of the Montreal Canadiens, and he was the team's coach for most of the 1920s and 1930s, when it won a number of Stanley Cups. The award given today to the most valuable player in the National Hockey League, the Hart Trophy, is named after this direct descendant of Aaron Hart.

For western Canadian Jewry, no team provided as much satisfaction as Winnipeg's YMHA softball team. Year after year it dominated every team it faced. But even in sports, the baleful anti-semitism of the period was unremitting. When the favoured Winnipeg YMHA football team went to Regina in 1936 to play for the Western Canadian Junior Championship, spectators invaded the field shouting, "Beat the Jews." The game was suspended as the YMHA players — who were in the lead — ran for their lives. Shortly thereafter Jewish officials decided to withdraw all their teams from organized sport. With the example of the Christie Pits riot before them, it seemed that some parts of Canada were too dangerous for Jewish athletes.

And certainly, all parts of the country remained closed to Jewish refugees. The world of the 1930s, said Chaim Weizmann, the most

Ben Yackubowitz, also known as
"Baby Yack."

influential Jewish leader of the period, was divided into two: countries
like Germany where Jews could not live and countries like Canada
which they could not enter. Indeed, of all the western democracies,
Canada had by far the worst record in providing sanctuary to Jewish
refugees fleeing the scourge of Nazism. While many small Latin
American countries accepted tens of thousands, and the United States
and even tiny Palestine over 100,000 each, vast and empty Canada
would allow in fewer than 5,000 between 1933 and 1945.

The Canadian government was fully aware of the anti-Jewish
feeling throughout the country. After all, many of its members shared

it. Indeed, Prime Minister Mackenzie King was obsessed with Jews. He dreamed of them often and filled his diary with his thoughts. While he saw Jews as "the People of the Book" and as somewhat "mystical," he was also capable of repeating — and believing — the most bilious anti-semitic slander. He was convinced that permitting Jewish refugees of "even the best type" into Canada would destroy the country. As he wrote in his diary: "We must seek to keep Canada free from unrest and too great an intermixture of foreign strains of blood." Jews, he feared, would not only pollute Canada's bloodstream, their admission would cause riots and worsen relations between the federal government and the provinces. Accepting Jewish refugees, he told his sympathetic cabinet, would undermine Canadian unity, alienate many Canadians, strengthen the forces of Quebec nationalism, and bring about bloodshed in the streets. King was influenced in these views by his Quebec lieutenant, Ernest Lapointe, who kept the bug in his ear about the dangers of alienating his province by opening Canada's doors to Jewish immigration, no matter how limited. Still, King was a consummate politician, the most successful in Canadian history. He prided himself on his ability to gauge the pulse of the nation. Had he believed there were votes to be won by admitting Jewish refugees he would likely have opened the doors wider.

At the same time King's deputy minister of immigration, Frederick Blair, a rabid anti-semite, was warning anyone who would listen that Jews were "cheaters and liars" who "destroyed" whatever countries they moved to. Along with other senior officials, including the country's leading diplomat and future governor general, Vincent Massey, Blair made certain that few Jews broke through the immigration barrier. As he boasted to the prime minister: "Pressure on the part of the Jewish people has never been greater than it is now and I am glad to say…that it has never been so well controlled. Fewer Jews are coming in than ever before."

Making up just over one per cent of the population, politically and economically impotent, overwhelmed by the horror of the Nazi rise

Jewish refugees gather in Zbąszyn, on the German-Polish border, after their expulsion from Germany, 1938.

to power and fearing a vicious anti-semitic backlash, Canadian Jews did little during the prewar years. By the late 1930s, there were few demonstrations or mass meetings and certainly no civil disobedience. Feeling frightened and marginal, Canadian Jews understood very well that any outburst could be used against them. The community would be branded as disloyal and some might even be deported. Though a few urged a more militant approach, quiet diplomacy and secret negotiations between the government and Jewish leaders were the order of the day. Although the community's spokesmen managed to wring some concessions out of the government — as a Jewish leader

Samuel Bronfman, *c.* 1939.

later put it, "Even crumbs are significant when the whole loaf is impossible, especially when every crumb represented a Jewish life saved from the Nazis" — on the whole they failed miserably. Even the horrors of *Kristallnacht* in November of 1938, when the Nazis destroyed thousands of synagogues, Jewish businesses and homes and arrested, maimed and murdered countless Jews, failed to move the Canadian government. The efforts of such pro-refugee groups as the Canadian League of Nations Society, such friends of the Jewish community as Senator Cairene Wilson, and some prominent clergymen made little difference.

These failures prompted a dramatic change in the Canadian Jewish Congress. Frustrated by its lack of success, prominent distiller Samuel Bronfman decided it was time to devote his enormous energies and resources to its revival. The son of early settlers in Wapella, Saskatchewan, Sam Bronfman was raised with a strong commitment to his fellow Jews. Indeed, his father was so determined that his children receive a Jewish education that he had brought with him a religious teacher from the old country. For years the family struggled to eke out an existence on the hostile prairie frontier. Eventually they achieved some success in the hotel and real estate business. It was in the production and sale of liquor, however, that the family fortune was made.

By the 1920s, Sam and his brother Allan had moved to Montreal, where they were actively involved in Jewish philanthrophy. While Allan was largely responsible for building the Jewish General Hospital, Sam was the lifeblood of a host of other Jewish institutions. Though generous with their money, the Bronfmans shunned Jewish organizations. Sam dismissed the Congress as "irrelevant and... useless" and felt that it was "doing the Jewish community more harm than good."

In August of 1938 the beleaguered president of the Congress, Sam Jacobs, died, worn out by his spirited but fruitless campaign in Ottawa to open Canada's doors to more Jewish refugees. Determined to select a president who would give the Congress an authoritative voice, Labour Zionist leaders approached Sam Bronfman. For them to consider the millionaire industrialist indicated the gravity of their concern. Yet Bronfman was different from most of his uptown colleagues. His immigrant background, his rural roots, his well-known commitment to Jewish causes and his generosity marked him, in Caiserman's words, as "one of us...a true man of the people."

Reluctantly Bronfman accepted the call. He, too, saw the need for a revivified Congress, and to take charge of its renewal he hired an energetic young lawyer, Saul Hayes. A brilliant choice, Hayes would provide the Congress with the professional expertise and political leadership it so desperately needed. Bronfman brought into the Congress other wealthy, uptown Jews who had hitherto stayed aloof from the organization but who were deeply involved in Jewish philanthropy. With Bronfman's commitment and funding, the new-found support in the more integrated sectors of Jewish society and especially Hayes' organizational talents, the Congress finally achieved stability.

Saul Hayes, *c.* 1950.

Significant as well was the new relationship between the Congress and the B'nai B'rith, the large American-based Jewish fraternal organization. It had first come to Canada in the 1870s and had lodges in most areas where there was a Jewish population. From the beginning these lodges were active in service, charity and community work, but they were most effective in public relations and in combating anti-semitism. Long before anyone else, B'nai B'rith leaders were heavily involved in anti-defamation and human rights work. In every region in the country, they had created organizations to fight discrimination and anti-semitism. Anxious to make use of their expertise and experience, and especially of their large and committed membership, Bronfman approached the B'nai B'rith executive with a proposal to create a common organization to combat anti-semitism. The times were too perilous and the situation of Canadian Jewry too precarious, he argued, for there to be divisions within the Jewish

Upper: Second World War recruiting poster published by the Canadian Jewish Congress.

Lower: Flight Lieutenant Sydney Shulemson, D.S.O D.F.C. Second World War.

community. On the issue of anti-semitism, he pleaded, Canadian Jewry must speak with one voice.

Though they had every right to disdain the upstart Congress for encroaching on their territory, B'nai B'rith leaders were totally forthcoming. They, too, realized that the unity of Canadian Jewry was far more important than the autonomy of their organization. They readily agreed to join the Congress in the creation of a National Joint Public Relations Committee to combat anti-semitism, to educate the Canadian public on its evil and to deal with and lobby government authorities over its control.

But as far as opening Canada's doors to refugees was concerned, neither the revitalized Congress nor the creation of the committee made any difference. Though Hayes, Bronfman, the Jewish members of Parliament and a few influential Jews were able to force some immigration permits out of a reluctant cabinet and Department of Immigration, they were powerless to change the government's policy. Canadian Jews could only watch in helpless frustration in June of 1939 as the *St. Louis*, a ship full of more than nine hundred German Jewish refugees, sailed from port to port off the coasts of the United States and Latin America looking for a place to drop its wretched cargo. Despite urgent pleas to the Canadian government, Mackenzie King replied that it was "not a Canadian problem." With King's response their last flickering hope for refuge was extinguished, and the Jews of the *St. Louis* headed back to Europe, where many would die in the gas chambers of the Third Reich.

With the onset of war, the Jewish community again mobilized. The Congress desperately urged eligible Jews to enlist in the services, and thousands did. As in the First World War, Jewish enrolment in the armed forces was among the highest per capita of any group in the country. Seventeen thousand joined up—about fifty per cent of those eligible for military service—and hundreds were decorated for bravery. The Jewish community raised large amounts of money through the Congress War Aid Executive

Jewish women sewing for the war effort, 1942. (Ottawa Jewish Historical Society 4-163)

to build recreation centres for off-duty soldiers, both Jewish and non-Jewish. The Congress also created a chaplaincy committee to make sure that there were enough Jewish chaplains to service the Canadian armed forces. It took some time, however, to convince the Department of National Defence that rabbis were necessary; only when the Congress provided a list of the large numbers of Jews in uniform did the department appoint Rabbi Gershon Levi of Montreal as Canada's first Jewish chaplain. Many others would soon follow.

Local Jewish communities from coast to coast also participated actively in the war effort. The Halifax community played host to thousands of Jewish servicemen during the war. In 1943, over four

Upper left: Rabbi Samuel Cass taking part in the first worship service celebrated on German territory by the 1st Canadian Army, 1945.

Lower left: Passover Seder for Canadian Jewish servicemen, held in the Maritimes.

Right: Letter from Chaplain Gershon Levi to the men in the service regarding Hanukkah celebrations, 1943.

CANADIAN MILITARY HEADQUARTERS

London, November 1943.

Dear Friend,

Here is another letter from your Padre, bringing you my warmest greetings for Chanukah, 5704 (Dec.22nd to 29th). Perhaps this letter will not reach you till after Chanukah, as many of our boys are even further afield than when I wrote you last. But you will know that my greetings are no less warm, and that I am no less eager to hear from you.

Chanukah is the Maccabean festival, the Feast of Dedication. It commemorates the victorious fight for liberty and freedom of conscience waged by our ancestors against the totalitarians of old. Led by Judah the Maccabee and his four brothers, our people rose against the tyrant Emperor Antiochus of Syria, and though greatly outnumbered, defeated the enemy in battle. On the 25th of Kislev, in the year 167 B.C.E., they recaptured Jerusalem and rededicated the Temple to the service of God. Their victory has always been an inspiration us Jews, and to all freedom-loving people. And today the spirit of the Maccabees lives again in those who fight to establish the Four Freedoms for mankind.

CHANUKAH CELEBRATIONS

If you are in Italy or North Africa, you may have little opportunity to celebrate Chanukah. Still, some of the boys have written me that they managed to observe Passover or the High Holydays with fellow-Jews in the British or American Forces, or with civilians, even as far away as India. You may be able to do the same. I would be interested to learn of your experiences.

In the United Kingdom, special Chanukah Services have been arranged, in conjunction with the Jewish Hospitality Committee, in centres all over the country. In most cases they will take place on Sunday afternoon, December 26th, and will be followed by a Chanukah Party.

In LONDON a service will be held at 1500 hours, 26 Dec., in the oldest Synagogue in the British Empire,- the 250-year old Synagogue in Bevis Marks, E.C.3. (near Aldgate). It will be followed by a tea and entertainment.

In ALDERSHOT a large service and Chanukah party will be held. Watch D.R.O's for the place and hour.

In BOURNEMOUTH, BRIGHTON, LEEDS, HARROGATE, DARLINGTON, GLASGOW - and scores of other towns, arrangements are under way for appropriate celebrations. Details can be secured from any Jewish Chaplain, or from your nearest Jewish Centre for the Forces.

(A reminder:- There is no special leave for Chanukah, and travel to London is strictly limited over that week-end).

That's all for now, except to say that I am always happy to hear from you. How are you getting on? Is your address changed? Are there any Jewish boys in your unit who are not in touch with me? Have you any requests? Let me know - your letters are always welcome.

May God Bless and Keep you, and may we all be able to light the Chanukah candles next year in our own homes.

Cordially,

Gershon

(S.Gershon Levi)H/Capt.
Jewish Chaplain
Canadian Military Headquarters.

#235 Shonie:
2 Dec 43 Darling: I was signing hundreds these circulars, when I discovered I had signed one as above! Honestly, I had already put it on the pile before I discovered the error he used 'dear friend' its none of business anyway it just shows

hundred men attended the community Passover Seder. Similarly the tiny Jewish community of Moncton opened a community centre which serviced thousands of Jewish men and women stationed at the nearby air base. Similarly, at the other end of the country, the British Columbia Jewish War Efforts Committee and the Federated Jewish Women of Vancouver heroically welcomed and took care of thousands of Jewish servicemen and women, not only from Canada but from the United States, Great Britain and elsewhere. Indeed, throughout the country, local Jewish communities — no matter how small — rushed forward to provide much-appreciated hospitality everywhere soldiers were stationed.

But even the outbreak of war had no impact on government policy. Of the hundreds of thousands of Jews who escaped the Nazis and made their way to Spain, Portugal, France, Belgium, Holland and Japan, Canada accepted a grand total of 500 between 1939 and 1945, though many of these refugees would have brought with them the skills and the capital Canada needed so desperately. The country did admit some 2,250 other Jews, but these were "internees," young German Jews shipped over from Great Britain for the duration of the war. For several years they were incarcerated in camps — often with Nazi prisoners of war — and kept as virtual captives. On their release, many left Canada as quickly as they could, though those who chose to remain made a distinct contribution to this country as scientists, scholars, artists and industrialists. They were a living reminder, a symbol, of how much Canada lost by keeping her doors shut so tightly.

Perhaps the most acute and poignant description of Canada in this period was provided by the condemned Jews in Auschwitz. They named the barracks where the food, clothes, gold, diamonds and other goods confiscated from the inmates were stored "Canada," because to them it represented luxury and salvation, a Garden of Eden in Hell. As well, however, it was unreachable, a completely sealed-off haven — as was Canada in the years between 1933 and 1945.

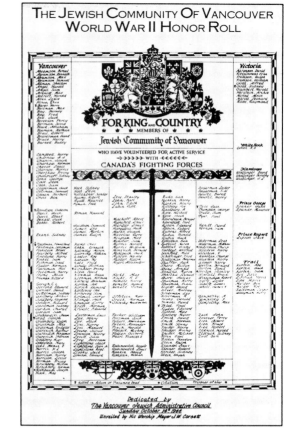

Upper: Second World War honour roll from the Jewish community of Vancouver.

Lower: Second World War grave marker in Europe.

CHAPTER NINE

NEW HORIZONS

1945 - 1990

It was April of 1945, and the war was drawing to a close. Over the past few months the liberation of Hitler's death camps had revealed to a skeptical world that events too horrible to be believed were not too horrible to have happened. On the instructions of his government, Georges Vanier, Canada's ambassador to France, joined American officials for a firsthand look at the recently liberated concentration camp at Buchenwald.

What Vanier saw sickened him. Worse, as a Canadian it made him ashamed. He wrote Prime Minister Mackenzie King detailing the ovens, the skeletal survivors, the mass graves, the "naked bodies piled up like so much cord wood." In a radio broadcast to Canada, Vanier condemned his government's indifference to the plight of the Jews. "How deaf we were" to their cries for help, he lamented.

If Vanier hoped that the revelations of the Nazi barbarities would improve Canada's hearing, he was sorely mistaken. When it came to Jews, the government would remain deaf—at least for a few more years.

* * *

News Release

From the Press Office of the
√ CANADIAN JEWISH CONGRESS
√ UNITED JEWISH REFUGEE AND WAR RELIEF AGENCIES
√ WAR EFFORTS COMMITTEE OF THE CANADIAN JEWISH CONGRESS

MONTREAL   1121 ST. CATHERINE STREET WEST   Tel. PLateau 6891

TORONTO OFFICE: 150 BEVERLEY STREET   WINNIPEG OFFICE: 401 CONFEDERATION LIFE BLDG.

H. M. Caiserman, the general secretary of the Canadian Jewish Congress, is en route to Poland. He sailed aboard the Canadian Pacific liner, the Empress of Scotland, from Halifax and arrived in London several days ago. Mr. Caiserman is the first representative of the Canadian Jewish community to be permitted to enter Poland.

Mr. Caiserman will be proceeding from London to Stockholm, Sweden, and thence to Poland where he will be devoting his efforts to an investigation of the conditions of the surviving Jews of Poland and to organizing the increased relief program of the Canadian Jewish community. In addition, Mr. Caiserman will do everything possible to locate the relatives of Canadian Jews who have survived in Poland and to restore contact between them.

Left: David Lewis (left) and A.M. Klein, Montreal, *c.* 1920s.

Right: Announcement of H.M. Caiserman's journey to Poland to survey postwar conditions, December 1945.

Left to right: David Rome, H.M. Caiserman and Sam Lipshitz, on the boat before Caiserman left for Poland.

Postwar Canada was booming. With most of Europe in ruins, Canada had emerged from the war with one of the world's strongest economies. Her food, lumber and manufactured goods were helping prop up the ravaged countries of Western Europe. Her fleet was one of the world's largest. And if there was any shortage in Canada, it was not of jobs, but of workers. It was clear that there would be no postwar recession as there had been twenty-five years before.

But where was Canada to get her workers? For sixteen years, since the onset of the Depression in late 1929, few immigrants had been allowed into the country. Now, with the economy on an up-swing, industry after industry was clamouring for labour and knew where to get it. In Europe hundreds of thousands of hungry men and women were pouring into displaced persons camps. Many among them were Jews who had escaped Hitler's Final Solution. They had no country, no home, no family to which they could return. Six million of their brothers and sisters had been murdered in history's most heinous crime. Those who had survived were now looking to start their lives again.

But Canada was not yet ready for them. In response to the demand for workers, the government allowed various companies to bring over miners, agricultural and lumber workers, even domestics, with but one caveat — no Jews. Canadian officials sensed that the country was not prepared to accept too many. A series of public opinion polls taken right after the war indicated that the majority of Canadians preferred almost any type of immigrant — including Germans — to Jews.

Thus, in the first two years after the war, as tens of thousands of refugees flooded into Canada, only a small percentage of them were Jews. Nor was much care given to screening those refugees who were allowed to enter. Since Canadian officials were mainly worried about keeping out Jews and Communist sympathizers, they found it convenient to favour those who had fought on the side of the Nazis; whatever else whatever else these might be, they were presumably non-Jewish and anti-Communist.

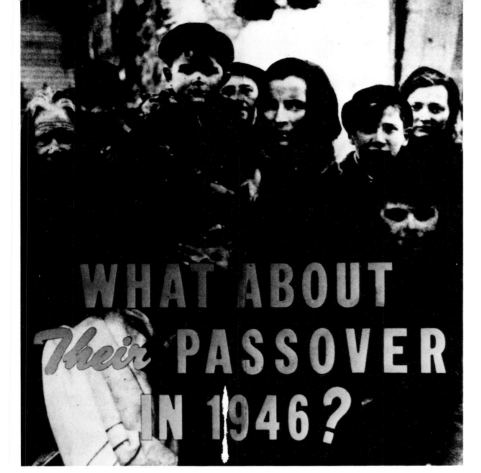

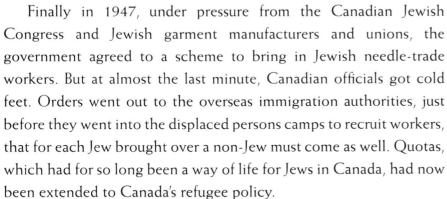

Left: Pamphlet issued by the Canadian Jewish Congress as part of their campaign for overseas relief.

Right: Immigrants sponsored by the Jewish Immigrant Aid Society arrive in Halifax.

Finally in 1947, under pressure from the Canadian Jewish Congress and Jewish garment manufacturers and unions, the government agreed to a scheme to bring in Jewish needle-trade workers. But at almost the last minute, Canadian officials got cold feet. Orders went out to the overseas immigration authorities, just before they went into the displaced persons camps to recruit workers, that for each Jew brought over a non-Jew must come as well. Quotas, which had for so long been a way of life for Jews in Canada, had now been extended to Canada's refugee policy.

There was one exception to this rule. In 1941 the Canadian government had approved a program to rescue one thousand Jewish refugee orphans from Vichy France. Unfortunately, the cabinet had dithered so long before accepting the scheme that by the time it was passed, there were no Jewish orphan children left in France; they had all been transported to Auschwitz. But the cabinet order was never

Upper left: War orphans en route to their new homes, *c.* 1947.

Upper right: Winnipeg group of war orphans at a baseball game, *c.* 1948.

Lower: John Hirsch (far right) was one of the war orphans who came to Winnipeg in 1949, assisted by the Canadian Jewish Congress.

rescinded and in 1947 it was revived. The problem was to find Jewish children — the Nazis had done their murderous job so efficiently that few had survived. Only by raising the age limit to eighteen could officials find the children they sought.

By the end of 1947 all the children — most well into their teens — had arrived in Canada. They were given a hero's welcome by an emotionally charged Jewish community, resettled in homes across the country and provided with whatever special help they required — all at the community's expense. Though for some the transition was exceedingly difficult, most thrived in their new homes.

Fortunately by 1948 Canadian attitudes towards Jewish immigration had begun to change. Mackenzie King had retired, Frederick Blair was dead and new leaders with new ideas and an expanded vision of the country's future began moving into positions of power. Many felt that Canada's hour of opportunity had finally arrived. With most of the western world's economies still devastated, Canada was on the brink of becoming a genuine world power. All she needed was more people. And so the doors were flung open, and during the next decade

Left: Toronto Jewish Youth Council packing clothes to send to Europe, *c.* 1946.

Right: Torah cover made in a displaced persons' camp in Europe and presented by the German-Jewish community of Montreal to the Canadian Jewish Congress in 1950, in recognition of the Congress' efforts to settle Jewish orphans in Canada after the war.

almost two million newcomers poured through, including thousands of Jews, most of them survivors of the death camps.

By the time of their arrival, the pervasive anti-semitism of earlier years had receded. The horrors of the Holocaust had shocked many Canadians; others were caught up in the dramatic struggle of the Jews in Palestine to create their own state. Though official Canadian policy was to support the British attempts to blockade Palestine and forcibly prevent Jewish refugees from entering, large numbers of Canadians sympathized with the plucky struggle of the beleaguered Jews in the Holy Land.

It was at this propitious moment that the Jewish leadership in Canada chose to launch an all-out offensive against discriminatory practices. Their efforts were fuelled by anger at the treatment of Jewish soldiers who were returning from overseas only to find

Left: Shipping of overseas relief sponsored by the Canadian Jewish Congress, *c*. 1946.

Right: Jewish refugees in Halifax, with Canadian Jewish Congress' Noah Heinish (far right).

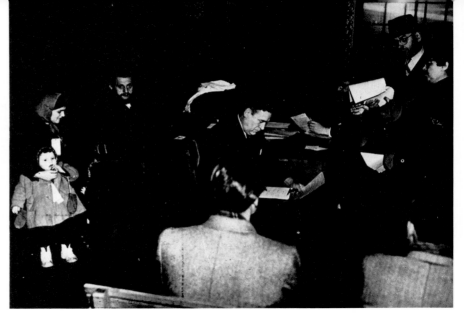

the same old restrictions barring their way. In a much-publicized incident, a veteran was fired from his salesman's job in Toronto when it was discovered that he was Jewish. Others found that skating rinks, swimming pools, golf clubs and hotels refused them admission, despite their heroic sacrifices on behalf of their country.

The Jewish Labour Committee, and the Joint Public Relations Committee of the Canadian Jewish Congress and B'nai B'rith took the lead in the campaign. Quiet diplomacy had been tried and found wanting. The young, energetic activists in charge of the campaign, particularly Kalman Kaplansky and Sid Blum of the Labour Committee and Ben Kayfetz of the Canadian Jewish Congress, determined that only direct lobbying and public agitation and education would work. Their strategy was to fight to remove restrictions not only against Jews but against all minorities.

Their campaign was given a boost by Mr. Justice Keillor MacKay of the Supreme Court of Ontario, who ruled in 1945 that the restrictive covenant clause barring the sale of property and houses to Jews and others was not in the public interest and therefore illegal. Though the case worked its way through the courts for another five years before the Supreme Court of Canada gave a definitive judgment, the first blow against discrimination had been struck. Others were soon to follow.

In 1947 the CCF government of Saskatchewan introduced the country's first human rights legislation. Four years later, responding to a well-orchestrated lobby by Jewish groups, the Conservative government of Ontario passed Canada's first fair employment law, followed three years later by fair housing legislation. In effect, by 1955 the province of Ontario had ruled that discrimination against any minority in hiring and renting or selling homes was illegal. Within a decade the federal government and most provinces followed suit; soon comprehensive human rights codes were adopted in Parliament and across the country. The 1982 Charter of Rights and Freedoms, which enshrined human rights in the Canadian Constitution, owes much to the pioneering work of Kaplansky, Blum, Kayfetz and their colleagues.

As these legal protections were put into place, an emboldened Canadian Jewry showed that it was no longer willing to accept the anti-semitism of an earlier period without a struggle. One of the major breakthroughs in the postwar period was in the profession of medicine. For decades it had been well known in the Jewish community — and probably outside it as well — that there were explicit quotas on the number of Jewish students accepted by the country's medical schools. Even worse, those few students who did manage to break through the barriers and get medical degrees were often deprived of the opportunity to practise as they wished.

It had not always been this way. In the mid-nineteenth century, Dr. Aaron Hart David, the scion of the two most prominent Quebec Jewish families, had been both general secretary of the Canadian Medical Association and dean of the faculty of medicine at Bishop's College. It would take another hundred years before there was another Jewish dean of medicine.

By the early 1900s, almost every medical school in Canada had a quota system. Jews were not the only group discriminated against; women and other ethnic minorities were also subject to severe restrictions. The Jewish press often carried stories of bright young

Canadian Court Upholds Racial Land-sale Restriction

Case To Be Taken To Further Appeal

Toronto, Thursday.

THE Ontario Court of Appeals has upheld a restrictive covenant barring the sale of land at a Lake Huron summer resort near Toronto to Jews or Negroes. Counsel for the appellants—Mrs. Annie Noble, the seller, and Mr. Bernard Wolfe, the purchaser—indicated that they would take the matter to the Supreme Court of Canada.

The first decision in a case of this sort, in 1945, completely upheld the right of the owner of such property to sell to a Jew. That decision, by Judge Keiller Mackay, was utilised by the United States Attorney-General in obtaining a decision from the U.S. Supreme Court, declaring that restrictive real estate covenants were unenforceable. In this case, Judge Mackay's principle was reversed by a provincial Supreme Court Justice, from whose decision the current appeal was carried.

In a written statement on behalf of the five-man court, which handed down a unanimous decision, Appellate Chief Justice Robertson rejected the arguments of the appellants that the covenant violated Canadian public policy. "To magnify this innocent and modest effort to establish and maintain a place suitable for a pleasant summer residence into an enterprise that offends against some public policy requires a stronger imagination than I possess," Judge Robertson declared. He added: "There is nothing criminal or immoral involved; the public interest is in no way concerned."

Rabbi Abraham Feinberg, Chairman of the Joint Public Relations Committee of the Canadian Jewish Congress, Central Region, and the B'nai B'rith, commenting on the decision, which he termed "shocking," stated: "The Court of Appeals excluded the principle of public policy from the restrictive covenant issue, and thus ignored a unique opportunity to affirm the spiritual onenness of Canada. I am convinced that public opinion takes a broader view than the learned judges."

News of the restrictive covenant barring the sale of land at an Ontario resort to Jews made headlines in the *South African Jewish Times*.

Jews with very high grades who could not qualify for admission, while non-Jews with considerably lower grades were accepted. Some students unable to enter medicine tried their luck in the faculties of dentistry, but there, too, rigid quotas existed. As the dean of dentistry of the University of Toronto explained in 1950, Jews lacked the necessary "muscle dexterity" to become qualified dentists.

Little could be done to force recalcitrant university officials to change their policies, but the Jewish community did come up with a strategy against the restrictions in hospitals: they built their own. Pioneering physicians A.I. Willinsky in Toronto and Alton Goldbloom in Montreal have detailed in their memoirs the difficulties they had in getting hospital appointments, and in admitting their patients to hospitals. Once admitted, Jewish patients were treated by doctors they did not know, whose language they might not speak. To counter these problems during the 1920s and early 1930s, the Jewish community established the Mount Sinai Hospital in Toronto and the Jewish General Hospital in Montreal. Efforts to transform a clinic in Winnipeg into Canada's third Jewish hospital foundered because of a lack of funds.

But the Winnipeg community showed its determination in another way. In 1944 the Avukah Society, an association of Jewish graduates from the University of Manitoba, led a campaign to expose the quota system at the university's medical faculty. At a meeting of the health committee of the legislature, the university's president and its dean of medicine squirmed in embarrassment as the restrictive policies were described in detail by Avukah members. Reading from internal university documents, they demonstrated that while Jews, women and other ethnic groups were subject to quotas, "preferred applicants…those of Anglo-Saxon, French or Icelandic origin" were regularly admitted with much lower grades. Under pressure from the legislature the medical school reluctantly agreed to change its policy, though the grumpy dean warned that the university would become known as a "Jewish University" and "promising" non-Jewish students would go elsewhere. The University of Manitoba was thus the first to rid itself of the odious "numerus clausus" (quota) system, and from 1945 on Jewish students as well as others from "non-preferred races" were admitted in increasing numbers.

Following the precedent of Manitoba, other medical schools began removing their restrictions, as did many hopsitals. Dr. Alton Goldbloom became head of the Children's Hospital in Montreal, and other Jewish doctors, long restricted to practising at the two Jewish hospitals, were soon regularly receiving staff appointments at non-Jewish hospitals. By the 1960s and 1970s, there were Jewish heads of departments, medical chiefs of staff, deans of medical schools and even a Jewish president of the Canadian Medical Association. Indeed, there was scarcely an area of medicine in which Jewish doctors did not achieve prominence.

Nor was the revolution in the status of Canadian Jewry restricted to the medical profession. Just as profound were the changes in the field of law. Though there were fewer restrictions on admission to law school, there were certainly many for Jews attempting to find jobs with established firms. Jewish gold-medal graduates throughout the country were forced to practise on their own. No Jews served on the bench, with the possible exception of an occasional local magistrate. In 1914 Samuel Shultz had been appointed to the county court in British Columbia, but it took thirty-one years before another Jew, Sam Factor in Toronto, was appointed. It was not until the early 1950s, with the elevation of Harry Batshaw in Quebec and Sam Freedman in Manitoba, that Canada had its first Jewish superior court judges. The latter also became Canada's first Jewish provincial chief justice in the 1970s. Since these appointments the changes have been dramatic. The last two decades have seen Jewish judges at all levels of the judicial system. Five provinces, British Columbia, Manitoba, Ontario, Quebec and Nova Scotia, have seen Jewish chief justices of either the Court of Appeal or the Supreme Court.

Bora Laskin.

Certainly no one better exemplified the striking turnabout in the legal system than Bora Laskin. In the 1930s this brilliant legal scholar returned to Toronto from Harvard University. Predictably he could not find a job. For several years he earned his living writing head-notes for a law journal. He was hired by the law department of the University of Toronto in 1940 only after the departmental chairman wrote a bizarre letter to the dubious university president testifying that, though Laskin was Jewish, he was nonetheless a "loyal British subject, loyal to our institutions and traditions...[who]...will not disgrace the University...[and who has] sworn on a bible before witnesses that [he is not] a member of any subversive movement."

Laskin quickly became one of the country's greatest law teachers and his example helped knock down the barriers for others. As a member of the Legal Affairs Committee of the Canadian Jewish Congress, he took the lead in fighting bigotry and racism throughout the country. By the 1970s he was on the Supreme Court of Canada and in 1975 he was appointed chief justice — a remarkable accomplishment for a child of Russian immigrants from Fort William, Ontario.

Bora Laskin's career symbolizes Canada's revolutionary transformation from a benighted, prejudice-ridden society to the progressive, open, multicultural nation it is today. But Laskin was not alone in his achievements. A fellow westerner, Maxwell Cohen, became one of the premier legal scholars in the country and dean of law at McGill University; recently he was appointed Canada's representative on the World Court. By the 1970s there were at least a half-dozen law schools with Jewish deans, and large numbers of Jewish faculty everywhere. Concomitant with the radical changes in the judiciary and the university, the country's large law firms actively began recruiting bright young Jewish law graduates. Within a generation, the barriers had been shattered.

Of all the vocations in prewar Canada, few were as bereft of Jews as university teaching and administration. During the 1930s, there was only a tiny handful of Jewish lecturers — no professors, no administrators, no deans, no chairmen of departments — throughout the entire country. Of the thousands of refugee scholars, teachers, scientists, artists, musicians and writers driven from German universities and conservatories between 1933 and 1940, only three or four were hired by Canadian universities. Indeed, just months before the outbreak of war, delegates at a conference of Canadian universities unanimously passed a resolution urging the government not to admit refugee scholars and to deport those already here, lest they accept positions "for which other Canadians might be qualified."

Universities not only discriminated against Jewish faculty, they also had quotas against Jewish students. Most notorious of these

David Croll.

was McGill's. For years it was an open secret that standards of admission were far higher for Jewish applicants than for anyone else. An examination of the correspondence of university officials from the president down makes it clear that they were determined to limit ruthlessly Jewish enrolment at McGill. They were worried that by accepting too many Jews McGill would become, in the words of one official, "the Yeshiva University of the North." So many Jewish students would qualify, said the university's principal, Sir Arthur Currie, that there would scarcely be any room for non-Jews. Despite the efforts of Sam Bronfman, who was one of the university's great benefactors, it was not until well after the Second World War that the quotas were dropped.

As restrictions fell by the wayside elsewhere in society, the universities soon fell into step. By the 1950s and 1960s, there were Jewish faculty in every university, as well as deans and departmental chairmen. And with the appointment of Max Wyman as president of the University of Alberta in 1966, followed a few months later by Ernest Sirluck's installation at the University of Manitoba, Canada had its first Jewish university presidents. Others would follow.

Ever since Ezekiel Hart, Canadian Jews had been — or had tried to be — active in the country's political life, mostly on the local level. It was not until 1935, when Windsor native David Croll entered the cabinet of Ontario, that a Jew was given a ministerial appointment. But Croll had less luck on the federal scene. On his return from the war, where he had attained the rank of lieutenant-colonel, Croll won a seat in Parliament, but the cabinet post most thought he deserved was denied. Neither Mackenzie King nor his successor, Louis St. Laurent, was prepared to have a Jew at the cabinet table. Croll was shunted off to the second chamber to become the country's first Jewish senator. Over the next forty years he would make a profound contribution to this country, but it could not be equal to what he would have made as a minister of the Crown. Another Jew from Windsor, Herb Gray, would become Canada's first Jewish federal cabinet minister, in 1969.

National Council of Jewish Women charity bazaar, 1948.

Since his appointment, there have been Jewish ministers in almost every federal cabinet.

In the postwar period Jews played a more prominent role in both the federal and provincial spheres. Throughout most of the 1940s and into the 1950s, the colourful labour activist Joe Salsberg sat as a Communist member of the legislature, where he contributed much to making Ontario a more open society. Conversely, another Communist, Fred Rose, who was elected to Parliament from Montreal, was later convicted of spying for the Soviet Union. When Salsberg was finally defeated in his riding of St. Andrews, it was by Allan Grossman, who became the country's first Jewish Conservative cabinet minister.

Perhaps no Jew contributed more to the political life of this country than a Polish immigrant brought up in the Yiddish-speaking ghetto of Montreal. The son of a garment worker, David Lewis won a Rhodes Scholarship to Oxford and returned to Canada in the late 1930s to become an architect of Canada's social democratic party, the CCF. For twenty years, it was largely through the indefatigable efforts of Lewis that the party survived. When the party was reborn as the

New Democratic Party in the 1960s, Lewis won a seat in Parliament and soon became the party's leader — the first Jew to lead a national political party in Canada.

In British Columbia, Dave Barrett became Canada's first Jewish premier in 1972, while in Ontario and Manitoba there were Jewish Opposition leaders. In Quebec, Victor Goldbloom, Alton's son, became that province's first Jewish cabinet minister in 1970. Indeed by the 1970s and 1980s there were so many Jews in various federal and provincial cabinets that few Canadians took any notice. The election of Nathan Phillips as mayor of Toronto in the 1950s did cause a stir, perhaps less because he was a Jew than because he was the first non-Protestant to occupy that position.

Along with advances in the political arena, Canadian Jews suddenly found influential positions available for the first time in the public service. There had always been some Jews in the federal civil service, but until the 1950s they had held only minor positions. The first Jew to "arrive" in Ottawa was Louis Rasminsky, in the Department of Finance in the 1940s. But year after year, Rasminsky was passed over for promotion until the late 1950s, when he was appointed to a position worthy of his talents and experience, governor of the Bank of Canada. By then a few Jews had been appointed ambassadors, but the real breakthrough came in the 1960s and 1970s when all of the barriers in the public service collapsed. Since then, Jews have been appointed to the most sensitive diplomatic and political postings. Jewish Canadians have over the past decade served their country as deputy ministers of a host of departments, including external affairs and finance, as ambassadors to the United Nations and the United States, as well as in a number of other key positions, including principal secretary to the prime minister.

By the 1950s, the nation's corporate boardrooms remained the last bastion not yet breached by Jews. Here the battle was tougher because the biases were more deep-seated and more difficult to confront. Legislation was of little use; what mattered were moral suasion and, more important, economic clout. When Sam Bronfman was invited to join the board of the Bank of Montreal in the 1950s, he was the first Jewish director of any of the country's major corporations in this century.

Gradually other Jews joined Bronfman around Canada's board-room tables. Although, as John Porter pointed out in his classic 1965 study of Canada's elites, *The Vertical Mosaic*, even in the mid-1960s scarcely any ethnic Canadians had broken into the country's establishment, Jews were gradually chipping away at this monopoly. The children and grandchildren of the immigrant workers of the turn of the century were rapidly succeeding in Canadian society. They were not willing to accept the restrictions of a previous generation; they were prepared to blast through the wall of prejudice that surrounded Canada's corporate elite.

Saidye Bronfman cutting the ribbon at the opening of the YM-YWHA, Montreal, 1955.

In the last two decades they succeeded. The Bronfmans in Montreal and Toronto (the children of Sam and Allen respectively), the Steinbergs, Reitmans and Pascals in Montreal, the Kofflers, Posluns and Wolfes in Toronto, the Cohens in Winnipeg, the Belzbergs in Vancouver and a host of others have all turned their small family businesses into giants of Canadian industry, and their success has led to corporate appointments. They have even taken control of some of the very trust and insurance companies that refused to deal with their parents and grandparents.

No rise up the corporate ladder has been more remarkable than that of the legendary Reichmann family of Toronto. Hungarian Jews who managed to stay one step ahead of the Nazis, the Reichmann brothers, Albert, Paul and Ralph, arrived in Canada in 1956 and through hard work, creative management and a large dose of risk-taking emerged as arguably the most influential industrialists in the country — all the while steadfastly maintaining their devout adherence to Orthodox Judaism.

One of the most significant corollaries to the rapid upward mobility of Canadian Jewry over the past three decades has been the phenomenal growth of Jewish philanthropy. According to recent studies, there are few more munificent communities in the world than Canada's Jews. Not only are their contributions to Israel and Jewish institutions proportionally among the highest anywhere, they have also been heavily involved in non-Jewish charitable activities. Canadian Jews have been in the forefront in funding the country's theatres, orchestras, universities, museums, art galleries, hospitals and other cultural and educational institutions, and have consistently given enormous amounts of time and money to almost every Canadian charity.

The Royal Commission on Bilingualism and Biculturalism, appointed in the 1960s, singled out the Jewish role in the development of Canadian literature as "outstanding" and "distinctive," and no one embodies these qualities more than the founding father of Jewish-Canadian literature, A.M. Klein. Born in the Montreal ghetto in 1909, the son of an immigrant garment worker, Klein spent much of his life as a part-time lawyer, editor of a variety of Anglo-Jewish journals, speechwriter for Sam Bronfman, and activist in Jewish and socialist politics (he once unsuccessfully ran for Parliament as a CCF candidate). But his real passion was poetry. In 1948 he won a Governor General's Award for his satirical yet poignant collection of poetry on Quebec, *The Rocking Chair*. His only novel, *The Second Scroll*, won him a wider readership. More important, he was, in the words of one scholar, "the founder of a whole dynasty of Canadian Jewish writers who studied him and were nurtured [and influenced] by him." Among these is a virtual who's who of Montreal's Jewish literati: Irving Layton, Leonard Cohen, Mordecai Richler and Ted Allan.

These writers form part of a long tradition of Jewish writing in Montreal. The country's first Jewish poet was probably Isidore Asher, a Scottish Jew who arrived in Montreal in the 1860s; before his return to Britain he published several highly praised volumes of verse. A few years later another British Jew, David Ansell, emigrated to Montreal and wrote a widely read book on the future of the British Empire. So appreciated were his ideas that he became well known in government circles in both Canada and England. He was appointed by Britain to be Canada's consul general in Mexico, a meaningless sinecure but one that probably made him Canada's first Jewish diplomat.

It was with the arrival of the Eastern European immigrants at the turn of the century that Yiddish writing flourished in Montreal. Prominent Yiddish authors and journalists were brought in to lecture, to teach and to write; some even made the city their home. Their presence, as well as the development of Yiddish schools and such cultural institutions as the Jewish Public Library, were the necessary foundation for the development of a generation of talented young Jewish writers in English.

Though some Winnipeg chauvinists may quarrel with this description — after all, their city with its vibrant Jewish life prompted one scholar to refer to it as the "Jerusalem of the New World" — it is clear that in the field of Jewish-Canadian literature Montreal stands alone.

But the Montreal ghetto was not the only place to produce a uniquely Anglo-Jewish literary culture. Jews in western Canada, who went through an entirely different experience, have also made a distinctive contribution. Adele Wiseman, Eli Mandel, Miriam Waddington and Jack Ludwig were products of this environment. So, to an extent, was the famed novelist Henry Kreisel, though he arrived in Canada from his native Austria during the Second World War as one of the internees shipped over by the British government. Over the past decade or two, other writers have begun adding to the rich tradition of Jewish-Canadian writing.

Though no discernible Jewish-Canadian school has emerged in the visual arts, sculptors such as Sorel Etrog, Gerald Gladstone and Stanley Lewis and painters such as Gershon Iskowitz, Aba Bayefsky, Lewis Muhlstock, Les Levine and Ghita Caiserman Roth have all included Jewish themes in their work. More distinctively Jewish is the music of some of this country's best composers, John Weinzweig,

Oskar Morawetz, Harry Freedman, Louis Applebaum, Srul Glick and
Milton Barnes.

The transformation in the status of Canadian Jewry over the past
generation has not been without its costs. Lost in the rise up the
social and economic ladder has been the world of the Jewish worker,
small-town storekeeper, farmer and radical. Their children, like
those of other Canadians, have become doctors, lawyers, academics,
accountants, civil servants, merchants and managers. If they did not
already live in large cities, most eagerly moved there to be close
to Jewish schools and institutions. They had no time for the old
ideological battles and the Jewish Communist became a relic of the
Cold War. In any case, the old divisions within the community have
largely disappeared, as downtown Jews have moved uptown and
taken over leadership positions.

Lost as well were the raucous dynamism and feistiness that
marked an earlier phase of Jewish life in Canada, stilled by the
trauma of the Holocaust and the fragility of the tiny new Jewish
state in the Middle East. The world had become too dangerous a
place for Jews to allow themselves the luxury of internal dissent and
divisiveness. The radicalism and class struggles of the 1920s and
1930s seemed sadly out of place in the changed circumstances of the
1950s and 1960s.

Jewish energies were now totally devoted to protecting the
State of Israel, to welcoming the influx of Holocaust survivors and
to breaking down the barriers in Canadian society. One Yiddish
pundit labelled postwar Jewry the *"sha shtill* generation," literally, the
silent generation, afraid to rock the boat for fear of sinking with
it. Unity and harmony were the watchwords. Thus Canadian Jewry
left community affairs in the hands of its leaders while at the same
time charging full steam ahead into a Canadian society that was
rapidly opening up. Only in the 1970s and 1980s — once Jews had
successfully achieved a new status, once anti-semitism had receded,
once Israel seemed relatively secure — was the community again

more tolerant of the dissent and pluralism that had been the hallmarks of an earlier period.

As the world around them changed, so, too, did the institutions and organizations within the Jewish community. And few changed as dramatically in the postwar period as the Zionist movement. Throughout the inter-war years, the renamed Zionist Organization of Canada confined itself largely to fundraising and to an occasional foray into political lobbying. Millions of dollars were raised, most of which went into purchasing the fertile Plain of Sharon for Palestinian Jews. But the organization's political endeavours were much less successful. Throughout the 1920s and 1930s, the leader of the Canadian Zionists, A.J. Freiman, would take delegations into meetings with the prime minister and other government officials to argue on behalf of the promised Jewish homeland. In particular, Freiman pleaded with his personal friend Mackenzie King to intercede with the British to open up Palestine to increased Jewish immigration. Every Jew admitted, Freiman argued, would be one less under the Nazi yoke. But King supported the British restrictionist policy and politely rebuffed every delegation's entreaties.

Once the Second World War began, Canadian Zionists adopted a more militant approach. Under the leadership of Montreal lawyer Harry Batshaw and Toronto financier Samuel Zacks, a massive public relations campaign on behalf of Palestine was launched. New committees were set up and the organization itself was revamped and renamed the United Zionist Council. Non-Jews were invited to play a more prominent role in the movement, but they, too, achieved little. A Canada at war had even less time for Jewish grievances than a Canada at peace. Only after the war, when the United Nations took up the problem of Palestine, did Canada evince some interest in what was to become of the promise made to the Jews in the Balfour Declaration — and only because a Canadian, Ivan Rand of the Supreme Court of Canada, was appointed to the United Nations Special Commission on Palestine.

May 14th 1948.

Labour Zionist Organization headquarters, Montreal, May 14, 1948, the day Israel was declared an independent state.

Meanwhile Canadian Zionists had pulled out all the stops. Through a high-profile group of prominent non-Jews, the Canadian Palestine Committee, it issued statements and press releases, sponsored radio broadcasts and bought newspaper advertisements. The committee gave Canadian Zionism a credibility it had not had in government circles for years. These activities certainly played a role in Canada's decision to recognize the Jewish state, but as historian

David Bercuson makes clear, Canada's decision was based on its own self-interest and not on the lobbying of Canada's Jews.

But it was not only in fundraising and lobbying for Palestine that Canadian Jews were selfless. Many also put their own bodies on the line. At least three hundred Canadian veterans — including some non-Jews such as "Buzz" Beurling, a Second World War flying ace, who had shot down more German planes than any other Canadian — volunteered to fight for the new Jewish state when it was attacked by five invading Arab armies in 1948. Organized by war heroes such as Flight Lieutenant Sydney Shulemson, the country's most decorated Jewish serviceman, and Major Ben Dunkelman, whose parents, David and Rose, were the backbone of Canadian Zionism for years, these volunteers performed yeoman service for the inexperienced Israeli army, and helped ensure its ultimate victory. A dozen Canadians, including Beurling, lost their lives so that the Jews might have a state.

For those who could not go over and fight, there were equally important tasks to be done at home. Aided by Alex Skelton, a sympathetic assistant deputy minister in the Department of Trade and Commerce, Zionist leaders were able to buy tons of surplus war materials — machine guns, mortars, even airplanes — through dummy corporations and ship them to a desperate Israeli army in crates marked "machine tools." Other Jews launched a number of fundraising campaigns. As a result, in just one year, between May 1948 and May 1949, nearly ten million dollars was raised for the new Jewish state — probably the most successful fundraising campaign in Canadian history to that time.

In the years since, Canadian Jews have contributed immense amounts of time, effort and funds to make certain that the tiny, fragile state would survive. During the Six Day War in June of 1967, when it appeared that Israel's Arab neighbours were prepared to follow through on their threat to push the Jews into the sea, Canadian Jewry, led by Sam Bronfman, reached deep into their pockets and in a matter of weeks raised over twenty-five million dollars.

Upper: First United Jewish Appeal mission to Israel, 1958. Left to right: Rabbi Reuben Slonim, Mrs. Nathan Phillips, Nathan Phillips, Bernard Weinberg. (Toronto Jewish Congress/CJC Ont. Region Archives 1217)

Lower: Advertisement in *Kanader Adler* for an event at the Montreal Forum commemorating the founding of the State of Israel.

INTERNATIONAL ARRIVALS LOBBY
AND TO DEPARTURE CONCOURSE

Sephardi Jewish immigrants from
Morocco, Haim Abenhaim family,
arriving in Montreal, 1960.

Over the past decade or two, the Zionist movement *per se* has lost its primacy in the community, although its tenets still command the loyalty of most Jews. Organized Zionism has become, in historian Michael Brown's phrase, "largely a spectator sport," as Diaspora Jews watch what goes on in Israel, cheering — or occasionally heckling — from the sidelines. Though some Canadian Jews may disagree with specific policies and activities of Israeli governments over the past few years, the community's commitment to the survival of the Jewish state has not wavered.

Yet many Jews feel that with the creation of the State of Israel the major part of the Zionist agenda has been achieved. Certainly much of the activity once the monopoly of Zionist organizations — education, fundraising, organizing trips to Israel — has been taken over by synagogues, the Canadian Jewish Congress, the B'nai B'rith and even the Israeli Embassy in Ottawa. A new organization, the Canada-Israel Committee, has taken over responsibility for lobbying. Thus, organized Zionism in Canada has become a victim of its own success. It made almost every Jewish institution so committed to Israel's survival that it has been left with little to do.

In the postwar period there were dramatic changes in Canadian immigration policy. With the world awash with refugees, a population-starved Canada once again opened her immigration gates in the 1950s. But for many of Canada's Jews, it was too late. Their families — mothers, fathers, sisters, brothers, aunts, uncles and cousins — had been wiped out by Hitler's murderous hordes. Thus for many of the country's Jews, whatever survivors did arrive became surrogate families. They were the only link to their own kin, to the towns, villages and *shtetls* that had been forever destroyed, to a culture that had disappeared.

No effort was spared to integrate them into Canadian society. The community's organizations, particularly the JIAS, the Congress' Refugee Committee, the National Council of Jewish Women, the *landsmanshaftn* and the Jewish Vocational Service, mobilized an all-out effort. The task was herculean. Buildings were bought to house the survivors; specially trained social workers were hired; special education programs were begun; employment bureaus were set up; individual Jews opened their homes to the refugees. It was as if Canadian Jewry was trying to compensate for its failure in the 1930s. In all, some forty thousand Holocaust survivors arrived in Canada.

Most survivors wanted little more than time to recuperate. Initially aloof from the Canadian Jewish community, they were not physically or emotionally ready to do more than rebuild their lives, and create new families and homes in their new land. Nor were they yet ready to talk of their experiences. It was not until the 1960s, partly as a result of some anti-semitic incidents sparked by a handful of vocal neo-Nazis, that survivors began to form their own organizations and to play a more active role in the Jewish community. Since then, of course, the survivors, either as individuals or through their organizations, have had a powerful impact within both the Jewish community and Canadian society in general. As living witnesses of the darkest moment in world history, they have inspired the community to move more forcefully against racists, to lobby for legislation banning hate propaganda, to pressure a reluctant Canadian government to prosecute war criminals, and to introduce Holocaust materials into school curricula across the country. In the fields of commerce, the arts and the law, survivors and their children have also made remarkable contributions to their adopted homeland.

Another group that has enriched Canadian life has been the Sephardi community. Since the 1950s some twenty thousand Francophone Jews from Morocco and elsewhere in North Africa have arrived in this country. Though most settled in Montreal, there are Sephardi communities in Toronto and other population centres. Like the Eastern European immigrants who preceded them, they set up their own organizations, schools, newspapers and synagogues, and likewise came into conflict with the community leadership. They, too, had their own language, customs, religious practices and way of life

Schwartz's Delicatessen, Montreal.

Canadian Jewish Congress Soviet Jewry Committee marches in Montreal.

that the Anglophone Jewish leadership found discomfiting. It became clear after some years that the Sephardi would not integrate into the community's English-speaking structure. Why should they do so in a Quebec that was becoming increasingly unilingual? Would it not be better for the Jewish community to maintain and encourage its own French-speaking minority?

Eventually, the umbrella organization of the Sephardi community agreed to become part of the Montreal community structure while retaining its autonomy on a wide variety of issues. Thus while creating a whole complex of communal institutions to mark their distinctiveness, they have joined with the Anglophone Jewish community on matters such as Israel and anti-semitism, which affect all Canadian Jewry.

Although the French-speaking Jewish population has thrived in the increasingly nationalist climate of Quebec, the English-speaking Jewish community has done less well. With the election of the separatist Parti Québécois government in 1976, many Jews decided that it was time to move elsewhere. Though the new government was not anti-Jewish — indeed it tried to reassure its Jewish citizenry — it was apparent to some Jews that their future no longer lay in a Francophone Quebec. Large numbers of them — mostly young professionals — left the province and migrated to more promising venues in Ontario, Alberta and British Columbia, or out of the

Jewish marriage contract or *ketubbah* given by the artist, Howard Fox, to his mother, born in the Soviet Union, and his father, born in Canada, on their 40th wedding anniversary in 1987. The depiction of Jerusalem, Toronto and Moscow are symbolic of the coming together of Jews from different lands.

country entirely. As a result of this exodus, and of the arrival of thousands of immigrants from Israel, South Africa and the Soviet Union, by the 1980s Toronto had replaced Montreal as the largest centre of Jewish population in the country.

Indeed internal migration has now become an ongoing phenomenon of Canadian Jewish life. Fully twenty per cent of Canada's Jews now live outside the province in which they were born. As the Jewish populations of the Atlantic provinces, Quebec and Winnipeg decline, those of Toronto, Ottawa, southern Ontario, Calgary, Edmonton and

Children lighting the Hanukkah candles.

Vancouver have grown almost exponentially. According to the most recent census figures today's Canadian Jewish population stands at nearly 330,000 (almost half of whom live in or near Toronto), a forty per cent increase since the end of the Second World War.

As each new group arrived — Israeli, South African, Latin American — it added a new dimension to Canada's Jewish mosaic. Most satisfying to Canada's Jews, however, has been the arrival of thousands of *refuseniks*, refugees from the Soviet Union. Since the late sixties, many in the community have been active in the Soviet Jewry movement. As they tried vainly to do for their brethren in the 1930s, they have lobbied, raised funds and organized demonstrations to pressure the Soviet government to permit Jews to leave the USSR. This time they have been more successful, and their government and their fellow Canadians have been more sympathetic. This time, as well, there is an Israel to take the bulk of the refugees.

The new multicultural Canada of the 1980s and 1990s is a far cry from the parochial country it was a generation ago. Multiculturalism is now an integral part of Canadian policy; diversity is encouraged. Protected against discrimination by legislation, encouraged to maintain their culture and heritage by government largesse, Canada's ethnic minorities are finally beginning to play their proper role in this country. Prejudice and hostility have given way to tolerance and respect. And in bringing about these changes few communities have been as instrumental as Canada's Jews. Either as individuals

234

or through their organizations, particularly the Canadian Jewish Congress and the B'nai B'rith, they have been in the frontlines fighting racism, attacking inequality and lobbying for more liberal immigration policies.

Yet ironically it is this new openness and absorbency of Canadian society, for which the Jewish community struggled long and hard, that may pose a real threat to Jewish survival. Today's Jewish leaders worry as much about the rate of assimilation as of anti-semitism. Together, the decline in fertility and the rapid rise of intermarriage, could create a demographic nightmare for Canadian Jews.

Despite these concerns the Jewish community is still vibrant and expansive. Jewish day-school enrolments are per capita the highest outside Israel. Though small, inner-city synagogues are closing, larger, more modern sanctuaries are being built in suburban neighbourhoods. New community organizations are coming into being and older ones are being revitalized. Paradoxically, while many worry about assimilation, the fastest-growing element of Canadian Jews is the ultra-Orthodox.

Canada's Jews have come a long way since Esther Brandeau's abbreviated stay some 250 years ago. Today's community, thriving, successful and integrated, can look back with pride at a long history of achievements and contributions in every sphere of Canadian life. From the early Quebec fur trader to the Cariboo gold miner and the prairie homesteader, from the immigrant garment worker, small-town storekeeper and itinerant pedlar to today's academic, professional and industrialist, the Jewish community has played a prominent role in this country.

It was not easy; Jewish history never is.

SOURCES

Much of this book is based on materials in the National Archives of the Canadian Jewish Congress and the Public Archives of Canada. As well, the following books and articles were consulted.

Chapter 1

Arnold, Abraham. "Series on Canadian Jewish History." *Canadian Jewish News*, 1972–77.

Bosher, John. *The Canada Merchants 1713–1763*. Toronto: Oxford University Press, 1987.

Marcus, Jacob. *Early American Jewry*. Philadelphia: Jewish Publication Society of America, 1951.

Rome, David. *Canadian Jewish Archives*. Vols. 15–25. Montreal: Canadian Jewish Congress, 1980–82.

Vaugeois, Denis. *Les Juifs de la Nouvelle-France*. Trois Rivières: Boréal Express, 1968.

Chapter 2

Godfrey, Sheldon and Judith. "The Jews of Upper Canada." *The Jewish Standard*, August to December 1989.

Ouellet, Fernand. *Lower Canada 1791–1840*. Toronto: McClelland and Stewart, 1980.

Sack, Benjamin G. *History of the Jews in Canada*. Montreal: Harvest House, 1965.

Chapter 3

Brown, Michael. *Jew or Juif? Jews, French-Canadians and Anglo-Canadians, 1759–1914*. Philadelphia: Jewish Publication Society of America, 1987.

Medjuk, Sheva. *The Jews of Atlantic Canada*. St. John's: Breakwater Press, 1986.

Rosenberg, Stuart E. *The Jewish Community in Canada*. 2 vols. Toronto: McClelland and Stewart, 1971.

Speisman, Stephen. *The Jews of Toronto*. Toronto: McClelland and Stewart, 1979.

Chapter 4

Klenman, Allan. "Pioneer Jews in Early British Columbia 1858–1878." Victoria: Unpublished, 1971.

Leonoff, Cyril. *Pioneers, Pedlars and Prayer Shawls*. Victoria: Sono Nis Press, 1978.

Rome, David. *The First Two Years*. Montreal: H.M. Caiserman, 1942.

Chapter 5

Belkin, Simon. *Through Narrow Gates*. Montreal: Canadian Jewish Congress, 1966.

Chiel, Arthur A. *The Jews in Manitoba*. Toronto: University of Toronto Press, 1961.

Gutkin, Harry. *Journey into Our Heritage*. Toronto: Lester & Orpen Dennys, 1980.

Leonoff, Cyril. *The Jewish Farmers of Western Canada*. Vancouver: Jewish Historical Society of British Columbia, 1984.

Neufeld, Timothy. *Jewish Colonization in the Northwest Territories*. Master's thesis, University of Saskatchewan, 1982.

Trachtenberg, Henry. *"The Old Clo' Move": Anti-Semitism, Politics, and the Jews of Winnipeg, 1882–1921.* Doctoral dissertation, York University, 1984.

Usiskin, Michael. *Uncle Mike's Edenbridge.* Winnipeg: Peguis Publishers, 1983.

Chapter 6

Cook, Ramsay G. *The Regenerators: Social Criticism in Late Victorian English Canada.* Toronto: University of Toronto Press, 1985.

Harney, Robert, ed. *Gathering Place: People and Neighbourhoods of Toronto: 1834–1945.* Toronto: Multicultural History Society of Canada, 1985.

Harney, Robert, and Troper, Harold. *Immigrants: A Portrait of the Urban Experience.* Toronto: Van Nostrand Reinhold, 1975.

Hart, A.D., ed. *The Jew in Canada.* Montreal: Jewish Publication, 1926.

Howe, Irving. *World of Our Fathers.* New York: Harcourt Brace Jovanovich, Inc., 1976.

Oiwa, Keibo. *Tradition and Social Change: Ideological Analysis of the Montreal Jewish Immigrant Ghetto in the Early Twentieth Century.* Doctoral dissertation, Cornell University Press, 1987.

Rome, David. *Canadian Jewish Archives.* Vols. 36–43. Montreal: Canadian Jewish Congress, 1986–88.

Silver, A.I. *The French Idea of Confederation.* Toronto: University of Toronto Press, 1986.

Tulchinsky, Gerald. "Immigration and Charity in the Montreal Jewish Community Before 1890." In *Social History,* 1983, pp. 354–80.

Wolofsky, Hirsch. *Journal of My Life: A Book of Memories.* Montreal: Eagle Publishing, 1945.

Chapter 7

Belkin, S. *The Poalei Zion Movement in Canada 1904–1920.* In Yiddish. Montreal: Labour Zionist

Movement, 1956.

Figler, Bernard. *Lillian and Archie Freiman.* Montreal: [Private], 1961.

Frager, Ruth. *Uncloaking Vested Interests: Class, Ethnicity and Gender in the Jewish Labour Movement in Toronto 1900–1939.* Doctoral dissertation, York University, 1986.

Kage, Joseph. *With Faith and Thanksgiving.* Montreal: Eagle Publishing, 1962.

Paris, Erna. *Jews: An Account of Their Experience in Canada.* Toronto: Macmillan of Canada, 1980.

Rosenberg, Louis. *Canada's Jews: A Social and Economic Study of the Jews in Canada.* Montreal: Canadian Jewish Congress, 1939.

Tulchinsky, Gerald. "A.M. Klein's Montreal," *Journal of Canadian Studies.* Vol. 19, no. 2: pp. 96–112. Summer 1984.

Chapter 8

Abella, Irving, and Troper, Harold. *None Is Too Many: Canada and the Jews of Europe 1933–1948.* Toronto: Lester & Orpen Dennys, 1982.

Anctil, Pierre. *Le rendez-vous manqué: les Juifs de Montréal face au Québec de l'entre-deux-guerres.* Montreal: Institut québécois de recherche sur la culture, 1988.

_____, and Caldwell, Gary, eds. *Juifs et réalités juives au Québec.* Quebec: Institut québécois de recherche sur la culture, 1984.

Betcherman, L.R. *The Swastika and the Maple Leaf.* Toronto: Fitzhenry & Whiteside, 1975.

Langlais, Jacques, and Rome, David. *Juifs et Québécois francais: 200 ans d'histoire.* Montreal: Editions Fides, 1986.

Levitt, Cyril, and Shaffir, William. *The Riot at Christie Pits.* Toronto: Lester & Orpen Dennys, 1987.

Rischin, Moses, ed. *The Jews of North America.* Detroit:

Wayne State University Press, 1987.

Rome, David. *Clouds in the Thirties.* 13 vols. Montreal: Canadian Jewish Congress, 1977–84.

Teboul, Victor. *Mythe et images du Juif au Québec.* Montreal: Editions de Lagrave, 1977.

Chapter 9

Bercuson, David. *Canada and the Birth of Israel.* Toronto: University of Toronto Press, 1985.

——————. *The Secret Army.* Toronto: Lester & Orpen Dennys, 1983.

Caplan, Usher. *Like One That Dreamed: A Portrait of A.M. Klein.* Toronto: McGraw Hill Ryerson, 1982.

Gutkin, Harry. *The Worst of Times: The Best of Times.* Toronto: Fitzhenry & Whiteside, 1987.

Kallen, Evelyn. *Spanning the Generations: A Study in Jewish Identity.* Toronto: Longman, 1977.

Kattan, Naim. *Juifs et Canadiens.* Montreal: Editions du Jour, 1967.

Lipsitz, E.Y., ed. *Canadian Jewry Today.* Toronto: JESL Educational Products, 1989.

Schoenfeld, Stuart. "An Invitation to a Discussion: A Perspective on Assimilation, Intermarriage and Jewish Identity in Ontario." Unpublished, 1987.

Smith, Cameron. *Unfinished Journey: The Lewis Family.* Toronto: Summerhill Press, 1989.

Trepanier, Esther. *Jewish Painters and Modernity 1930–1945.* Montreal: Saidye Bronfman Centre, 1987.

Waddington, Miriam. *Apartment Seven.* Toronto: Oxford University Press, 1989.

Waller, Harold. *The Canadian Jewish Community: A National Perspective.* Philadelphia: Temple University, Centre for Jewish Community Studies, 1977.

PICTURE SOURCES

Many thanks to the following archives and archivists for their valuable research assistance: British Columbia Archives and Records Service, Delphine Castles and Leni Hoover; Canadian Jewish Congress National Archives, Janice Rosen; City of Vancouver Archives, Carol Haber; Fortress of Louisbourg National Historic Park, Kenneth Donovan; Holy Blossom Temple, David Hart; Jewish Historical Society of British Columbia, Cyril Leonoff, Marlene Mitchell and Stanley Winfield; Jewish Historical Society of Western Canada, Bonnie Tregobov; Jewish Public Library, Carol Katz; Fort Michilimackinac, Keith Widder; McCord Museum Archives, Pamela Miller and Nora Haig; McGill University Archives, Phebe Chartrand; National Archives of Canada, Lawrence Tapper; Ottawa Jewish Historical Society, Shirley Berman; Saint John Jewish Historical Museum, Marcia Koven; and Toronto Jewish Congress/Canadian Jewish Congress, Ontario Region Archives, Stephen Speisman.

For reasons of space the following abbreviations have been used:

AO: Archives of Ontario, Toronto
BCARS: British Columbia Archives
  and Records Service, Victoria
CJCNA: Canadian Jewish Congress National Archives
CMC: Canadian Museum of Civilization
CTA: City of Toronto Archives
CVA: City of Vancouver Archives, Vancouver
JHSBC: Jewish Historical Society of British Columbia
JHSWC: Jewish Historical Society of Western Canada

JPL: Jewish Public Library
MTRL: Metropolitan Toronto Reference Library, Toronto
NAC: National Archives of Canada, Ottawa
OJHS: Ottawa Jewish Historical Society, Ottawa
PANS: Public Archives of Nova Scotia
SJJHM: Saint John Jewish Historical Museum
TJC/CJC-ORA: Toronto Jewish Congress/Canadian Jewish
  Congress, Ontario Region Archives, Toronto
YIVO: YIVO Institute for Jewish Research

Front Cover: CMC, loaned by Beth Tzedec Reuben and Helene Dennis Museum.
Frontispiece: Toronto Jewish Congress Archives–Shuls Project by Sheldon Levitt, Lynn Milstone and Sid Tenenbaum.
Back Cover: Clockwise from upper left: CMC, loaned by Beth Tzedec Reuben and Helene Dennis Museum; CMC, loaned by Ronald Finegold; CMC, loaned by Social Action Committee, Temple Israel, Ottawa; CMC, loaned by Gershon and Rebecca Fenster Museum of Jewish Art.

———————————————————— CHAPTER ONE ————————————————————

Display page: University of Toronto Map Library; *1:* NAC (C-107626); *2:* Fortress of Louisbourg National Historic Park, Environment Canada, Canada Parks Service; *5:* Royal Ontario Museum, Canadiana Department (940 x 54); *6:* Bibliotheque Nationale, Cartes et Plans, France, GeC, 5019; *7:* PANS; *8, left:* PANS; *right:* PANS; *9:* PANS; *10:* NAC (C-135628); *11, upper:* NAC (C-134140); *lower: The Jew in Canada; 12: The Jew in Canada; 13, upper:* William L. Clements Library, University of Michigan; *lower:* CMC, loaned by Mackinac State Historic Parks, Mackinac Island, Michigan; *14, left: The Jew in Canada; right:* MTRL, J. Ross Robertson Collection (T 16328); *15, upper:* MTRL, J. Ross Robertson Collection (T 15674); *lower:* McCord Museum; *16:* CMC, loaned by Gershon and Rebecca Fenster Museum of Jewish Art; *17, upper:* NAC (C-24562); *lower:* McCord Museum, Notman Photographic Archives (MP154 (16)); *18: The Jew in Canada; 19, upper:* Service de ciné-photographie, Musée de la Province de Québec; *lower left:* McGill University Archives (PR 015498); *lower right: The Jew in Canada; 20:* McCord Museum, Hart Papers (M21359).

─────────────── CHAPTER TWO ───────────────

Page 22: JHSWC, *Journey into Our Heritage,* Harry Gutkin; *24, upper left: The Jew in Canada; upper right:* NAC (C-135626); *lower: The Jew in Canada; 26: The Jew in Canada; 27:* McCord Museum, Hart Papers (M21359); *28:* NAC (C-12090); *32:* CJCNA (PC1/6/364); *33, left:* McGill University Archives (PR 015511); *upper right:* McGill University Archives; *lower right:* McCord Museum, Notman Photographic Archives (19, 799-13 II); *34:* McGill University Archives; *35:* McCord Museum, Notman Photographic Archives (MP154 (17)).

─────────────── CHAPTER THREE ───────────────

Page 36: The Jew in Canada; 37: The Jew in Canada; 38, upper: CJCNA (PCI/6/583); *lower:* CJCNA (PC1/1/23); *39, upper left: The Jew in Canada; upper right: The Jew in Canada; lower left: The Jew in Canada; lower right: The Jew in Canada; 40, left:* CMC, loaned by Dr. Robert Levine and Marion Greenwood; *right:* MTRL, J. Ross Robertson Collection (T 14910); *41, upper:* NAC (C-18507); *lower: The Jew in Canada; 42, left: The Jew in Canada; right:* CMC, loaned by Annette Wolff; *43:* CTA (SC 498-2-N); *44:* University of Toronto Archives; *45, left: The Jew in Canada; middle: The Jew in Canada; right: The Jew in Canada; 46:* Holy Blossom Temple Archives; *47, left:* Holy Blossom Temple Archives; *upper right:* Holy Blossom Temple Archives; *lower right:* CTA (SC497-26-N); *48, upper:* CMC, donated by Hy Goodman; *lower:* CMC, donated by Hy Goodman; *49:* MTRL (T 14459); *50, upper left:* SJJHM; *middle:* SJJHM; *right:* SJJHM; *51, left:* SJJHM; *right:* SJJHM; *52:* CMC, Beth Tzedec Reuben and Helene Dennis Museum.

─────────────── CHAPTER FOUR ───────────────

Page 54: BCARS (HP10110); *55:* BCARS (HP4173); *56:* BCARS (HP25310); *58:* BCARS (HP14233); *59:* JHSBC (265); *60, left:* JHSWC (JHS 1689); *right:* BCARS (HP4350); *61:* NAC (C-5005); *62:* JHSWC (JM 1875); *63, left:* BCARS (HP7281); *upper right:* BCARS (HP3063); *lower right:* JHSBC (470); *64: The Jew in Canada; 65:* CJCNA (PC1/6/8) and Provincial Archives, B.C.; *66, left: The Jew in Canada; right:* BCARS (HP15100); *67:* JHSBC (34); *68:* JHSWC (JM 1736); *69:* JHSWC (JM 702A), *Journey into Our Heritage,* Harry Gutkin; *70:* NAC (PA-26365); *71, upper:* CVA (DIST.P.30 N.19, portion of); *lower:* CVA (BU.P.662 N.545); *72, upper left,* JHSBC (37); *upper right:* JHSBC (1); *lower:* JHSBC (497); *73:* CVA (BO.P.56 N.17).

─────────────── CHAPTER FIVE ───────────────

Page 74: JHSBC, Cyril Leonoff; *75:* JHSWC (JHS 314), *Journey into Our Heritage,* Harry Gutkin; *76:* NAC (PA-13008); *77:* JHSWC (JM 2087); *79:* JHSWC (JM 920); *80:* JHSWC (JHS 1201, JM 727); *81:* JHSWC (JM 646); *83:* JHSWC (MG1 A1-3); *84, upper:* JHSWC (JM 2025); *lower:* JHSWC (JM 2720); *85, upper left:* JHSWC (JM 2248), *Journey into Our Heritage,* Harry Gutkin; *upper right:* JHSWC (JHS 2719); *lower:* JHSWC (JHS 1559); *86, upper:* JHSWC (JM 195); *lower,* JHSBC, C.E. Leonoff; *87, upper left:* CJCNA (PC12/0C/9.102); *upper right:* CJCNA (PC12/0C/9.103); *lower: The Jew in Canada; 88:* JHSWC (JHS 3381, JM 1167); *89, upper:* CJCNA (JCA M-1); *lower:* CMC, donated by Lawrence Tapper; *90, upper:* JHSWC (JM 198); *lower:* YIVO; *91: Journey into Our Heritage,* Harry Gutkin; *92:* JHSWC (JHS 408); *93:* JHSWC (JHS 1860); *94, upper left:* NAC (C-27462); *upper right:* NAC (C-27450); *lower:* NAC (C-27461); *95, left:* NAC (C-27598); *upper right:* NAC (C-27459); *lower right:* NAC (C-27458); *96:* NAC (C-27526); *97, upper left:* NAC (C-27605); *upper right:* JHSWC (JHS 1394, JM 94/./2); *lower:* NAC (C-27513); *98, upper left:* JHSWC (JHS 492, JM 588); *upper right:* NAC (C-27619); *lower:* JHSWC (JHS 526), *Journey into Our Heritage,* Harry Gutkin; *99:* NAC (C-27464); *100:* JHSWC (JHS 3144); *101:* JHSWC (JHS 1812, JM 184).

─────────────── CHAPTER SIX ───────────────

Page 102: JHSWC (JHS 523); *104: The Jew in Canada; 105:* MTRL, J. Ross Robertson Collection (T 11147); *112:* Dorothy Freiman Alexandor; *113: The Jew in Canada; 114, left:* OJHS (1-079); *right:* OJHS (2-018) and NAC (4636); *115, upper:* OJHS (1-075); *lower:* OJHS (2-036); *116, upper:* Hotel de Ville, Montreal (D-95-11); *lower:* CMC, loaned by Allan Sonny Rubin and Leon Rubin; *117:* AO; *118, upper left: The Jew in Canada; upper right:* CJCNA (PC3/1/26A); *lower:* TJC/CJC-ORA; *119, left:*

CTA (James 679); *right*: CTA (SC3 E8 Box 1 File 5 pg 26); *120*: CTA (James 8029); *121, upper*: CTA (James 291); *lower*: MTRL (T 1152); *122*: JHSBC (7); *123*: JHSWC (JHS 1775); *124*: CJCNA (PC1/5/35 A.5); *125, upper*: TJC/CJC-ORA (1171); *lower*: JPL (84-193); *126*: JHSWC (JHS 1659); *127, upper*: JHSWC (JHS 870); *lower*: JHSWC (JM 3392); *128, upper*: TJC/CJC-ORA (253); *lower*: *The Jew in Canada*; *129*: NAC (C-135433); *130*: *The Jew in Canada*; *133*: TJC/CJC-ORA (3054); *134*: MTRL (T 33794); *135*: MTRL (T 33795); *137*: TJC/CJC-ORA (13); *138*: AO (Acc 21210-2222); *139*: AO (Acc 14361-508); *140*: AO (Acc 14361-126); *141*: AO (Acc 21210-5).

CHAPTER SEVEN

Page 146: OJHS (4-018); *147*: YIVO, Alter Kacyzne; *148*: YIVO, Alter Kacyzne; *149*: CJCNA (PC1/6/7231); *150*: *The Jew in Canada*; *151*: JPL (83-018); *152, left*: NAC (C-135629); *right*: Glenbow Archives, Calgary (NA-5350-1); *153*: TJC/CJC-ORA (2913); *154, left*: *The Jew in Canada*; *right*: JHSWC (JHS 1054); *155, upper*: CJCNA (Caiserman PP2); *lower*: TJC/CJC-ORA (1911); *156, upper*: CJCNA (PC1/4/1C); *lower*: JHSWC (JM 1911), *Journey into Our Heritage*, Harry Gutkin; *157*: *The Jew in Canada*; *158*: JPL (83-141); *159*: JHSWC (JHS 791), *Journey into Our Heritage*, Harry Gutkin; *160, left*: OJHS (1-174), NAC (PA-122816); *right*: Glenbow Archives, Calgary (NB 24-1); *161, upper left*: CTA (James 2206); *upper right*: *The Jew in Canada*; *lower*: *The Jew in Canada*; *162*: CJCNA (2A 1919/27); *163, upper*: CJCNA (A6 1919); *lower*: CJCNA (ZA 1919); *164*: *The Jew in Canada*; *166, upper*: JHSWC (JHS 2431); *lower*: JHSWC (JM 3390); *167*: CMC, loaned by Mrs. Lawrence Bilsky; *168, upper*: CJCNA (P89.2.2 in L42); *lower*: *The Jew in Canada*; *169*: AO (Acc 14361-24); *170, upper*: AO (Acc 14361-88); *lower*: AO (Acc 21210-1); *171, upper*: AO (Acc 14361-100); *lower*: JHSWC (JHS 3149); *172*: TJC/CJC-ORA (55); *173*: JHSWC (JHS 763); *174*: JHSWC (JHS 720); *175*: CTA (James 616); *176*: Foote Collection, Manitoba Archives (N-2762); *177*: Manitoba Archives.

CHAPTER EIGHT

Page 178, clockwise from upper left: CMC, loaned by CJCNA; CJCNA; CMC, loaned by CJCNA; CJCNA; CMC, loaned by CJCNA; CJCNA. *179*: *The Evening Telegram*, August 1, 1933; *180*: CTA (G&M 30791); *181, left*: CJCNA (PC1/1/5.3); *right*: CJCNA (PC1/1/5.10); *183*: CJCNA (PC1/3/771); *185*: CJCNA; *187*: CJCNA; *188*: JHSWC (JM 1913); *189, upper*: Manitoba Archives; *lower*: *The Jew in Canada*; *190*: CJCNA (PC1/3/40); *191*: *Journey into Our Heritage*, Harry Gutkin; *192, upper*: CJCNA (PC1/3/77 K.1); *lower*: CJCNA (PC1/3/74D); *193, upper left*: JHSWC (JHS 2739); *upper right*: JHSWC (JM 3389); *lower*: Manitoba Archives; *194*: TJC/CJC-ORA (4980); *195, upper*: AO (Acc 21210-27); *lower*: AO (Acc 14361-198); *196*: AO (Acc 21210-31); *197*: Canada's Sports Hall of Fame; *199*: Canada's Sports Hall of Fame; *201*: YIVO; *202*: CJCNA (Bronfman PP); *203*: CJCNA (PC1/6/286); *204, upper*: CJCNA (CJC FA3-Enlist); *lower*: CJCNA; *205*: OJHS (4-163); *206, upper left*: NAC (PA-174315); *lower left*: CJCNA (PC1/6/161); *right*: NAC (C-135436); *207, upper*: Royal Canadian Legion, Shalom Branch178, Vancouver; *lower*: CJCNA (PC1/1/6A.3).

CHAPTER NINE

Page 208: NAC (C-70429); *209*: CJCNA; *210*: CJCNA (Caiserman PP6); *211, left*: CJCNA (FA.3 Passover); *right*: JPL (84-149); *212, upper left*: CJCNA (PC1/1/20 C.1); *upper right*: CJCNA (PC1/2/63A.2); *lower*: JHSWC (JHS 186, JM 412); *213, left*: CJCNA (PC1/6/56); *right*: CMC, loaned by CJCNA; *214, left*: CJCNA (PC1/6/13); *right*: CJCNA (PC1/2/63A.Z); *215*: NAC (C-135434); *218*: CJCNA (Laskin PP1); *220*: CJCNA (Croll PP1); *221*: CJCNA (PC3/1/6); *223*: CJCNA; *228*: JPL (83-446-1); *229, upper*: TJC/CJC-ORA (1217); *lower*: CJCNA; *230*: CJCNA (PC2/1/7A.4); *231*: CJCNA, Alan Kaufman; *232*: CJCNA (PC1/2/74.A.); *233*: CMC, donated by Howard Fox; *234*: JHSWC (JHS 3385, JM 175).

INDEX

Page numbers in italics refer to illustrations and/or captions on the page indicated.

ACKNOWLEDGEMENTS

The words in this book are mine although many of the insights come from others. In particular, like all Canadian Jews, I owe much to a small group of non-professional historians who have expended considerable time and effort, in countless archives, museums, libraries and even graveyards, attempting to trace and detail the Jewish presence in Canada. These men and women, whose love of their people and their country is evident in almost every phrase they write, include the dean of Canadian Jewish historians, David Rome, as well as Abe Arnold, Sheldon and Judy Godfrey, Harry Gutkin, Julius Hayman, Ben Kayfetz and Cyril Leonoff. They are the real pioneers in the writing of the history of the Jews in Canada.

There are others who made this book possible and to whom I am deeply grateful: Andrea Bronfman, who is the driving force behind the exhibition which provided the impetus for the book; Malcolm Lester, who proposed the project to me; Professor Craig Brown, for his valuable reading of the manuscript; Avram Shtern and Janice Rosen at the Canadian Jewish Congress National Archives, who assisted with the research; Sandra Morton Weizman, guest curator of the "A Coat of Many Colours" exhibition; Catherine Yolles, who shepherded the book through its many phases; Anne Holloway and Bernice Eisenstein, who edited the manuscript; Lorraine Johnson, who located the photographs; and Pronk&Associates for the design of the book.